THE
UNDERBOSS

THE
UNDERBOSS

The Rise and Fall
of a Mafia Family

GERARD O'NEILL
& DICK LEHR

ST. MARTIN'S PRESS, NEW YORK

Janet and Brian and Shane
Bernadette and Nicholas

Design by Claudia Carlson

Library of Congress Cataloging-in-Publication Data

O'Neill, Gerard.
    The underboss : the rise and fall of a Mafia family / Gerard
O'Neill and Dick Lehr.
        p. m.
    "A Thomas Dunne book."
    ISBN 0-312-02619-6
        1. Mafia—Massachusetts—Boston—Case studies.
    2. Angiulo family.   3. Criminal investigation—Massa-
chusetts—Boston—Case studies.
    I. Lehr, Dick. II. Title.
    HV6452.M42M346   1989
    364.1′06′074461—dc19   88-30825
                                                      CIP

FIRST EDITION

10 9 8 7 6 5 4 3 2 1

ACKNOWLEDGMENTS

For a story that first ran in *The Boston Globe* and is now between two hard covers, we would like to thank the following people: Publisher Bill Taylor for his ongoing support of The Spotlight Team's efforts; Editor Jack Driscoll for supporting the idea of turning the Mafia series into a book and for his helpful suggestions after reading the manuscript; Sal Micciche for his advice, legal and otherwise; Christine Chinlund, a Spotlight Team colleague who worked on the Mafia project, for her writing suggestions on the final draft; Spotlight researcher Mary Elizabeth Knox for her invaluable fact-checking and historical research; former *Globe* reporter Richard Connolly for advice along the way from a journalist who specialized in covering the Mafia; Kevin Cullen, a *Globe* reporter who helped make the original newspaper series a success; Charles Everitt, president of the *Globe*'s *Pequot Press*, who helped two novices find their ways; Bernadette Rossi Lehr for her suggestions after reading the drafts more times than she bargained for; the *Globe* library staff for their unstinting cooperation; John and Nancy Lehr for their steady interest in the book; Harry Goldgar for first showing a seventeen year old the pleasures of writing; and, finally, several persons in law enforcement and on the fringes of the underworld who unfortunately cannot be named publicly. They know who they are.

1

COLD PORK CHOPS

At 9 P.M., about halfway through her meal at Francesca's restaurant in Boston's North End, a short, perky
brunette told her husband she was going to check in
with their babysitter to make sure the kids were okay.
Dressed casually in jeans and sweater, she bounced her
way among the tightly packed formica-top tables to
the pay phone.

"This is Mrs. Jones," she said. "Are the children all
right?" Because no one was standing near the phone,
there was no need for elaborate code talk. She quietly
added: "One, four, and five are here. Two and three are
not." As someone approached, she said her good-byes
with a flourish of good cheer. "We'll be home shortly,"
she chirped to the babysitter. She hung up and wove
back to her seat, smiling sweetly.

The reassured mother was, in fact, an FBI agent. Her

cryptic message told the case agent, Edward Quinn, that Mafia Underboss Gennaro J. Angiulo (number one) and two of his four brothers were at the small Italian restaurant just a few blocks from the bureau's downtown Boston office.

On the other end, Quinn made a brisk announcement to an assembled battalion of agents: Jerry, Frank, and Mike Angiulo had ordered supper and were to be arrested before they could finish. He knew that the oldest brother, Nicolo, was ill and at home in Revere. Nick could be grabbed the next day. But it was number three—Donato Angiulo—who worried him the most. Danny was unaccounted for and could wind up in Italy or parts unknown if the FBI didn't get him that night. Quinn ordered a team of six agents to find the dangerous Mafia lieutenant.

The agents headed out to smother the North End, looking for Danny's 1978 black Cadillac, especially around his hangouts, the Café Pompeii on Hanover Street and the Knights of Columbus hall on North Margin Street. Even after nightfall on this September 19, 1983, the unseasonable mugginess from several straight days of ninety-degree heat lingered. The twilight breezes that swept off the inner harbor were less refreshing than sticky.

Almost as an omen, the month had been a harsh one in Boston. Major developments on the three fronts of interest in a parochial city—politics, sports, and religion—all brought bad news. The local media was dominated by the police commissioner's struggle with alcoholism; another late-season collapse by the Red Sox; and the unexpected death of the city's spiritual leader, Archbishop Humberto Cardinal Medeiros.

But those events occurred on the city's beat, the public side that any resident or visitor could monitor easily in the newspapers or television. Less detectable was the pulse of Boston's underworld, that subterranean life where day is night—a time to rest—and night is day—a time to work: hustling numbers; staging craps, barboot games, and Las Vegas nights; taking sports bets; collecting loan-shark payments; and, on occasion, ruling that somebody's life must come to a brutal finish.

In the North End, Mafia ruler Gennaro Angiulo had sought out a cool spot from the kind of stifling heat that left shirts dark with city grime and arms wet with perspiration. For a late supper, he and two of his brothers had gone to Francesca's Restaurant on North Washington Street to take up their regular table in a back room.

His night had begun routinely enough. He and his brothers discussed their various illegal enterprises and then made the short walk from the Mafia boardroom at 98 Prince Street to the favored restaurant. It was a route that took them along streets and past buildings that hadn't changed in more than a century—despite Boston's new skyline of skyscrapers that rose in the shimmer of summer heat just a few blocks from their neighborhood. It was a route that took them past tenement buildings where their mother and father first lived as teenagers when they arrived from Italy eight decades earlier.

The small eatery was situated on one of the boundaries of their thickly settled North End neighborhood, with its narrow alleys and dark streets that were labyrinthian even for a city not known for making much street sense. But this was where the 64-year-old Jerry Angiulo and his brothers felt safe. Here they were born and, for nearly three decades, this was where they controlled a ruthless criminal enterprise considered among the most profitable in the country.

The North End was already an Italian stronghold when the Angiulos' parents arrived in the neighborhood in the early 1900s, where they ran a market on Prince Street. And that was the street where the Angiulo boys grew up and where Jerry, with a knack for numbers, realized how millions could be made from efficiently run rackets. Jerry became a commuter in the late 1950s from his mansion in the North Shore community of Nahant, but he always kept his headquarters in the spit of land that jutted out between Boston Harbor and the Charles River Basin. He didn't budge from Prince Street even though the old neighborhood, by 1983, found itself pressured by the economic revival that was changing the face of most of the city's downtown.

But the North End stubbornly resisted the change. There remained the generational and interlocking relationships among neighbors. Most important to the Angiulos, there were still many pairs of eyes and ears looking out and listening in, providing a seemingly airtight network that insulated the mobsters from outsiders.

It was a home court advantage that agents of the Federal Bureau of Investigation had long considered as insurmountable as that enjoyed by the Celtics basketball team in nearby Boston Garden. The North End was the Angiulos' defense against an alien and fast-changing city, and when it came to Mafia business, the brothers stuck closely together in their old confines. Frank "Cat" Angiulo, one of Jerry's younger brothers, who served as an accountant for the myriad bookmaking operations, lived on Prince Street directly across from the office. In fact, Frankie was such a homebody that he never even ventured the few blocks to the famous Quincy Market, the sprawling commercial marketplace that had emerged from the ruins of a warehouse district in the late 1970s.

In many respects, Gennaro Angiulo, the Mafia chieftain who was seated apart from the other diners at Francesca's, had led a charmed life. He'd made millions and, for those keeping a scorecard, he was way out front in that endless game of evasion with the authorities that every mobster must take seriously. Since the early 1960s, the nimble-minded Mafia boss had been targeted by every level of law enforcement—city, state, and federal. He'd outwitted them all— serving only two thirty-day prison terms despite a résumé that included trials for murder and laundering money stolen in an armed robbery as well as countless grand jury probes. Both prison terms came after the notoriously hot-tempered Angiulo lost his cool during challenges on his turf. The first was in 1966 for assault after he objected to the presence of an Internal Revenue Service agent outside his North End office and slapped the man as two bodyguards stood watch. The other was in 1973 when he assaulted a coastguardsman who dared to board his yacht to inspect it for minor boating violations.

Those skirmishes aside, the compact, silver-haired Mafia autocrat was legendary for his ability to skirt the government's maneuverings, thwarting every move it made. For years, when trouble came, he used his analytical mind to stay one step ahead of prosecutors, interrogating underlings who appeared before grand juries or were questioned by police. What did they ask you? Who asked the question? What did you say? Angiulo combed his underlings' memories for any small clue to help him fashion countermoves that might include trying to bribe a juror, paying off witnesses for their false testimony, or even killing them if they could not be counted on. But even now, as he sat to discuss business with Frankie and Mike over dinner, Jerry Angiulo sensed the latest FBI offensive was unlike any he had faced before. There had been strong indications this round would be different.

"I smell a RICO," Angiulo had been telling his brothers for a couple of years now. He was referring to the Racketeering Influenced and Corrupt Organizations law, the organized crime–fighting tool that had been around since 1970 but had only recently been dusted off and used by the Organized Crime Strike Forces around the country. Angiulo's senses had been heightened in the first six months of 1981, after a federal grand jury was convened, and many of his bookmaking offices had suffered a series of raids that had rankled and confounded him.

Enraged at apparent breakdowns in security, he began worrying constantly about the law that made it a crime to operate a criminal outfit. In angry lectures that bordered on tirades, he hounded his brothers about the RICO threat. "They will take your fuckin' head off," he pronounced once about the power federal agents had, now that they were armed with RICO. "Nobody's ever been able to beat it yet," he complained in another endless monologue to Frankie in which he mixed his personal analysis with readings from the statute. Despite his persistent efforts to find an escape clause in the legalese, Angiulo, in calmer moments of clarity, concluded, "The law was only written for people like us."

As he dined at Francesca's Restaurant, these were the kinds of concerns that nagged at Angiulo, that had intensified during the past twelve months, ever since his suspicions about the feds and RICO had been confirmed. On August 3, 1982, Jerry, his brothers, a leading *capo de regime* and brutal enforcer named Ilario M. A. "Larry" Zannino, and sixty other mobsters had been notified that for nearly four months in 1981 their conversations had been tape recorded. Now a new federal grand jury was hearing evidence against the family. But none of the Angiulos knew when the blow from the FBI would come. And for reasons no one fully understands, none of them fled the country.

So they kept up their routines, which included dinner at Francesca's. On this particular night, Jerry ordered pork chops. Frank and Mike Angiulo both had linguini with clam sauce. Unknown to them, two pairs of FBI agents, posing as married couples, sat at separate tables among the other diners. After "Mrs. Jones" called Quinn at 9 P.M. at the squad room, the rug was permanently pulled out from under the Angiulos. For the Mafia in Boston, nothing would be the same again.

In Quinn's possession was Jerry's arrest warrant, the result of the mob boss's secret indictment, along with warrants for Angiulo's four brothers, Capo Zannino, who had been hospitalized earlier that day, and another aging capo named Sammy Granito from Revere.

Since 1978, the veteran FBI agent, whose hair was now graying slightly, had been in charge of "Operation Bostar," which was designed to topple the Angiulos. In Quinn, the bureau had chosen an Irishman who was Angiulo's polar opposite—the God-fearing son of a Boston police lieutenant, graduate of Boston College High School and Boston College, and ex-Marine. Busting bank robbers and mobsters was the kind of work Agent Quinn preferred. It's what the bureau did best and it was work without any gray areas, only a bold, bright line between the good guys and bad guys. There weren't the perplexing ambiguities that surface in some of the bureau's other domestic activities, such as the ones Quinn faced firsthand during a stint in New York in the 1970s. The devout Catholic had been part of a team of agents staking out a church to arrest radical priest Daniel Berrigan, who never did show up. Give him a bank robber or mobster any time.

Hanging up the phone, Quinn surveyed the squad room of the almost thirty agents he had mobilized for this moment: The seven-year battle of wits and stamina was about to end. Somewhere along the line, the mission against the Boston Mafia had been reduced to its simplest terms—Ed Quinn versus Jerry Angiulo. Or at least Angiulo saw it that way starting back in 1981, when he began asking his brothers who this Quinn guy was, and what his family situation was. He learned that Quinn, after more than a decade in the bureau, had been transferred back to his native Boston in 1978.

It was the kind of Angiulo talk that put Quinn on notice, causing the agent to worry that Angiulo was unpredictable enough to violate one of the unwritten rules among agents and the mob that innocent family members were off limits. So one day in April 1981, knowing he would meet Angiulo in federal court, Quinn wired himself on the hunch that he'd capture a threat made to a federal agent.

"You know," Jerry said, approaching Quinn near the courthouse elevator accompanied by his attorney and his son. "I know that you know me, and most certainly I know that I recognize you, but I can't remember your first name."

"Yeah, well my name is Agent Quinn."

Jerry smiled. He loved to spar. For the next several seconds, the two went back and forth, playing a word game, until Angiulo boarded the elevator. "Be careful," he told the agent.

Then, returning to his office in the North End, Angiulo relished the retelling of this face-off with Quinn. " 'I know who you are but I can't remember your first name,' " he told his capo Larry Zannino, quoting from the conversation. "What was his fuckin' answer? Tell him." He gestured to his son and his attorney, but then answered his own question. " 'My name is Mr. Quinn.' 'Oh, I know that.' Now he knows I'm hitting on him. 'What I want to know is your first name.' Like, nice and easy I'm sayin' to him, you know I wanna know, you cocksucker, where you live, Quinn, that's what. He knows it."

In the years to come, the two would go nose to nose countless times. By 1987, the case did indeed boil down again to Quinn versus Angiulo. In Massachusetts Superior Court, where Jerry was on trial for ordering a gangland execution, Quinn would stand in the witness box, arms folded, while Angiulo sat alone at the defense table. Quinn would testify that as a result of the FBI probe and subsequent legal proceeding he had met Angiulo "at least 100 times." When Quinn sidestepped a question from the mobster's lawyer, Angiulo, from his seat, would mutter "son of a bitch."

So a face-to-face exchange that hot summer night in 1983 was something both men had been working toward for years. For Boston, the city's biggest bust would have an apt finish: Quinn and Angiulo, each man playing a prototypical part in an age-old conflict that began when the North End first filled up with immigrants from southern Italy as the second-generation Irish moved out, sniping as they left. In some ways, the arrests were acts of historical destiny: Boston was the perfect setting for the final interplay between Irish cop and Italian mobster.

Having received the call from the restaurant, Quinn then gave last-minute instructions to some twenty agents before they all headed down to the garage of the John F. Kennedy Federal Building and launched the caravan that would mark the beginning of the end for Gennaro Angiulo and his crime family. Quinn sent one team to Revere to arrest Capo de Regime Sammy Granito at his home, and another to the Lynn Hospital to find Larry Zannino. The final plans for Jerry Angiulo's arrest had involved a certain amount of protocol to acknowledge those who'd played key roles in the long and exhausting probe. Two agents had been assigned to arrest each mobster: he and Pete Kennedy would take Jerry; John Connolly and Bill Regii would take Frank; Nick Gianturco and Bobby Jordan had Mike. The six had been among the central cast in the FBI's Operation Bostar.

To take care of coordinating with the Boston police,

Quinn also had Eddie Walsh, the veteran Boston Police deputy superintendent who had been hounding mafiosi since the 1950s and attributed Angiulo's supremacy to "the three B's—balls, brains and bucks." Quinn made sure to invite John Morris, the former boss of the squad who had conceived the bugging plan and oversaw its implementation but, between the bugging and now, had been transferred to run another squad. Morris, thankful for being "invited," nonetheless felt somewhat left out, an observer rather than a guiding force on this night.

Within ten minutes of leaving their office, their eight cars having snaked past Boston Garden and into a dark, narrow alley behind the restaurant, FBI agents flooded Francesca's dining room.

Quinn was the first agent through the door. As the other agents fanned out to make sure no young up-and-comer tried something foolish to save the Angiulos, Quinn kept his eyes focused straight ahead on the mobsters' table in back. In the end, it would take a matter of seconds. But just as waterlogged timber is double in weight, these seconds, soaked in years of FBI sweat, passed in a kind of slow time.

Looking up, Angiulo spotted Quinn. "Mr. Quinn," he called out, referring to the agent as he had in their first encounter.

Quinn's response had four parts:

"Mr. Angiulo.

"FBI.

"You're under arrest.

"Stand up."

Quinn already had the handcuffs out. He pulled Angiulo's arms behind him. The other agents moved in on Frank and Mike.

"There is no reason for that," Angiulo snarled. He tried to move his hands in front. Of course he had known for months that this was coming—the FBI had the tapes, which contained even his own prescient insights about his outfit's mounting slip-ups and vulnerabilities. "You know what happened?" he once asked Larry Zannino. "Gennaro Angiulo fell asleep." But even if he knew Quinn's appearance was inevitable, it didn't mean he had to suffer the indignity of having his hands cuffed behind his back.

Quinn would not budge. He always applied handcuffs in back. This way the person could not raise his hands or try any other move. It was the way Quinn had been taught. "That's the rules, and this is how you go," Quinn told him. No exceptions. He pulled back Angiulo's arms and snapped on the cuffs.

Now Angiulo led a different kind of entourage past the other tables of the restaurant—the major figure in a Mafia roundup that included five associates. With military dispatch, the multiple arrests had taken two minutes. A waitress in the kitchen missed the whole thing. Hangers-on just sat there stunned, their mouths open for a full moment after the lightning operation was over and the Angiulos had been herded out to unmarked Fords. The restaurant then exploded into a hubbub. Minutes later, six agents handcuffed Danny Angiulo two blocks away as he walked to his car. Within hours, reporters from all the newspapers and radio and television stations in Boston would be scrambling for details of what became the most sensational organized crime story in the city's history.

But Jerry Angiulo was not one to go quietly. He may have had to tolerate Quinn's handcuff rules on that particular summer night, but it didn't mean he had to stop playing the wiseguy. As he left, the always defiant Angiulo sought the last word. Over his shoulder he vowed angrily to anyone within earshot, "I'll be back for my pork chops before they're cold."

2

THE MOB IN BOSTON

After an arduous birth and stunted childhood, the back-water Boston Mafia came of age the day in 1931 when Irish gang leader Frankie Wallace staggered into a dingy third-floor office in the North End. He died there of a single bullet wound to the heart while a secretary literally shrieked bloody murder.

It had been a quickly planned killing, an impromptu addendum to what was supposed to be a peace parley on how best to split up liquor hijacking and the hundreds of cases of booze coming over land and by sea for the speakeasies of New England.

Though Wallace didn't know it, negotiations had ended that morning when, in a telephone conversation with his North End counterpart, Wallace ruled out any compromise on who would get what. As leader of the best-known crime gang in the city, he was coming over from the Irish stronghold of South Boston to dictate terms, not divvy up the pie. His Gustin Gang was to be cut in on all liquor unloaded on the shoreline in and around South Boston, and the gang's convoys were not to be raided. Or else.

But when Wallace and two henchmen strode briskly into the Testa Building three days before Christmas, seven mafiosi were behind closed doors on the third floor. When Wallace banged on the door of Joseph Lombardo's C and F Importing, the guns roared for several seconds. Barney Walsh, one of the Gustins, tried to escape down the stairwell but was cut down and died on his face on the second-floor landing. The terrified third gang member, Timothy Coffey, survived by hiding in an office up the hall, not coming out until the police arrived to mop up after the blood-splattered, epochal event on Hanover Street. Wallace staggered down the hall to the law office of Julian H. Wolfson and careened through the door, landing like a ragdoll on a foyer chair, then toppling half over, his head on the floor.

Prior to the Gustin Gang ambush, the Boston Mafia had been viewed as the puny pushcart peddlers of organized crime, a bush-league embarrassment compared to Al Capone's Chicago and Lucky Luciano's New York. But when Frankie Wallace began to reach too far and demand too much, the Italians knew they were facing a subsistence future in a flagrantly Irish city. They would either have to settle for smuggling by fishing boat and minor gambling in the North End—or take some action. The barrage in the Testa Building was their resounding answer.

The audacious execution of the preeminent Irish mobster on alien turf at high noon, while war veterans packed Christmas baskets for the poor children of the North End on the floor above, meant Boston's underworld would stay balkanized. The Mafia won because it didn't lose. There would be no Boston overlord, and the warring factions would retreat to their ethnic enclaves where they would stay put for decades, leaving the Mafia firmly in charge of the North End and with its fair share of Boston bootlegging.

During the Depression era and World War II, the Mafia was able to expand slightly its loansharking and gambling network into other small pockets throughout the city, most prominently in East Boston, another former Irish stronghold that became an Italian neighborhood after World War I. In this post-Gustin era, the uneducated but stately Joseph Lombardo became a major figure in the mob, a *consigliere* and then an eminent elder statesman, sharing power with an older, better connected man from Sicily who had arrived in 1920 with a special imprimatur from the Old World. Together, they ran a laissez-faire gambling operation in Boston until it fell into the eager hands and facile mind of Gennaro Angiulo, a North End native who was 12 years old when the Irish gang leaders were murdered around the corner from where he lived.

Lombardo's bold action gave the Mafia the time it needed to take hold and even prosper in Boston's wildly competitive crime market, one that was structured by the order in which immigrant ships arrived. The Irish came first in the mid-nineteenth century and controlled politics and the waterfront within a generation. Jewish mobsters, whose forebears arrived near the end of the century, were dominating the speakeasies of the Roaring Twenties. For the Italians, still bunched into one of Boston's poorest neighborhoods, the demise of the Gustin Gang was a propitious event. It gave the Mafia prestige and room to grow in the wild gestation period for crime in America known as Prohibition. Never again would the Mafia be denied its fair share.

In what became a familiar pattern in Mafia cases, Timothy Coffey, the surviving member of the ambushed Gustin trio, refused to testify before a grand jury, taking the Fifth Amendment in both of his appearances. Only three Italians—Lombardo, Frank Cucchiara of the North End, and Salvatore Congemi of the North End—were held on probable cause. They were not indicted by the grand jury after Coffey refused to testify, and no other witnesses could be found. Along with Lombardo, Cucchiara rose in the ranks, going on to be Boston's only representative at the infamous mass meeting of the national Mafia at Apalachin, New York, in 1957.

But Lombardo became an almost mystical figure, a man of respect who could arbitrate the endless childish squabbles among his underlings over money and territory. Known as J.L., he had the bearing and manner of leadership, a combination of street toughness and old-world gentility that makes those who remember him nostalgic for his era.

His importing business was on the North End's main thoroughfare, historic Hanover Street, once home to Cotton Mather, Benjamin Franklin, and Revolutionary War cabals—and then to successive generations of immigrants who jammed into squalid tenements that replaced manors. By the time of the Gustin Gang shooting, Hanover Street was a vivid symbol of a motley era, a bustling, congested, and dangerous section of town dominated by the wares and violence of the Prohibition era. Gunfights were so common on this street of saloons and small businesses that it had become known as the "shooting gallery." After Wallace bled to death in the third-floor law office, Lombardo disappeared for nine days. He then surrendered on his own terms rather than suffer the indignities of being arrested. He knew the only evidence to put him at the scene was an Irish policeman who tried to sell Lombardo tickets to the policeman's ball in the Testa Building two hours before all hell broke loose at C and F Importing. If no one talked, there would be no case against him.

Lombardo and his bodyguard walked into Boston police headquarters on New Year's Eve. "I'd like to see Superintendent Crowley," he said to the desk sergeant. "Who's calling?" he was asked. "Tell him Joe Lombardo would like to see him," he said quietly.

Questioned on his whereabouts the day of the murders, the 36-year-old Lombardo apologized repeatedly for his lack of cooperation—but firmly declined to answer. "I don't want you to think I'm sassy, Superintendent," he said, "but I'm not going to answer any questions." He never did, not one, and was released for good in March. He would run gambling and the satellite industry of loansharking for decades as second in command to Filippo Buccola, an older and more patriarchal Sicilian. They never took a backward step.

While the Mafia remained hemmed into the mono-lithically Italian North End, it had salvaged its self-respect and solidified its hold. You could do little better in the ethnic free-for-all that shaped the Boston underworld. It had also benefited from the dissension in South Boston, as the Gustin Gang never fully regained its footing following Frankie Wallace's sudden death. Named after a rough-and-tumble Southie street, the Gustins survived in name only, its members gradually drifting apart during the 1930s, free-lancing here and there, sticking close to home, working the docks for pilferage or even wages.

Boston's underworld remained splintered into the 1960s, much as it had been since the end of the nineteenth century, a nexus of ethnic villages with political power vested in the Irish because they were the first off the ships and had a natural instinct for politics, a passion alien to the xenophobic Italians who came later. The Irish have dominated Boston politics since they took City Hall at the turn of the century.

When hard times in Southern Italy precipitated an exodus in the 1880s, the first arrivals in Boston were outnumbered by the Irish by a 60–1 margin. By the time of the Gustin Gang, the Irish population advantage was down to 2-1 but it still meant there were only 90,000 Italians in a city of 780,000.

Another immigration that shaped Prohibition-era crime in Boston was the influx of Eastern European Jews in the 1890s. They were relegated to the North End, East Boston, and the West End but would have a disproportionate influence in the speakeasy and rumrunning end of the city's underworld.

By the 1930s, despite the steady increase in the Italians and Jews, Boston remained an Irish town, with politics and patronage firmly in hand from the bastion of City Hall. The Yankees of the *Mayflower* and after had retreated to Beacon Hill, where they had to make do with controlling state government and making life as difficult as possible for Irish mayors. They studiously ignored the rabble in the North End, deigning only to sell off a Bullfinch-designed brick church just off Hanover Street to the Catholic diocese, which formed an instant parish of five thousand persons in the mid-nineteenth century and called the building St. Stephen's.

Perhaps because of all the adversity, the Mafia found a home. Small and lean, the group was able to prosper without the cyclical cataclysms of New York and Chicago and Detroit. In other waterfront cities, the Mafia families had larger numbers, control of pier pilferage, and far less competition from rivals. They were able to expand far more quickly from Prohibition gluttony and then frantic Depression-era gambling. Their staple became the false hope of the long-odds lottery. But the price of boundless expansion elsewhere was blood in the streets and major police investigations. Boston would have neither until the 1960s, a free ride of thirty years.

The frenetic Prohibition growth in other cities had a downside Boston was spared. In Chicago, Al Capone made $50 million a year until he was brought down by federal agents in 1934. In New York, the "Castellammarese War" left scores dead and two violent changes of leadership in one six-month period in 1931. In New Orleans, the Sicilians controlled the docks before the turn of the century, but the early start there brought a probe by the city's police chief—and lynchings of Sicilians when the chief was murdered for doing the job too well.

But all the early spadework was a prelude to the seminal event at the end of Prohibition that shook the Mafia to its core: the bloodletting in New York in 1930–31 that reverberated throughout the decades, with vendettas lasting to early graves. It was an upheaval that Boston was able to sit out, just watching to see which side won the vicious battle.

It began, as it always seemed to, when greed and vanity took hold of a dominant leader who decided to become the only leader. The don of Manhattan, a squat, insatiable man of legendary appetites named Joseph Masseria, became distrustful of the burgeoning and feisty Sicilian contingent in Brooklyn. He demanded a loyalty oath that was summarily rebuffed. Masseria had one of the Sicilians shot dead and held another for ransom. But it only hardened the resistance of the Sicilians led by Salvatore Maranzano, who, like many of the men in Brooklyn, were from the same small village in Sicily known as Castellammarese. The loyalty oath was all it took to set off months of mayhem, an ugly war of attrition that pitted a generation of leaders against each other. Masseria's allies were Charles "Lucky" Luciano, Vito Genovese, Joe Adonis, Carlo Gambino, Albert Anastasia, and Frank Costello. The Sicilians had Joseph Bonanno, Joseph Profaci, Thomas Lucchese, Joseph Magaliocco, and Stephano Magaddino of Buffalo. Off and on, the Mafia's all-star line up would be at each others throats forever more.

The tide turned against Masseria in early 1931 after he had lost fifty men to the better organized and slightly more fanatical men of Sicily. Luciano, the shrewdest and most practical of them all, saw bootlegging profits decline during the prolonged feud and urged peace on the pigheaded Masseria, but Masseria had abandoned the balance sheet for the body count. Luciano struck a deal with the other side: amnesty for Masseria's head.

The first phase of the war ended on April 19, 1931, at Scarpato's restaurant on Coney Island. Seconds after Luciano left the table to go to the men's room, gunmen moved quickly into the dining room, showering the bloated Masseria with bullets, killing him instantly. After the funeral, Maranzano held a meeting with five hundred men at a Bronx hall, outlining a family structure of capo, sottocapo, capo regime, and soldier that exists to this day. But there was a fatal flaw in Maranzano's new constitution: It provided for a dictator with the title of *capo di tutti capo*, the boss of all bosses. And he gave the job to himself.

Maranzano, who was spellbound by Caesar and had an apartment full of books about the Roman Empire, would be dead in six months, another murder traceable to the fine hand of Luciano. This time, though, Luciano used imported killers, Jewish gangsters who posed as New York detectives and swept right into Maranzano's real-estate office, flashing phony badges at guards in the anteroom. They shot him four times and, for good measure, stabbed him six times in the stomach. Luciano took over, presiding at a more democratic commission set up to establish policy and arbitrate disputes. He brought a measure of evenhanded predictability to the Mafia, stressing cooperation among the families and getting loyalty in return.

While Boston was a sideshow to these seismic events, the reign of Luciano, with its emphasis on respect and negotiation, helped shape the two dominant leaders of a generation in New England, a 45-year-old fight promoter in Boston named Filippo Buccola and a young ex-convict in Providence named Raymond L. S. Patriarca. The marching orders shifted slightly from "do this or else" to "ignore these rules at your peril." Buccola was more flexible than the obdurate Patriarca, who was a fair but ferocious man when crossed.

The Boston Mafia's slow development was due in part to the city's long tradition of hovels and hostility for whoever was last off the boat. From the mid-nineteenth century on, many of the new arrivals started out in the North End, which early in Boston history became an abandoned ghetto with no political power and little sanitation, an ostracized island of tenements for immigrants who had nowhere else to go. It was a ghastly place of disease and crime, a wretched slum where three out of every ten children died before the age of one, giving Boston the highest child death rate in the United States. Yet, in the 1840s, the North End was where most immigrants in Boston began a hard life in a new country.

The evolution of the North End is the story of lost grandeur. In the beginning, which in Boston means the seventeenth century, it was the first and most elegant neighborhood, home to Cotton Mather and wealthy merchants who built spacious manor houses. But the area raced downhill after the Revolutionary War, with business and the upper crust moving inland, leaving the waterfront to the riffraff and inexorable decay. It stayed an immigrant's nadir for more than a century, a separate island of unremitting misery.

The dark narrow streets of the North End, long a protective cover for organized crime, lie on what was once sparsely settled marshland where deteriorating manors were converted into ramshackle apartments. At the turn of the eighteenth century the area was becoming a miasmic rooming house, a forbidding waterfront of warehouses, saloons, and brothels. Within a few decades, the potato crop failure in Ireland disgorged emaciated and unskilled farmers on its shore like so many bedraggled swimmers. By 1855, more than half of the North End's population was Irish—14,000 of 26,000. The Irish began moving out after the Civil War, first to escape the wretched tenement life, and later the incessant conflicts with the newly arrived Italians, who began to come in numbers in the 1880s.

By 1895, the Italian population of the North End tripled. There was a steady stream of Eastern European Jews as well, most of them from Russia, who settled in small blocks near where the Angiulos grew up. Gennaro always was able to do business more readily with Jewish bookies than Irish gangsters.

As the Irish withdrew from the North End, seeking the better housing and jobs of newer neighborhoods such as nearby South Boston, they turned their voluble social networks into potent ward politics. They left the North End on bad terms and kept it that way. It was in the North End where the Italians and Irish gangs of Boston first clashed. This was to be an enduring enmity, one that carried over to a young Gennaro Angiulo growing up there in the 1920s.

The tension between the two dominant ethnic blocks in Boston dates back a century and persists to this day. In the 1880s, they fought each other in the street over menial jobs and the last crammed apartment in a fetid tenement that housed up to fifty children. The Irish left the North End as a retreating army might, sniping as they pulled out, leaving nasty wounds that were remembered in the street again and again when Caesar and Giovannina Angiulo set up house on Prince Street in 1915.

The North End remained isolated and spurned while the rest of the city's population exploded and assimilated, while other neighborhoods teemed with newcomers and new ventures. From 1850, when the immigration wave began in earnest, until the birth of the last Angiulo brother in 1927, when the influx into Boston crested, the city's population had increased nearly 600 percent, peaking at close to 800,000. The growth took place all around the North End, which not only lagged far behind, but actually receded as the city swelled. It may as well have been a village in Sicily, sealed off by jagged mountain passes.

Omen or coincidence, Angiulo's birth in 1919 dovetailed with the real beginning of the Mafia in America: the Eighteenth Amendment to the Constitution, which banned alcoholic beverages. Although the law went on the books, it did not go into effect until a year later. Perversely, it became the lifeblood of a fledgling urban crime organization that had been getting by on extortion, theft, and neighborhood gambling.

Angiulo's birth took place in the city's most tumultuous year in the modern era. First, there was a bizarre tragedy only blocks from Angiulo's house. When Giovannina Angiulo was six months' pregnant with her third child, whom she would name Gennaro after her father, a huge storage tank with 2.2 million gallons of molasses burst on Commercial Street, which ran along the outer edge of the North End. A 15-foot tidal wave of goo swept aside everything in its path, drowning twenty-one persons, destroying a fire station, and pushing horse-drawn wagons into the harbor. Then, six months after Angiulo's birth, militant Boston patrolmen went on strike after negotiations to form a union broke down. Within days, the festive mood of the populace turned ugly. Crap games on the Common escalated into rapes in Scollay Square alleys and hallways. Governor Calvin Coolidge sent in troops to restore order, broke the strike, and, with nearly unanimous public support, fired one thousand policemen who had let the city sink into chaos. The patrolmen's action was denounced as a national crime by President Woodrow Wilson and condemned from pulpits around the city, but didn't cause a ripple in the impervious North End, which remained a cloistered place, little different from an overcrowded village south of Rome. The dialect, dress, customs, manner, and cooking were no different from back home. Women wore black, men furtive looks. Unmarried women, no matter the age, were always under the surveillance of concerned parents and even cousins three streets over. North End residents looked inward or out to sea, and the secretive ambiance seeped into Angiulo's character, becoming an indelible part of his makeup.

This mentality persists today, with many older Italians such as the Angiulos sticking to themselves, seldom venturing from their street or even their homes, some wearing a permanent pallor of the house-bound. Much of the second generation turned their backs on Boston's Irish politics or Brahmin culture, preferring the familiarity and comfort of old-world ways. An entire neighborhood resisted assimilation throughout the twentieth century.

Before the Angiulo brothers went to jail, it's likely that none of them ever walked the five blocks to the city's spiffy showplace, the refurbished Faneuil Hall marketplace of smart shops and expensive restaurants and singles' bars. As often as not, the brothers ate supper in their office on Prince Street, firing up four burners on a stove large enough to service a small restaurant.

Even in 1981, when the North End was partly gentrified into a high-rent district and Italians shared power at every stratum in the city, Angiulo still rubbed the Irish wound, lashing out at the dogged FBI team on his tail led by the son of a Boston cop, Ed Quinn of Dorchester. After Quinn popped up all over a grand jury case against the family, Angiulo saw him more as an Irish tormentor than an FBI agent. "Quinn, Quinn all over again," he said to an underling in his office on Prince Street. "You know Quinn at all? . . . Thin-looking motherfucker . . . Did you ever see those guys from South Boston that wear the scully caps from the fucking docks? Thin, thin guys, black beardish. Always with a dark beard. Without the beard on and the fucking eyebrows, you know the Irish, the real Irish, that's Quinn."

Irishmen on the docks were bad enough. But put them in a police uniform and it defined Angiulo's lifelong nemesis: a horde of Irish cops. His disdain was boundless. In his view, policemen were psychotics who took the job to act out their aggressions. "You have to be a special guy to be a cop to begin with," he told an Italian court officer who passed along information to the family from Boston's Suffolk County Courthouse. "He's disturbed up here and once they get the feel of it . . . That's why all Irishmen are cops. They love it. Alone they're a piece of shit. When they put on the uniform and they get a little power, they start destroying everything."

The Boston Mafia took hold in such a milieu, though none of its leaders until Angiulo was born in the North End—or even lived there. They did business in the cafés during the day but slept elsewhere, much as generals stay in separate camps.

Just as their predecessors began by exploiting the peasants of Sicily in exchange for ephemeral protection against conquering armies, the Boston Mafia lived off the factory workers and street vendors of the North End, parasites operating just below the surface of daily commerce, holding out usurious loans and the false hope of the Italian lottery number. Boston's Mafia stabilized at the entry level, not reaching the Roaring Twenties until the 1960s.

It never did cut into the Irish monopoly on waterfront pilferage and union jobs and it had to struggle during prohibition to keep pace with Jewish gangsters who set out to control the liquor for their speakeasies in downtown Boston and elsewhere. The bulk of it came overland from Canada, and the Irish controlled most of the liquor brought in along the waterfront. The North End Mafia had to make do with an occasional boatload of liquor smuggled in at night, dumped on North End docks along with the catch of the day, and loaded onto a ragtag convoy of trucks for distribution to the speakeasies of Tremont Street and beyond.

The better conditions for growth—and the man to manage it—lay to the south of Boston, in the far smaller but mostly Italian city of Providence, Rhode Island. The man for the times was Raymond Patriarca, who had put in a long, hard apprenticeship during Prohibition, running prostitutes and hijacking trucks, learning the ropes as an associate and then member of the New York Mafia, which he purportedly joined in 1929.

While Angiulo would make it as a born bookmaker, Patriarca would rise to the top by being, in the words of one Massachusetts state policemen "just the toughest guy you ever saw." In Providence, he was able to take advantage of a large Italian population and ready access to politicians and police. In the late 1930s, he was able to bribe his way out of prison on armed robbery charges by paying for a pardon. Several decades later he received early parole from a Rhode Island state prison on a murder conspiracy charge after a letter was written on his behalf in 1973 by then Speaker of the

House, Joseph A. Bevilacqua. The letter stated Patriarca was "a person of integrity and, in my opinion, good moral character."

Over the years, Patriarca became the tail that wagged the dog, the driving force behind the New England Mafia, a brutal man who nevertheless had the leadership and management skills to oversee what would become a billion-dollar business. By the early 1950s, it was simply impossible to be a major figure in crime in New England and not have to deal with Patriarca. Big-time gamblers needed his race wire or layoff bank, and career armed robbers had to go through him to launder money or goods.

The man Patriarca replaced as New England don, Filippo "Phil" Buccola, was not as suited to make the leap from prohibition to big-time racketeering. He was a Sicilian who ran the North End with a firm, even hand and was tough enough to protect his turf. In fact, he was believed to have been forced to flee from vengeful rivals in Sicily after a murder in Palermo, arriving in Boston with impressive credentials and persuasive old-world ties. But he just didn't have it in him to expand, to push for new business and territory, knowing that the one who reached too far for dominance in Boston was the one who got killed. Like Frankie Wallace.

When Buccola's name appeared in the Boston newspapers—and it wasn't often—he was referred to as a local sportsman, a boxing manager and promoter who also owned racehorses. He showed up on the back pages for contesting charges of tax fraud and nonpayment dating back to the 1920s. And, when it didn't make any difference, he was named as the one-time head of the New England Mafia by Cosa Nostra turn-

coat, Joseph Valachi, who testified before Congress in
1963. The newspapers said Buccola had retired to Italy.
Close enough. He had been back in Sicily for a decade,
running a chicken farm outside of Palermo with baby
chicks imported from New Hampshire. The life suited
him, and over the decades (until his death in 1987 at
the age of 101) he kept his hand in Boston's underworld,
sponsoring a few of the Sicilians who came to the United
States in the mid-1980s, a secret influx that replenished
the Mafia's decimated ranks with troops who avoided
the flashy wiseguy life in favor of a work ethic and drug
profits. In many ways, they became just like the de-
pendable, loyal soldiers that arrived as immigrants when
Buccola first started out in Boston at the dawn of Prohibition.

Born in Palermo, Buccola was an educated man and
an adventurer who attended the Universita degli Studi
in Palermo and another school in Switzerland and who
traveled to Russia before the Revolution. After he came
to the United States in 1920, he had a meteoric rise,
something that was undoubtedly prearranged before he
left Sicily.

His timing could not have been better. He was an
experienced leader arriving at the age of 34 on the eve
of Prohibition from a relatively well-off Sicilian family.
He was head man within a few years and was formally
sanctioned as head of the New England Mafia by the
newly formed Luciano Commission in 1932, according
to an FBI summary of a bugged conversation in Patriarca's office. Most of the other Mafia leaders, in contrast,
had immigrated as much younger men from impov-
erished families and came up through the ranks. It also
seemed that the avuncular Buccola treated his power
in the comfortable way of someone who was used to

it, lacking the insecurity of most of his peers who had to fight or crawl for it.

Buccola's ostensible business was promoting boxing matches and his dream was to manage an Italian to a world championship. The closest he came was having one of his fighters, Odonne Piazzo, fight unsuccessfully for the middleweight title in 1932. Indeed, the mobsters of that era were all tied up in the Boston boxing scene, with Buccola and Charles "King" Solomon, the head of the Jewish bootlegging and nightclub scene, both having stables of fighters. They were hands-on managers who frequently were in the corners when their fighters were in the ring. They not only shared an avid interest, they had the same partner in some fight deals—an Irishman to even out the ethnic triumverate of the day. Daniel Carroll of South Boston shared an office on School Street with Buccola. Carroll was also so close to Solomon that he would race to Boston City Hospital after Solomon had been fatally shot in a speakeasy in 1933.

No one knows for sure, but old hands in the North End and some in law enforcement today say Solomon was murdered because he openly denigrated Italians and was moving to cut them out of the bootlegging— or cheat them of the hard-won prerogatives gained by the Gustin Gang ambush. Solomon was also about to go to trial on bootlegging charges, something that made his various partners nervous about their own vulnerability. But, at the time, Boston police dismissed the murder as a random killing done by down-and-out Irish free-lancers who were simply after the big wad of cash Solomon always carried. Whatever the reason, it left Buccola undisputed champion.

When Solomon was murdered, the only measure of

his wealth on paper was an indictment for operating a $14 million rum-running network. He was a period piece, a character from a gangster movie to the very end, railing at the "dirty rats" who shot him, as he fell on a nightclub table. He was everything Buccola was not. He was flashy, an expensive dresser with an expansive smile. He had swarthy good looks and was frequently seen with showgirls at night clubs, including the Cocoanut Grove, which he owned and which would be gutted in 1942 by Boston's worst fire disaster.

If the Solomon hit came out of the North End—and most police who have worked the Boston Mafia shift think it did—then it showed Lombardo had learned a lesson in the year that elapsed after the Gustin Gang ambush: no direct participation. When Maranzano, the boss of bosses, was killed in September of 1931, Luciano had used four Jewish gangsters to do the job. "King" Solomon was killed by a 28-year-old petty thief named James P. "Skeets" Coyne, who fired three shots after five accomplices crashed into each other to get out of the Cotton Club speakeasy at four in the morning. There were no Italians and none of the group was directly affiliated with Irish gangs.

The shooting took place after Solomon and two dancers from his club joined the Cocoanut Grove bandleader for an early-morning jazz jam with black musicians in Roxbury. Solomon arrived at about three in the morning of January 24, 1933, and danced twice with one of the women before he had the waitress break a $50 bill. Across the dance floor were six Irish toughs in a booth, nursing drinks. After Solomon had been there an hour, one of the men went to his table and told him a friend wanted to see him in the men's room.

The next scene is from a James Cagney movie. According to the trial testimony, when Solomon got up and headed for the men's room, four of the men followed him, one of them saying, "Keep going, we've got you covered," as they got to the lavatory door. A waitress testified that when she was in the adjoining kitchen to pick up an order, she heard Solomon protest through the wall: "You've got the money. What more do you want?" Coyne replied "You've been asking for this," followed by three shots. The four men inside raced to a waiting car. Coyne, apprehended in Indiana a year later, was sentenced to ten to twenty years after he pleaded guilty to manslaughter. The rest were acquitted of robbery and murder charges.

The Solomon and Gustin Gang murders were the types of solutions that would later become a matter of routine for Patriarca. Avaricious rivals and insubordinate minions were ordered killed with brisk "do it" commands. It happened a dozen times a year. But in Boston of the 1930s, such drastic action by the Mafia was rare. It came only after a dire threat to take something away from the Italians; it was never used to grab something new. Boston became a city where the Mafia gradually gained the upper hand but not total control.

By several accounts, Buccola was a savvy man who never overplayed his hand or stayed too long in the game. He was flexible as long as you didn't push him in a corner. He wasn't in the fight game for nothing, but he also had a temperament that meshed with his time and place. Buccola even looked the part. He wore suits and bow ties and rimless glasses, giving him a country doctor appearance. He was not hard to distinguish from his dark, glowering peers and is remembered, perhaps through the shimmer of time, as the last of the dignified dons. He gets the ultimate accolade: "A man you could talk to."

One North End operative used Buccola as a metaphor for the days of his youth when there was some gentility in the process, the right mix of magnanimity and firmness. Buccola was the Don of the Second Chance who said go and sin no more. You take that corner to take bets and you get this corner to sell your after-hours pints. The operative viewed Buccola as a patient, slightly weary man of goodwill whose demeanor still let you know he was not to be crossed. An old friend recalls him simply as The Great White Father.

Surprisingly, Buccola never lived in the North End, although he preferred to hold court there, usually at the Florentine Café at the corner of Hanover and Prince streets, where he was often seen with Lombardo. Buccola lived in apartments around Boston until he married an Irish nurse named Rose Hogan who came from Charlestown and worked at a local hospital. They moved to Newton Center in 1934 and had a live-in maid. The couple's last ten years in Boston were spent in an apartment on Beacon Street, just outside of Kenmore Square. Records indicate they left Boston in 1954. This is also the year the FBI says Patriarca formally took over the New England family.

He would return at least one more time on Mafia business, coming back in 1957, shortly before the national commission meeting in upper New York State turned into a fiasco when a police raid forced scores of mafiosi to flee on foot through the woods near the small town of Apalachin. The Boston representative, Frank Cucchiara, was there with a message given him by Buccola from founding father Lucky Luciano, who had been living in Italy since being deported at the end of World War II. Before Buccola flew to Boston, federal agents claim that he and Luciano had conferred in Rome about the commission meeting, which had been called in part to sanction Genovese's control of Luciano's old family.

Buccola had intermittent influence in Boston over the following decades. Most recently, he had sponsored some Sicilian Mafia members who came to Boston in the mid-1980s to help shore up the depleted middle level of the mob arriving with the same kind of entrée that had helped Buccola get his start sixty-five years before.

A North End friend, who has visited Buccola in Sicily several times, last saw him in the mid-1980s. Buccola had had breathing difficulties but had been in otherwise good health, even in his late nineties. The friend said Buccola always spoke fondly of Boston, especially its hospital care, noting that his wife returned for an eye operation in the 1960s. She died in Palermo in the early 1970s.

It was Rose, the friend said, who urged Buccola to return home to a summer house that had been built after World War II. When he left, he was sixty-eight years old, had no children, and saw the Mafia attracting more and more national attention from congressional investigators. Buccola may have seen the handwriting on the wall before any of them, perhaps sensing danger in the rapid rise of ruthless men such as Patriarca and Angiulo. In any event, he decided it was time to go.

The house he had built was a six-room villa in a small section of Palermo known as Villagio Ruffini at Piazza Marie Consultirce. It was on a five-acre lemon tree grove and a bigger home than he had asked for because the money he had sent to build it went so far in Sicily.

He replaced the lemon trees with ten chicken coops, gradually building a small business into a major one, starting at a time when the only chickens you could find in Sicily were scrawny ones pecking away in backyards. He added an incubator building and then a slaughterhouse in the 1960s, using seven small vans to deliver eggs and chicken parts to restaurants and retail stores. A store he started in the seventies with the son of a niece expanded into a small supermarket. He never had to borrow money from a bank.

The old friend, who has profited from Boston real estate, kidded Buccola about not taking his advice to invest in property, not even buying his own home in the United States. Buccola was a renter. "I'd tell him," the friend said, "well, they just sold your old apartment building on Beacon Street for a million dollars." He said Buccola had just laughed and gestured toward his chicken farm as evidence of his wise use of money.

On the last visit before his death, Buccola had asked his old friend about the trouble the Mafia was having in Boston with federal prosecutors. Someone got careless, he was told. Buccola simply nodded, saying nothing more about it, much like an accomplished old ball player who is still interested in the game but only as an elusive memory.

3

THE RISE OF GENNARO ANGIULO

Like most Mafia leaders, Raymond L. S. Patriarca faltered when he was asked what he did for a living. He blustered about being a small businessman who was maligned by press and police, a scapegoat kicked around Rhode Island for twenty years. But he could never tell you what it was he did to make money.

When he was pressed about his résumé at a congressional hearing into organized crime, Patriarca sputtered and digressed. The subcommittee counsel zeroed in again. Could you tell us, Mr. Patriarca, what jobs you held as a young man? At the 1959 hearing, Patriarca finally said he had no job from 1932 until 1944, which was true enough if you agree that armed robber, hijacker, and prisoner are not bona fide occupations. He added that in 1944—the year he got out of jail for robberies in Massachusetts—he went to work as a counterman in a small Providence restaurant. After a year at that job, Patriarca said, "I think I played the horses until 1950." After he stopped playing the horses, he also happened to become the Godfather of New England and to select a fast-talking numbers man from Boston as his sottocapo, or underboss.

Patriarca smiled on Gennaro Angiulo of the North End after Angiulo trekked to Providence with an envelope full of "tribute" money, seeking the privilege of running the Mafia gambling franchise in Boston, an untapped reservoir that had never come close to its potential. Patriarca quickly saw that Angiulo was the pepper pot needed to shake Boston out of its backwater doldrums. They would go on to be the odd couple of the New England underworld for nearly three decades, with Patriarca the low-key company man and mediator and Angiulo the flamboyant provocateur out for himself.

The partnership brought Boston's Mafia to a new vista. It became organized and opportunistic, evolving into the most successful money-making operation of its size in the country. Although Boston's diverse underworld factions were too entrenched for Angiulo to subdue, he was able—with Patriarca's help—to gain financial primacy over the rabid rivals that made up the city's tumultuous crime network. Boston became the Wall Street of New England.

One thing was clear from the start: no Ray, no Jerry. Angiulo's power would always rest on his access to Patriarca. And his access came down to cash. The Patriarca-Angiulo alliance was strictly financial, a matter of money talking. Angiulo's power base was rooted in Patriarca's monopoly over the race-results wire and the numbers layoff that afforded bookies an insurance policy against big losses. An abrasive man, Angiulo was not particularly liked or respected. But he had Raymond—as long as Boston gambling money kept flowing down to Federal Hill in Providence.

Even before he formally petitioned Patriarca for the job, Angiulo had already been proving himself, instilling a system into what had been a bad blend of amorphous gambling territories and little accountability. Once he began making biweekly deliveries to Providence, Angiulo would quickly jump ahead of enforcers with more seniority and more scalps on their belts. In fact, Angiulo had no scalps, never having "earned his bones," or killed a man to become a "made" Mafia member. It was something that would always hurt him with his peers. Money—not muscle—got him baptized into La Cosa Nostra.

Patriarca was the personification of both sides of the Mafia equation for success: He had the brawn and brain to run the equivalent of a multinational corporation with finesse and ruthlessness. He had come up the hard way, a Horatio Alger story without a shred of glamour or nobility to it, but a remarkable rise nonetheless.

Born in Worcester in 1908 to immigrant parents, he escaped from a local jail in Massachusetts when he was twenty, bought his way out of prison when he was thirty, and was heir apparent to the don of New England when he was forty. The soldiers and associates soon learned that Patriarca was more than just resourceful, he was also utterly ruthless when he had to be. Cross him and he would have you killed—not ostracized or roughed up, but dead in a gravel pit or car trunk.

His rise was similar to many of the New York City dons of the same era; they were born in the United States to parents from hardscrabble villages in Sicily or southern Italy who left around the turn of the century because there was little food and no work. As Patriarca told the Senate subcommittee, when he was seventeen and his father Eleuterio had just died, he "drifted a little." Over the next half century, he was arrested or indicted twenty-eight times, convicted seven times, and incarcerated four times, serving a total of 11 years, more than half of it on a murder conspiracy charge late in his life. He was plagued by indictments on old capital crimes right up until his death, at 76, in 1984. He was fatally stricken at the apartment of a woman friend who sold real estate in Providence.

After getting off the front line of crime after World War II, he became a Godfather to the core, with nothing too minor for his consideration if it involved a suppli-cant who would remember the favor when the time came. For all his sinister looks and sullen ways, Pa-triarca had a deft sense of public relations. Despite his hostile appearance, he was urbane compared to other top mobsters. Unlike Angiulo, he had a polished way with the police and public. While he ducked the press, he always had a smile and wave for neighbors on his nightly walk and police who cruised by his office. An-giulo used to glare and spit on the sidewalk when he saw most policemen.

Patriarca had the paradoxical personality of the most feared leaders: friendly but deadly. He was so smooth and correct in his personal dealings that people forgot how vicious he really was. His snap decisions on death contracts were one of the reasons he could drive home all alone at the same time every day without fear for his safety.

On matters Angiulo would have sneered at, people felt free to petition Patriarca. He regularly sorted out domestic and family disputes in his Providence office, patching up such things as a feud between two brothers that was ruining their local auto body business. In another example, he showed sensitive judgment by declining to order a friend's daughter home to her father after he determined she was a divorced woman who was old enough to be on her own. The rest of the time he ran a billion-dollar business.

Except for the occasional supplicant, the daily agenda was made up of a parade of the faithful bearing tithes —cold cash for the middle drawer in the dirty back room of a cigarette vending-machine business in a run-down section of Providence. It could be the receipts from a wholly owned subsidiary or the rent from a franchise. In a complex maze of interests, he completely controlled some markets, especially those involving gambling, loansharking, and pornography, and dabbled in others such as truck hijacking and drug traffic in which free-lancers negotiated fees to do business. As a member of the ruling Mafia commission in New York, he also had some national investments, holding hidden interests in two Las Vegas casinos and pieces of deals in Florida and Philadelphia.

By the 1960s, Patriarca had come light years from his first encounter with notoriety—an egregious prison pardon in 1938 that became a resounding political blunder, culminating in the impeachment of a Massachusetts Governor's Councilor. Patriarca was pardoned for armed robbery after serving less than three months of a three-year sentence, setting off a maelstrom that doomed a crusty caricature of corruption, Councilor Daniel Coakley. When Patriarca received the pardon, he appeared to be just another armed robber and three-time loser. In fact, he was a streamlined comer in the Mafia whose street smarts and toughness had made him a favorite in New York, mostly with major figures in the Genovese and Profaci families. He was their "can do" man in New England.

Over the years, Patriarca appeared most involved in the affairs of the Profaci family in South Brooklyn, which was badly shaken in the 1960s by an insurrection that climaxed with the assassination of family leader Joseph Colombo in 1971. One of Patriarca's top assistants in Rhode Island had been sent to New York to help shore up the Colombo regime—to no avail. The New York connection in Providence was further cemented by Patriarca's number two man, Henry Tameleo, who was a veteran of the Bonnano family from Brooklyn.

Patriarca's frequent contact with Genovese family leaders seems to have been over jurisdictional matters, with New England divided along the Connecticut River. The Genovese family controlled such major cities as Hartford, Springfield, and Albany, while Patriarca had most of Worcester and exclusive control in Boston, Revere, and Maine.

Patriarca's ascendency in New England was formalized in 1944 when, recently released from jail in Massachusetts, he was transferred to Buccola's regime as heir apparent. By 1950, he had eclipsed Buccola, who was in semi-retirement before leaving the United States for good in 1954.

Patriarca's trademark would be murder and political influence. As later FBI digests would show from a secret bug in his office from 1962 to 1965, his political contributions and payoffs gave him a sub rosa entrée with governors, legislators, and judges in Rhode Island and Massachusetts.

Patriarca was as different from the benign Buccola

as Lenny Bruce from Jack Benny. The changes in pace and tone he brought were profound. The axis would tilt toward Providence forever more. Of course, he had advantages that Buccola never did—strong New York connections and a small, largely Italian city as his base. By the mid-1950s, nothing east of the Connecticut River moved without his curt okay.

The final obstacle to absolute power for Patriarca was eliminated with the shooting death in 1952 of the only real rival left—the tough and defiant Carlton O'Brien of Providence, who was a major bootlegging figure along with Charles "King" Solomon of Boston. Like most of the rum-running hierarchy, O'Brien moved into gambling during the Depression and World War II, eventually controlling the invaluable race-results wire and several betting parlors. When he died of two shotgun blasts in the early morning hours, Patriarca had a clear field—and exclusive control of the wire. Mafia control of the wire meant more money for the coffers, as winners bet again when they get fast results.

Unlike Buccola, who seems to have started at the top, arriving from Sicily in 1920 and taking the reins quickly, Patriarca had paid his dues. His inestimable respect came from the way he had proved his mettle.

Not so with Jerry Angiulo. While both he and Patriarca shared the same background of poor immigrant parents from southern Italy who had raised their children in hand-to-mouth households, Angiulo was a diminutive youth who would make it on stealth rather than strength.

When Angiulo returned from Navy duty in 1947 at the age of twenty-eight, he was just another guy driving a delivery truck on the streets of the North End, one of six sons of Caesar and Giovannina Angiulo. They had come over from small towns in southern Italy just after the turn of the century, meeting and marrying in the North End, then moving into an apartment on Prince Street in 1915.

The Angiulos lived in a sparse household on a tightly packed, narrow street of five-story brick tenements, but the family was no worse off than its blue-collar neighbors. They all nudged the poverty line. The subsistence life, however, left Angiulo with a permanent obsession with money. Decades later, when he was reminiscing with his top capo de regime, Larry Zannino, shortly after they worked out the details on murdering a malcontent, Angiulo said, "When you were born broke like all of us were, you know, money becomes very important."

It was a rare understatement. Throughout his career, the pint-size Angiulo was a cunning man obsessed with the power and pleasure of money. It was his elixir, the core of his life. His power to command payments was primordial. No excuse was good enough, no punishment too severe, for it would be money that would transform his crowded, Spartan home on Prince Street into headquarters for the Mafia, not far from the corner café where Buccola often had held court and from the office building where seven mafiosi had gunned down the leader of the Gustin Gang from South Boston.

Angiulo was his mother's son; he inherited her nimble mind and sharp tongue as well as the name of her father. Giovannina Angiulo was an inveterate card player who would take on all comers in the neighborhood while she ran the family grocery store with one hand. In later years, when the neighbors kowtowed to all her sons, she zoomed up Prince Street in a Cadillac and just dumped it in the middle of the road, bustling into the family home known as the Dog House. Flunkies ran out to park the car by a curb.

Having grown up around the corner from the Gustin Gang ambush site, Angiulo saw how the insularity of his neighborhood made it a place where the mob always felt safe, where tobacco stores, groceries, and funeral parlors were usually fronts for gambling operations where loans could be had and bets put down. He saw retail shops run from the backs of trucks and half-pints for sale in doorways after the bars closed. Strangers were always noticed immediately on these streets, the object of an informal house-to-house surveillance. It was a perverted crime watch, a reverse alarm system.

Policemen were negotiable hazards in such a place, potential allies for a price. Some of the men who broke the rules were killed and, after the grisly deaths, denounced on the street as dirty bastards who deserved it. It was a paranoid and violent world that was also a perfect breeding ground for a prospective Mafia leader.

Angiulo is remembered by high school classmates as a mischievous, outspoken teenager who loved an audience and who had a cutting edge to his humor. He made fun of certain kids to make the other kids laugh. One classmate, who was in his homeroom at Boston English High, recalled Angiulo as an extrovert who "wouldn't hesitate to get out of the chair and say something to the teacher." The yearbook lists his ambition as "criminal lawyer." The classmate said, "Well, he got halfway there . . ."

After the Navy, where Angiulo won some battle awards in World War II duty in the Pacific, he found his way quickly into the North End's gambling network. He drove a truck days and worked in Consigliere

Joe Lombardo's "horse room" at night, taking bets and saving his money, biding his time.

According to some gamblers on the fringe, Angiulo's ambition got the best of him in the late 1940s when he was taking in bets for the Lombardo operation. Some of the money failed to turn up and Angiulo had to go on the lam for a while until his parents made good for it. When all was forgiven and Angiulo could walk along Prince Street again with impunity, he immediately began figuring the angles, using the equivalent of insider trading to parlay his knowledge of fixed horse races into a quick bankroll. He graduated from the horse room to the job of runner for bookies in Roxbury and the North End. He would need some luck, but he was on his way.

At the same time, about four miles away, a shy, soft-spoken boy named Edward Quinn, who would spend much of his adult life as an FBI agent in pursuit of Angiulo, was a first-grader at St. Margaret's elementary school in Dorchester, near Edward Everett Square. It was an Irish neighborhood of triple-decker apartment houses with driveways and backyards, giving it an almost rural flavor compared with the jam-packed five-story tenements and sunless streets of the North End.

Quinn's father, Arthur, a gentle, dignified man who was a Boston policeman for thirty-eight years, was always home for supper at 5:30, eschewing the barroom stop on the way home for a few drinks with the boys. He liked his beer but he liked it at home. It was a strongly Irish Catholic family that did things together. Arthur never missed a basketball game, even though it was only church league stuff. Sometimes he was the only parent in the gym. There was not enough money for two weeks at Cape Cod in the summer, so they would go to Nantasket beach outside of Boston for the day or make the hour-long walk to Malibu Beach in Savin Hill, carrying their beach chairs. It was not a big thing, but when Ed Quinn was in grammar school, he was always vaguely aware that his father was a policeman. It pleased him.

But to Angiulo, the only good Irish cop was the antithesis of Arthur Quinn, the one he could put in his back pocket, the one who would take the money and look the other way when there was a crap shoot, bar-booth game, numbers office, or after-hours drinking spot in his precinct. Angiulo and his brothers would know such men and prey on their weaknesses for money, alcohol, and, occasionally, women.

The ever-watchful Angiulo got his chance for the big time because of the fitful presidential ambitions of a somewhat obscure U.S. senator from Tennessee, Estes Kefauver, who began seeking a national audience by taking on organized crime in televised hearings in 1950. It was the first real, hard look at the Mafia on a national level and it terrified old-timers such as Buccola and Lombardo, who saw the klieg lights as the end of their subterranean world. They overreacted to the periodic announcement of Kefauver hearings in Boston—hearings that were scheduled but never took place. Lombardo ordered the gambling in town shut down and Buccola, at his wife's behest, retired to Sicily by 1954.

Ironically, the ultimate impact of the Kefauver scare was to make the New England Mafia stronger. To some extent, it pushed aside the old leadership, leaving Pa-

triarca firmly at the helm and giving Angiulo the opportunity to take gambling in Boston out of the petty
cash category and into the big time.

Previously, Angiulo and his brothers had been run-
ners for bookies who took bets almost as an avocation.
They usually combined it with some other business:
a restaurant, pawn shop, or candy store. Angiulo became the centripetal force that brought the disparate
elements together. He made gambling a full-time,
streamlined business.

In 1950, when Lombardo ordered all Mafia and independent books to shut down, or operate without a
central layoff bank and no police protection, Angiulo
went to him with a simple proposition: Let me run
your books and take the fall if there's trouble. J.L. gave
him the go-ahead. The Kefauver plague passed when
the congressional hearings focused on bigger fish in
more established cities such as New York and Chicago,
giving Boston an inadvertent boost.

But the Lombardo shut-down edict was a double-
edged sword to the "independents," or those bookies
who were loosely affiliated with the Mafia. They paid
tribute to do business in exchange for not having to
worry much about mob shakedowns or police raids.
During the Kefauver threat, they lost some of Lombardo's protection but gained even more freedom to
operate. All that ended with Angiulo. He became the
bane of the independents, a scheming dictator always
looking for ways to squeeze them for more money. His
approach to bookies was that they operated at his suf-
ferance. They had to pay him "rent" for their tele-
phones and a percentage of the take or he'd have the
phones yanked off the wall. The old regime's philos-

ophy was much more live and let live—as long as you didn't cheat.

Angiulo was cunning and insatiable, a master at setting himself up as the arbiter of disputes he caused. He sent thugs around demanding more of a cut from independents and then commiserated with the frantic bookies when they came looking for justice from the underboss. With studied munificence, he would tell the petitioners he would call off the dogs, that it must be a mistake. But, do me a favor, he would say, just pay a little more so no one will lose face.

Lombardo had been tough but straightforward, treating underlings with a modicum of respect. Decades later, a bookie would remember Lombardo slapping one of his men for abusing the waiters at his restaurant in the North End. The soldiers were amusing themselves just for the macho hell of it and Lombardo put an end to it. "I can get along without you coming in here," he told the soldier, "but I can't without my waiters." Angiulo never learned the value of loyalty and never had the restraint of true leadership. It would hurt him in the end.

But in the post-Kefauver era, Angiulo moved quickly to merge his gains into a network, picking up the business of some dropouts and slowly encroaching on Irish, Italian, and Jewish independents. It appeared he pacified Lombardo by making him more money at less risk by steadily increasing business. Through some basic management and hard work, the amorphous numbers and horse-betting operations in Boston coalesced into a whole. One of Angiulo's innovations was ingenious in its simplicity: He turned casual bettors into small-time bookies by offering them a quarter back on each dollar bet they placed, providing an incentive to collect and deliver bets to a central spot for reimbursement. Angiulo was a creative hands-on manager and gambling was his only active business until he opened a lounge in Boston's adult entertainment district, the Combat Zone, in 1961. He ran gambling offices in person and there was always an Angiulo brother there when money was to be counted.

The older Mafia leaders never really understood the intricacies of the numbers business, but Jerry and his younger brother Frank did. They figured out ways to monitor heavy betting on certain numbers and how best to lay off bets to avoid rare big payouts in the longshot number lottery that was based on parimutuel handles from certain racetracks.

Angiulo also could adjust to adversity. In the late 1950s, when a series of police raids occurred around afternoon collection time, rather than shut down for a while as Lombardo would have done, he moved back the "turn-in" time to midnight. He frequently ran the operation until four in the morning.

While he could be engaging when it suited him, Angiulo was usually intemperate and cutting, a leader remembered by the rank and file as a bully who ranted and raved, who shouted "you understand American?" when he was through talking and just wanted the job done. One associate was overheard on an FBI wiretap saying that he never really talked to Angiulo because he was always yelling and never listening.

The closest thing the family had to a velvet glove was Nicolo Angiulo, the first-born son who was three years older than Jerry. He was the family fixer, even from the early days, the one who showed up at the courthouse when a soldier or associate was being arraigned or sentenced. A former federal official who pursued the Angiulos for years viewed Nick as the keeper of the police payment "pad" because "he got results." Nick became the consigliere and Jerry gave him a wide berth.

But business expansion was Jerry Angiulo's exclusive purview. In addition to being the master of the "numbers," he ran two other betting operations. At night, he and his brothers had a boiler room–type system in the North End that handled dog-race betting, with about fifteen men taking bets on eight races at fifty cents a race. His younger brother Danny would bring the workers sandwiches and pay them from a roll of half-dollars. The Angiulos had a similar operation during the day for horse races. All told, the brothers had about fifty office workers taking different kinds of bets. Lombardo, now richer with less work, was in semi-retirement, more concerned with his horse farm in Framingham than the numbers business in Boston.

By the late 1950s, one last hurdle remained for Angiulo. Though he was a born bookmaker who had hustled Boston into a sensible system, he was still stuck with free-lancer status. He was not a so-called Friend of Ours, a Mafia member. As such, he was fair game for made members short on cash. Leg-breakers such as Larry Zannino, a Patriarca favorite, began to prey upon the vulnerable Angiulo, shaking him down regularly, even roughing him up when he refused to pay.

The Angiulo solution, according to police and underworld accounts, was to stuff $50,000 in cash in an envelope and bring it down to Patriarca in Providence, promising him at least $100,000 a year for the right to run Boston. With a successful track record and cash on the table, Angiulo prevailed. They struck a deal. Patriarca made a call to Boston, perhaps calling off a dog he had put on the hunt in the first place. Zannino, who had had up to two hundred loan sharks working for him, became an obsequious enforcer for Angiulo after they had been competitors, crisscrossing each other in Boston's low-rent district, the South End, both chasing the same people for money. Angiulo controlled the Lebanese bookies in the area and they and their customers were loan-shark customers of Zannino. For starters, Raymond's imprimatur meant Angiulo would get the South End payments first instead of last. And paying up was the name of the game. By the early 1960s, Boston's underworld had become so rabid that it seldom "stopped the clock" on debtors who were bled dry, by letting them pay just principal and not interest. Other cities stopped short of killing those hopelessly behind on the theory that a dead man can't pay. Not in Boston. At least in this one area, the Mafia and Irish gangs worked in symbiotic harmony. Mafiosi lent surplus gambling money to Irish hoodlums for 1 to 2 percent a week and they, in turn, put it "on the street" at 3 to 4 percent a week. Law enforcement estimated that the victims of two out of every three murders or maimings in Greater Boston were people unable to keep up with debt services of up to 400 percent a year.

Although it is unclear exactly when Angiulo got "baptized" as a member of La Cosa Nostra, it appears to have been sometime before he turned 40. Angiulo joined Patriarca at a meeting in New York with Vito Genovese, the Ivan the Terrible of the national Mafia, not long before Genovese went off to jail for good in 1959. The New York luncheon meeting would have definitely been a members-only affair. It was a daunting moment for Angiulo, who was making his first trip to the big leagues. Genovese was the titular overseer of New England and Angiulo had to fork over some of the riches recently extracted from the Irish gangs in Boston, simply as tribute to the dominant don of the day. Although it was the kind of thing he demanded for himself routinely, he didn't like it a bit.

Angiulo recalled the meeting with angst in a conversation secretly recorded by the FBI in his Prince Street office in 1981. He was still tremulous over an incident more than two decades old. "Vito looked at me," he told a visitor about the request for tribute, which had left the normally loquacious Angiulo tongue-tied. "It'll be done, Vito," was all he could say. The memory of having to be docile and to give up money still grated. "Right now I got a fucking knot in my stomach," he said to the visitor.

It's likely his searing experience with Genovese prompted him to tell Patriarca, when they were ruminating about Mafia family history one day in 1963, that it was better to have a small, manageable family like theirs than the tangled branches down in New York City. He sounded the rube. But, even if he didn't know it, he was lucky to be invited to New York. He was in his thirties, the head of Boston gambling, rubbing elbows with Patriarca and Genovese and thirty other high-level mobsters in a New York restaurant. Ten years earlier, he had been on the lam, with Joe Lombardo's men looking for him.

By 1961, Angiulo had extensive investments in real estate, owned a small hospital in Boston, and had interests in two car dealerships in Lynn and a country club in Worcester County. He had two business addresses, adding his new Combat Zone lounge to the longstanding Prince Street office. He named the lounge

Jay's after himself and used a basement room there as an office and apartment for most of the 1960s. His typical day was a whirlwind that began after noontime, when he left his Medford home, where he lived with his wife, Anna, and two children. He commuted the fifteen miles south to Boston, starting the day on Prince Street, moving on to Jay's Lounge around supper time, and heading home at two or three in the morning.

Once sanctioned by Patriarca, he had moved strongly against the independent bookies, setting up a system in which Mafia enforcers were assigned to bookies, collecting half their receipts as the price of letting them operate and, in turn, giving half to Angiulo, who gave half to Patriarca.

About a year after Angiulo opened Jay's Lounge, the downstairs office was illegally bugged by the FBI, which was racing to get intelligence on the the Mafia in Boston and other major cities. Notoriety was not far behind. In 1963, the cocky street kid was publicly identified in congressional hearings as Patriarca's underboss. Neighbors were asked by reporters about the Angiulos, but were told that they kept to themselves, with Jerry a virtual phantom, a ghostly face in a Cadillac that flashed by children walking home from school. No one ever saw him come home at night.

Just as Angiulo began dividing his time between the Combat Zone and Prince Street, Ed Quinn began Boston College as a self-effacing economics major who was vaguely interested in a business career. He went there on a scholarship he won from the Wianno Country Club on Cape Cod, where he had caddied for three summers. The scholarship paid half of the $800 annual tuition and he needed every cent of it. Quinn had a strong if inchoate sense of duty and was drawn to the military; his interest was heightened by letters from his older sister Elizabeth, an Air Force lieutenant stationed in Paris. He signed up with the Marines his junior year and went to Quantico training camp that summer, graduating from college in 1963 as a second lieutenant. There were stories in the local papers about the three lieutenants in one family, with his father being one of the commanders at Division Three in Mattapan.

Ed Quinn's second stop in the Marines was at Da Nang in Vietnam, and though it was early in the fighting—1963–64—he saw a lot of action as part of a helicopter squad ferrying South Vietnamese troops to battle. On his first day there, twelve men in his company were killed. He thought more about getting out alive than what he would do in civilian life.

While Quinn was stationed in Da Nang, the FBI in Boston was frantically trying to catch up with Angiulo, marching to new directions from Attorney General Robert F. Kennedy that forced J. Edgar Hoover to drop his obsession with Communist infiltrators in favor of rooting out Kennedy's Enemy Within. They put illegal bugs in Patriarca's office in Providence and Jay's Lounge in Boston just to find out where things stood and who was who. They found Angiulo was far more than just one of Boston's bigger bookies: He was the major moneymaker who fed the coffers in Providence and grabbed a piece of everything that moved in Greater Boston.

The Patriarca bug told them as much about Angiulo as any of the New England Mafia figures, especially about his constant squabbles with rivals and his connections with corrupt policemen in the Boston department and the Massachusetts state police. But, because the tap was illegal and for intelligence gathering only, it gave them leads and not evidence. The best the FBI could do with it was devise a careful game plan with the certain knowledge it was up against a wily foe.

The tap revealed that the one town Angiulo couldn't crack was Revere, the Dodge City of the East, a place of endless feuds long dominated by a bootlegger and gambler named Louis Fox, who had dealt directly with Patriarca from the beginning. Angiulo had put Boston gambling under tighter centralized control, but was never able to absorb the fiercely anarchical frontier city of Revere, a mad violent vortex that had been half Jewish bookies and half Italian since the end of Prohibition.

When Fox died in 1963, Angiulo tried to muscle in —but ran headlong into hard-nosed Phil Gallo, the deputy police chief who, to underline the inimitable nature of Revere, was both a police officer and heir to Fox's empire. Gallo was a man of legendary chutzpah who chased bikers out of town like the marshals of the Wild West banished gunslingers. He would ask the motley crew whether it would like to clear out before or after the fire he was expecting in their modest quarters. During their feud over Angiulo's encroachment, Jerry's Cadillac was shot up one morning on Huntington Avenue, where Angiulo owned some property and was staying with his girlfriend, Barbara Lombard (she became his common-law wife after his 1963 divorce).

Angiulo could never crack Revere because mobsters there had direct access to Patriarca, who was apparently satisfied with his cut from Revere and felt some obligation to old allies in the city. Angiulo would have to make do with Boston and the slow, steady expansion against its indigenous Irish gangs and other, more vulnerable "independents."

According to FBI digests of the Patriarca bug, Angiulo had much more success in cultivating high-level police contacts than in taming Revere mafiosi. The bug laid bare the vital role of political corruption in protecting the varied interests of the New England Mafia. It was a fragile two-tiered system built on personal rather than institutional relationships.

Patriarca's contacts were primarily at a level high enough for him to influence legislation and get favorable treatment from courts for his troops. He was on a first-name basis with high Rhode Island officials, had fast access to a handful of judges in Rhode Island, Massachusetts, and New York, and dealt regularly with politicians in Massachusetts and Rhode Island on legislation or in using them to make overtures to parole boards.

Yet over the life of the bug, which was in his office from 1962 to 1965, the political contacts didn't yield Patriarca many tangible results. He worked mightily to get extra racing dates for a Massachusetts track he and others had a hidden interest in, even putting $225,000 in an escrow account for payment to legislators when the deal was signed by the governor—but the legislation was just too flagrant to fly. He also persistently sought the early release of his favorite tough guy, Zannino, but Massachusetts prosecutors put too much heat on the parole board to get that done, even with the winsome, redoubtable governor's councilor,

Patrick "Sonny" McDonough, on the case. Patriarca and McDonough had a secret meeting in Boston on the parole issue to no avail.

In Boston, the lower tier of authority belonged to Angiulo, where he followed the maxim that all politics is local. He cultivated Boston police wherever he could with the limited objective of protecting his gambling networks from raids that cost him money and manpower.

Building on traditional access to Boston police, Angiulo had strengthened the network greatly in a short time. A little over a decade after Lombardo gave him a half-hearted go-ahead to run some Boston gambling while the heat was on, Angiulo's police pad included Carl Larson, a major in the state police, and Herbert Mulloney, a high-ranking officer in the Boston police department. One of the FBI summaries had Angiulo moaning about Mulloney returning a $500 Christmas envelope to an East Boston mobster as insufficient funds. Angiulo reported the hold-out got Mulloney $1,000, along with $2,500 he had already received from the North End. Mulloney worked in the department for ten more years, retiring in 1973 to become a security consultant. He died in 1985. Unlike Larson, there were not widespread suspicions about Mulloney while he was on the force. He was viewed by state police as an effective cop who happened to be soft on gambling.

Major Larson was a different proposition. He sought Angiulo out as his Revere contretemps became known in police circles through informants. Larson apparently saw it as a chance to increase his retainer, agreeing to tip Angiulo about pending state police raids there. Angiulo said Larson called his brother Nicolo with the proposition and that Jerry jumped at it, telling Patriarca that he would pay Larson $200 a month to get protection for a crap game he owned in Revere. Angiulo called Larson a "cute s.o.b." who would only agree to final details in a face-to-face meeting with him at a house of a friend of his in Newton. Larson set up the meeting for 5:30 P.M. by calling Nick and saying only "Hiya. Will that guy be around tonight?" "Yes" meant the meeting was on.

When the meeting took place, Angiulo also asked for protection for a three-nights-a-week crap game in Chelsea for $500 a month and the transfer of a state policeman, who was the brother of a Boston bookie, to the intelligence division that developed information on organized crime.

Larson, now deceased, is remembered by state policemen as a strange, intimidating man, a hulking 6-foot-6-inch major known with little affection as Big Daddy. Back in the days when all state policemen lived in barracks, he would almost always eat alone. Once in a while, he would ask a trooper to join him—but he would barely say a word. He was a master at getting into the locker room without setting off a door alarm. Suddenly, he would just be standing there, making everyone nervous. It ended for Larson when one of his Revere tip-offs was too blatant, when he was readily isolated as the leak. Because the evidence from an illegal bug in Patriarca's office was too tainted to use against him, Larson was able to retire and take a job as head of security at a corporation on Massachusetts' high-tech belt along Route 128.

One rare public manifestation of the Angiulo family's cozy relationship with the Boston police occurred when Jerry's mother Giovannina died in 1975 at the age of 82. With the district deputy superintendent directing traffic in uniform, a forty-seven-car procession wound its way through the North End. Four patrolmen on motorcycles escorted the hearse and mourners, which included twenty-nine underworld figures from four states, to the cemetery. The deputy superintendent was reassigned out of the North End following the funeral and ensuing publicity.

In addition to police connections, the other major element in Angiulo's burgeoning wealth was his unprecedented exploitation of so-called suckers, the non-Mafia employees who took most of the risks and did much of the dirty work. Summaries of conversations secretly recorded in Patriarca's office in the 1960s and the FBI transcripts from Prince Street in the 1980s paint a portrait of a merciless mercenary who used people and threw them away.

And it was not just suckers who had to worry about being ripped off. In July 1963, when the mafioso owner of a Revere nightclub was shot, Angiulo told Patriarca in a recorded conversation that he went to the hospital and talked to one of the man's sons. Although the mobster recovered, the son had told Angiulo that it looked like his father was going to die. Angiulo said he considered going to the man's home with an associate and robbing it while his family was at the hospital, the implication being that the nightclub owner owed Angiulo money anyway.

His pursuit of money was nothing short of predatory. FBI agents overhead the following exchange at Jay's Lounge in the 1960s when the death of an old-time Boston mobster was reported to Angiulo by an underling. At first, it appeared Angiulo was shocked and grief-stricken. He can't be dead, Angiulo exclaimed. But he is, the foot soldier said. Jerry then ordered his man to call the hospital to make sure. The soldier balked, saying only family members can get patient information. "Then tell em you're a member of the family. . . . He can't be fuckin' dead. He owes me $14,000."

Even his own family was not completely safe from his cut-throat greed. Angiulo and his younger brother Danny once battled so vehemently over property that listening FBI agents just waited for guns to go off.

"You gonna kill me?" Angiulo angrily challenged Danny on one of the brother's rare visits to 98 Prince Street.

"Kill you for what?" responded Danny, who was a brutal loanshark enforcer and the toughest brother in the family.

"Kill me, you cocksucker. . . . You're the guy who does all that," said Jerry.

"You're fucking right I do," responded Danny, referring to Jerry's failure to "earn his bones," or kill someone to become a "made" Mafia member.

"Go ahead, what are you waiting for?" Jerry needled.

"You ain't worth it," said Danny wearily, ending the rancor for the moment.

Just one small window on the family wealth emerged in the 1980s when federal agents found that the Angiulos were using a local bank contact to illegally launder cash in amounts over $10,000. Between 1979 and 1983, the two Angiulo holding companies, Huntington Realty and Federal Investments, obtained more than $7 million in cashier's checks from the Bank of Boston, with more that $2 million of the checks purchased with cash in amounts above $10,000 apiece. These should have been reported to the IRS and were not because the family had managed to get itself put on an exempt list for large transactions.

But on the street, away from the high finance, only Nick Angiulo seemed to have any real rapport with the rank and file. He would be there with solace or money when they were arrested or sent off to jail. He saw to it that families got some cash each week while the breadwinners were behind bars, paying the price for gambling raids. While Nick worked at building morale, Jerry would have none of it. There was no sympathy or concern from Jerry for "suckers" doing time. And if there was a hint that these underpaid men might talk, his solution was simple: kill them.

From the beginning, he was hard-hearted and utilitarian. His view was crystalized in a conversation with his brothers that was bugged by the FBI in 1981 in the aftermath of a massive gambling raid. Fussing about having to pay troops when they went off to jail for refusing to implicate the Angiulos, he told his cohorts that spending eighteen months in jail was the least the lower-level workers could do. "You know something," he said. "We sent suckers to do eighteen. We gave 'em $300 a week and all they used to get was $90 to go pick up one envelope and you know most of them come out and they were all fucking rich. . . . If they can't do eighteen fucking months, they don't belong around here anyway. That's my opinion."

This rapacious sentiment was the main reason that Boston, under Angiulo, became both bonanza and rat's nest. It may have made the most money per capita of Mafia cities, but it also had the highest number of informers. Single-handedly, Angiulo had turned Boston into one of the most lucrative—and dangerous—places for the Mafia to operate in the country.

Jerry's self-interest was evident from the start. As

often as not, when he made his biweekly trips to Providence to deliver his tribute, the agenda included some trouble in the ranks caused by the prickly, expansion-minded underboss from Boston. As events unfolded, it became clear that Angiulo was quick to move on another man's turf, pick a fight, and then scurry down to Providence as the injured party. The issue was usually who pulled the fast one here: Jerry or the other guy. In the few years between Angiulo getting sanctioned as Boston leader and his opening the Combat Zone lounge in 1961, he got giddy with power. He began strutting around with a bodyguard like Frank Sinatra prowling through a Vegas casino at three in the morning, just looking for someone to displease him.

When the feds began to play catch-up in the early 1960s, the first trouble for the Angiulos came from the IRS, which attached some of their property held by a real-estate trust—a claim the family has apparently never had to satisfy. Despite the family's millions, there is no discharge of a federal tax lien for $262,000 filed in 1967. Criminal charges of tax fraud were skirted largely through the destruction of records and the Angiulos seemed home free—until Jerry lost his temper. He slapped an IRS agent with two bodyguards present and had to serve a month in jail for it—the first time he was incarcerated in fifteen years of hustling bets and numbers.

He now had a potentate's persona and was getting difficult to live with, both in Providence and at home. He was divorced in 1963, with allegations in court that he beat his wife. For much of the 1960s, he was in and out of hot water with Patriarca for making waves in the Boston gambling scene. By that time, he had moved

from Medford to a two-story Tudor home in the exclusive East Point section of Nahant, a jewel of a house
overlooking the water. It had a kidney-shaped swim-
ming pool and a back lawn that swept to the sea and
it was right around the corner from the church where
one of Franklin Delano Roosevelt's sons got married
in 1938.

He had become Little Caesar, a short, scrappy satrap
who used his mercurial mind as a weapon in a world
of slow-witted brutes. His rapid rise, based on business
acumen and moxie, left him preening his feathers and
hopelessly insecure, especially about his physical
prowess in the ultimate land of machismo. He came
to demand absolute fealty to head off even a glimmer
of disrespect, which was much worse than bad form—
it undermined his self-image as infallible tycoon. Jerry
Angiulo was perhaps more conscious of his image than
most politicians and movie stars. The only restraint in
his life was Raymond Patriarca.

Always on stage, always conscious of being watched,
Angiulo, particularly in his court appearances, was a
poser who would glare at jurors, berate his lawyers,
study notes with affected interest. One state investigator who worked the Mafia beat for decades has concluded all mafiosi are actors, even the dees and doses
guys, playing out a bad movie in which real people get
hurt. "I haven't met a wiseguy yet," said the detective,
"who wasn't an actor. When they go to prison and
they're doing time they have one goal—to get out. They
meet with the sociologist and they pick up the buzz
words and then when they go before the parole board,
they use all those phrases. The person listening thinks
they've learned something about themselves. They've
learned how to act. That's how they intimidate and

control. Jerry with his ranting and raving—that's part of an act. He wasn't that tough a guy. He's an actor."

Angiulo performed regularly for Patriarca—and occasionally wore out his welcome. Several times in the three years of the Patriarca office bug, Raymond had to pacify high-level mobsters livid at the heavy-handed abuse they got from Angiulo after he decided he had been cheated or had not been shown proper respect. At one point, Patriarca was ready to throw Angiulo to the wolves over a vicious argument Angiulo initiated with the sons of an old rival of Patriarca's from Worcester. They were all in a country club in central Massachusetts and Jerry had decided he was getting cheated. He resorted to profane name-calling so infuriating and humiliating that the brothers went to Patriarca seeking permission to kill Angiulo. Next time it happens, Patriarca told them, you can kill him with my blessing. Angiulo was summoned to Providence the next week and given the hard facts—he apologized profusely to the still smarting brothers.

The other blunder around this time was vintage Angiulo. He had a headstrong encounter with a major Jewish gambler from Brookline who, apparently unknown to Angiulo, had strong ties to the Genovese family and was involved in large-scale odds-making and layoff networks across the country. He was a major leaguer not to be trifled with. But Angiulo trampled over some of the Brookline bettor's prerogatives in Revere, clashing over loan-shark debts. It sullied an older, stronger allegiance of Patriarca's and he moved against Angiulo immediately, summoning both men down to Providence for a formal hearing after the conflict was brought to his attention by elder statesman Joe Lombardo.

It all started when the Jewish gambler walked into Jay's Lounge demanding rather than requesting to see Jerry over the Revere matter. Angiulo was not there, but several of his associates were present when the Brookline man banged the door on the way out. Angiulo was wild and, in a puerile tit-for-tat, sent one of his brothers and his bodyguard, Peter Limone, to the gambler's hangout, where they mouthed off in profane and prejudiced epithets. The ground rules set by Patriarca telegraphed the outcome: Angiulo was not to holler, swear, or abuse the Jewish gambler. Each would make his case and Patriarca would then retire to make a decision. The final decree was "let the Jew be" and the word was soon out in Revere that Angiulo had been rebuked.

The telling difference between the two top leaders was crystalized in their contrasting grand jury appearances in the mid-1960s, when authorities were probing whether there really was a Mafia at work in New England.

On a fall day in 1963, Patriarca outfoxed the waiting press corps at the Providence courthouse by pulling into a parking lot alone in a Volkswagen, not the Cadillac the reporters were all expecting. He slipped in a back door and then chastised the prosecutor for besmirching his good name. He told his underlings back at the office that he took "the ball" away from the assistant district attorney immediately. He said he denied he was part of La Cosa Nostra and complained that his family was suffering needlessly from all the foolish talk, that his son had been forced to drop out of the University of Rhode Island and that his wife had enough trouble with cancer. On the way out, he was spotted and simply stared his famous stare of deep disdain at the photographers before driving away alone. The grand jury report said there was no evidence of organized crime in Rhode Island, though some gambling did occur here and there from time to time.

A year later in Boston, Angiulo and his brother were summoned to a grand jury with a similar purpose. Jerry arrived with a retinue and high-priced lawyer and played to the media crowd awaiting the underboss's appearance. He jousted with photographers, who kept their distance. "What do you think we are, monsters or something?" He jawed with the newsmen the way he did with FBI agents he spotted in North End restaurants or on the street. He lingered in the spotlight that Patriarca ducked.

Angiulo agreed to pose for a television cameraman. He took off his glasses, removed the cigarette from his mouth, adjusted his tie, and dusted off his blue suit. "My tie straight?" he asked jocularly. "Wait'll I say something to make me smile . . . cheese, cheese." He stopped suddenly with a look of concern. Does that thing have sound? he asked the cameraman. Assured it did not, he resumed his chant of "Cheese, cheese, cheese" as his brothers huddled with the lawyer in a corner. "Wait a minute," was his final instruction. "If you are going to take my picture, take my good side."

Angiulo was in the catbird seat in the early sixties, his gambling empire now firmly entrenched in the North End, West End, East Boston, and parts of Revere, Roxbury, and the South End. Independents in and around Boston paid escalating tithes to get strong-arm men off their backs and to get access to Patriarca's monopoly over racing results and layoff banks. The Angiulo gambling network had followed the exodus of Italians to such bedroom communities as Medford, Watertown, Waltham, and Newton.

A couple of months after Jerry Angiulo hammed it up for the Boston press at the courthouse, Marine Lieutenant Ed Quinn came home to Dorchester from Cherry Point, North Carolina, for Christmas leave. He had six months left to serve and not a clue about what he was going to do with the rest of his life. The first night home, a new neighbor came over for a drink. He turned out to be an FBI agent and, with Arthur Quinn smiling over his shoulder, talked to Ed about the bureau. He was back the next day and they talked some more. The agent left an application behind. "Why not?" Quinn thought as he headed back to North Carolina. It had stirred his sense of duty.

4

CATCH UP

*It is better to die on your feet, than to live
on your knees, and know your concepts
are sound,
Than to try to run, hide and scurry, out of
fear, of the dirt, the earth and the ground.*

The crude couplet from "Boston's Gang War" was
penned by Joseph Barboza, a beefy, sleepy-eyed exe-
cutioner for the Boston Mafia who almost brought Jerry
Angiulo down. The poem was his macho motto—and
self-imposed death sentence.

Born to a Portuguese family in the Massachusetts
fishing port of New Bedford, Barboza was part of the
Boston underworld's caste system, one of the highly
expendable "suckers"—non-Mafia employees who were
routinely exploited by the Angiulos. They were quasi-
wiseguys who got the dirty work and were packed off

to jail with false camaraderie and $300 a month—if they were lucky. Sometimes, to eliminate any chance of prosecution, the sucker was killed after carrying out a difficult murder contract. No witness, no problem. For close to a decade, the high-flying Angiulo had used such men and thrown them away.

But Joe Barboza was different, and he tried to explain why. The poem, one of many, was his groping way of saying his pride was more important than his life and that, if double-crossed, he would take on the mob, regardless of the odds. Barboza was transformed by Mafia treachery into an informant who began talking with the same zeal that motivated him when he murdered people—to be the best. He'd killed more than twenty foes for the Mafia, and when he finally switched sides to become the government's hit man, he wanted to go all the way: knock off the entire Mafia leadership, from Angiulo in Boston to Patriarca in Providence.

In law enforcement's first major go-round with the leaders of New England's underworld, Barboza ended the Mafia's free ride. Before Barboza "flipped" in 1967, no one had laid a glove on the wily Angiulo. The 1963 congressional hearings in Washington, D.C., featuring Joe Valachi's testimony—along with the intelligence gathered from secret buggings of various mafiosi around the country, including Angiulo in Boston and Patriarca in Providence—only served to document how far law enforcement had to go. Until then, they'd simply established that the Mafia was a tight, ruthless organization that had been prospering just below the surface of society for thirty years.

In the early 1960s, Attorney General Robert F. Kennedy, drawing on his years as a labor racketeering investigator for a Senate subcommittee, forced the FBI to shift its emphasis from Communist infiltration to the Mafia. The change could be measured in numbers. The New York office of the bureau went from four agents working on La Cosa Nostra in 1959 to one hundred and fifty by 1962. The FBI office in Boston was not any different, establishing its first Organized Crime Squad in the early 1960s, with Dennis Condon, a home-town product from Charlestown who'd mostly worked on bank robberies, being the first Boston agent handed the ticket on Gennaro Angiulo.

The reaction by law enforcement coincided with Angiulo's emergence from a decade in the city's shadows. He found himself suddenly thrust onto the main stage, publicly identified as underboss. From then on, any mention of his name carried the tag, "reputed Mafia boss." But he hardly suffered from all the exposure; he sailed through the early part of the decade, expanding his empire by fueling the self-destructive penchant of the Irish gangs and ducking the escalating interest lawmen had in him. By 1965, the best thing federal authorities had gotten on the crafty mafioso had been the assault of an IRS agent who dared to question him on Thatcher Street in the North End. Angiulo first told Patriarca he would fight the charge by paying fake eyewitnesses for false testimony. But he eventually cooled off and copped a plea that netted him a mere thirty days.

Condon, other FBI agents, and state and city police were scrambling in those days to devise strategies to penetrate the Angiulo sanctuary as well as to control the region's sudden surge in Irish gangland violence that had started in August 1960 when one gang member insulted the wife of a rival gang member after drinking beer all day at Salisbury Beach. The back alleys of Somerville and Charlestown became battlegrounds, with the death toll hitting double figures in the early 1960s and rising exponentially. At first the underworld chaos was encouraged by Angiulo as something he could exploit to his benefit. But things were getting out of control and Raymond Patriarca was threatening to "declare martial law" in Boston. Angiulo had fueled a fire he couldn't put out.

One typical victim was a middle-aged burglar named Teddy Deegan, who in March 1965 was ambushed and gunned down in an alley in Chelsea in the middle of the night. But not all the victims were Irish—in June the next year, the corpse of ex-boxer and wiseguy Rocco DiSeglio was found slumped in the front seat of a car abandoned in the suburban town of Topsfield, north of the city. DiSeglio had been shot three times in the head. He was quickly dubbed the thirty-second gang victim. There were few leads.

Not much the feds tried seemed to be working. The FBI had been gathering plenty of inside information that provided the bureau with its first sketches of the Mafia structure in Boston, but most of what they got was simply information, not evidence that could be used in court. They tried raiding the gambling operations on a regular basis, but the tactic was only a small bother to the mobsters, simply driving the Angiulos farther into the recesses of their North End neighborhood and causing the family to become even more subterranean.

It seemed that the harder the FBI tried to penetrate Angiulo's world, the more elusive the mobster became. Early in 1965, Boston police hauled him in along with several other suspected mob leaders to question them about the gangland war, but the cops had nothing on

Angiulo. He refused to answer any questions and, by dawn, was back on the street.

The strategy that finally produced some results was getting mobsters to turn on the organization. The FBI had detected a dent in the Mafia's armor: the growing number of unhappy "suckers." Angiulo and Patriarca had sent legions of these characters onto the front line, encouraging them to think they were big shots—until it no longer served their interests.

Starting in late 1966, Condon and his partner, Paul Rico, began feeling out the most ferocious in the Mafia's coterie of killers, Joseph "Baron" Barboza, nicknamed "The Animal."

In the end, Barboza became the best of the bunch. He was Boston's Joe Valachi—an inside guy who told all, with the added punch of firsthand accounts of specific crimes, such as the murders of Teddy Deegan and Rocco DiSeglio. He became the government's first big break: a Frankenstein whom Angiulo and Patriarca had created and then cast off. But, unwittingly, Barboza also served to heighten Angiulo's growing aura of invincibility, because the one major mafioso the informant's web was unable to ensnare was the bob-and-weave Angiulo.

The Mafia liked what it saw when it first recruited Barboza during the mid-1950s, when the young tough guy was serving yet another state prison term. A second-generation Portuguese-American, Barboza had gotten a head start in crime as the son of a two-bit boxer and convict who drank, chased women, and abandoned his wife and four kids when Joe was 12.

From the beginning, Barboza was like a revved-up

Chevy: always running others off the road, burning rubber, causing havoc, and leaving tracks wherever he went. He slugged anyone or anything that got in his way. At age 13, he and his older brother were arrested after a spree of vandalism—knocking out signals on the streetcar system in New Bedford. By 1949, the 17-year-old led a gang that broke into homes and small businesses, stealing money, watches, liquor, and guns. At some of the restaurants the gang burglarized, police found pastry cream dripping from the ceiling. The food fights provided the Barboza gang with a nickname, Cream Puff Bandits, and revealed a leader still straddling the fence between being a kid and a killer.

The hardening came with hard time. Sentenced to the Concord Reformatory for 5 years in 1950, Barboza led a wild break-out in the summer of 1953 that was the largest in the prison's 75-year history. Barboza and six others, having guzzled whiskey and popped uppers, overpowered four guards and raced away in two cars. They beat up people, cruised the bars in Boston's Scollay Square, wandered to Lynn and Revere, and were finally nabbed at a subway station in East Boston. The party lasted barely twenty-four hours.

"I don't remember much about the escape," was the party line a hung-over Barboza gave to police. It was the first time the public got a hard look at the muscular convict, whose dark, wavy hair, deep-set eyes, and thick lips were the prominent features of his oversize head. "I was drunk—drunk from capsules and liquor. I'm not going to tell you where I got the stuff, but I had goof-balls and liquor the day of the escape." That November, awaiting trial for the prison break, Barboza slugged a guard in the prison cafeteria. Three months later, he was at it again. He greeted a guard entering his cell with a table to the guard's chest.

The prison escape earned Barboza a stay at Walpole, the maximum security prison. It was there that the Mafia took an interest in the surly convict, and it was for the Mafia that he mostly worked after his parole in 1958. Barboza did some boxing too, worked as a dockhand, even as a clerk in a fruit store, but he excelled at killing. He was a fixture in East Boston, particularly in a bar at the corner of Bennington and Brooks streets, which became known among wiseguys as Barboza's Corner. He never became a Mafia soldier—his ethnicity barred that—but within eight years, during the escalation of the gangland war, he earned a reputation as one of the state's real killers.

He also earned his nickname—Animal. The episode behind that name occurred at a Revere club popular with mafiosi, particularly Henry Tameleo, a powerful underworld figure who served as adviser to Raymond Patriarca. Barboza was at the club drinking and carrying on when an older Italian patron who did not enjoy Barboza's crude behavior told him so. Barboza approached the man and slapped him hard across the face. Tameleo, seated not far away, shouted angrily, "I don't want you ever to slap that man. I don't want you to touch anybody with your hands again." Barboza, brooding at the bar, suddenly leaned over and bit the man's ear. "I didn't touch him with my hands," he snarled at Tameleo.

By January 1966, Barboza was big-time—often representing him now was the famous criminal lawyer F. Lee Bailey. But he was also facing big troubles. The law was constantly on his heels. For disturbing the peace one night at the same Revere nightclub, where he slugged a detective, Barboza received a six-month sentence.

More ominous, however, was his increasingly shaky position in the underworld. Before the nightclub debacle, he'd been shot at while standing outside his home in Chelsea. Police believed there'd been other attempts. Someone wanted him dead, and the headstrong Barboza wasn't helping matters. Brimming with reckless power, he was having trouble playing by the Mafia's rules. One time he'd gone into a nightclub on Stuart Street in Boston, where the owner paid Angiulo for protection, and told the owner to make payments to him too. The word on the street was that Mr. Angiulo wasn't pleased.

By mid-1966, the unrelenting attention Barboza got from the law only made his standing in the outfit more tenuous. He'd become the rope in a tug-of-war between law enforcement officials who were trying to nail the killer and an underworld trying to shield itself. But if Barboza had any lingering doubts about his fall from Mafia grace, they had disappeared by October. He'd worn out his stay with Angiulo and Patriarca, and the moment he was back in police custody the two let go of their end of the rope.

Barboza himself realized this in early October 1966, after he and three local hoods were picked up on weapons charges while cruising the Combat Zone in Boston. In their car, police found an army M-1 rifle, a loaded .45-caliber automatic pistol, and a knife. Once again, the law had enough to tie up Barboza's time. The others were released on a low bail, but Barboza's was set at $100,000, and the Animal couldn't post it.

Barboza sat behind bars, confused that neither Angiulo nor Patriarca had sent anyone down with money to spring him. In fact, he'd heard it was the Mafia that tipped off the cops that he was riding around the Zone armed and ready for business. Fortunately for Barboza, others had not forgotten him. One of the guys nabbed with him, Arthur C. "Tash" Bratsos, a 36-year-old loan shark from Medford who'd made his far lower bail, began hitting up other wiseguys around town for Barboza's. Helping was 27-year-old Thomas J. DePrisco, Jr., known as an enforcer, or "stalker."

Then the Mafia sent Joe a message.

It came after he'd been in jail for more than five weeks. Bratsos and DePrisco, continuing to press people on behalf of Barboza, had raised $59,000. One November night, the pair visited the Nite Lite Café, a mafiosi hangout on Commercial Street in the North End. The bar was managed by Ralph "Ralphie Chong" Lamattina, a soldier in the Angiulo family who was assigned to Capo de Regime Larry Zannino. Lamattina, like Bratsos, lived in Medford; in fact, the two were neighbors—Ralphie lived in the house behind Tash's.

But that meant nothing. Barboza's two fundraisers had gone to the wrong place after midnight looking for financial aid. Bratsos was shot twice in the back of the head. DePrisco was shot four times. The Mafia, in an awkward attempt to have police think the murders were the work of Irish gangsters, dumped the corpses in the back seat of Bratsos's black Cadillac and abandoned the car in South Boston. No one was fooled. The slayings were counted as the thirty-ninth and fortieth in the ongoing gangland violence, and police, acting on a tip, were able to search the Nite Lite while the corpses were still warm. Police found Ralph Lamattina in the café. Someone had tried using solvent to wash blood off the sidewalk out front. Inside, the walls were pocked with bullet holes and the carpet was wet with blood. A spent bullet and bullet casing, tested later, were shown to have been fired from the murder weapon.

Throughout that day and the next, police rounded up thirty wiseguys for questioning. News of the murders shook Barboza. Not only were his pals dead, but the $59,000 was missing. The afternoon the bodies were discovered, he was taken to Boston City Hospital for a toothache. He was under heavy police guard; his hands were manacled and his eyes hidden behind dark, wraparound shades. As Barboza climbed out of the police vehicle, a photographer immediately snapped his picture. Barboza flipped out, screaming at the press and the police. He dove back into the car, demanding to be returned to the Charles Street Jail.

Monitoring all of this were the FBI's Condon and Rico, for Barboza's mounting troubles coincided with the bureau's decision to actively cultivate informants. Barboza, in their mind, was a prime candidate. They began to visit the Animal in jail, telling him he'd become a sore spot to the organization; that he had no future with it; that he was a marked man; that his friends were marked men; and that, during the FBI's secret bugging of Patriarca, the boss had several times mentioned Barboza in less than favorable terms.

But converting Barboza was not easy. The process took time, almost six months, during which Barboza vacillated wildly between promising to help and refusing to believe the Mafia had dumped him. From jail, he wrote Angiulo and Patriarca notes, with the initial ones demanding an explanation for the murders and the stolen bail money and the later ones containing explicit threats about whom he would bring down if he cooperated.

During those six months, both sides—the Mafia and the law—acted in ways that encouraged Barboza to roll over. Three weeks after the two fundraisers were knocked off, Barboza's pal, Joe Amico, was gunned down in Revere. Amico was no fool; he'd gone into hiding immediately after the Bratsos and DePrisco hits. But the Mafia tracked down the 24-year-old just before Christmas.

Condon and Rico talked to Barboza about his dead friend. The next month, in state court, Barboza was convicted on the weapons charges after a 10-day trial. In late January 1967, he was sentenced to a 5-year term at Walpole. Condon and Rico went to Walpole to see him. In February, Ralph Lamattina pleaded guilty to being an accessory after the fact in the murders of Bratsos and DePrisco. The prosecutors insisted Lamattina knew who did the actual killing, but "Ralphie Chong" wouldn't talk. The Mafia soldier was sentenced to 10 to 14 years.

Eventually, Lamattina did "talk," albeit years later in a conversation secretly recorded by the FBI. In April 1981, he commiserated with Zannino about the messy handling of the hits late one night at their North End club. "Remember when we did that work in, in, in the Nite Lite?" Lamattina asked Zannino and soldier John Cincotti. The trio tried to recall who worked that night. Cincotti had been behind the bar, but was sent home before the shooting started.

"Yeah, we made you go home," Zannino told Cincotti.

"Made everyone go home," Lamattina said.

"I threw everybody out of the joint," Zannino said.

The gist of the discussion was that the murders could have been executed better—maybe they should have burned down the café afterward, or maybe the bodies should have been left inside and the police summoned immediately, instead of dumping the bodies in Southie and attempting to clean up. Zannino concluded that their major mistake was shooting Bratsos and DePrisco inside the café. Ralphie would never have gone to prison if the killing were done outside. "It shouldn't have happened inside his joint," Zannino said. "No reason for it. . . . Once they get on the sidewalk, crack them and fuck them and walk away."

But, following orders from Patriarca back in February 1967, Lamattina pled guilty and refused to aid curious federal agents trying to pry inside information from him. The feds, however, could turn elsewhere—Barboza was finally providing the FBI with solid intelligence about the Mafia. Over the next several months, he began telling them about the slayings of burglar Teddy Deegan in 1965, boxer Rocco DiSeglio in 1966, and a Providence bookie named Willie Marfeo. The feds convened a grand jury, and newspaper stories began hinting that major organized crime cases were brewing.

In protective custody, the volatile Barboza was not easy to babysit. To one state police investigator, Barboza was only the second criminal he'd ever dealt with who frightened him—not that Barboza threatened him, it was Barboza's look. The first was the Boston Strangler, Albert DeSalvo. The investigator had met Barboza in a motel on Route 1 in Foxborough in order to question him. He found Barboza seated directly in front of the television watching Johnny Carson on "The Tonight Show." Barboza, unshaven, wore a T-shirt with a pack of cigarettes rolled in one sleeve and a baseball cap on his head, backward.

The trooper stood there watching Barboza watch Carson. Carson's guest was Truman Capote and the two talked about Capote's book *In Cold Blood*. The author noted that one of the killers he'd written about had inscribed the words *love* and *hate* on his knuckles. Capote explained that, to him, the tattoos suggested a homosexual slant—a comment that prompted a sudden reaction from Barboza. He took the chair he'd been sitting on and swung it through the television screen. Then he turned to the trooper, who spotted immediately that the Animal had the words *love* and *hate* tattooed on his knuckles.

By June 1967, Barboza began dropping his bombs. The first came on June 20: Patriarca, Tameleo, and another mobster were indicted in federal court on charges of conspiring to kill Marfeo. The second fell August 9 when Angiulo was one of four mobsters accused in state court of organizing the DiSeglio killing. Had he been convicted on charges of conspiracy and accessory before the murder, Angiulo could have gotten the death sentence. The final dropped that October—Tameleo, Angiulo bodyguard Peter Limone, and four others were charged in state court in the Deegan murder. In Boston, the FBI finally had a chance to get Jerry Angiulo, along with the top man, Patriarca, and other assorted wiseguys.

In court the day after his indictment, Angiulo, sporting heavy, dark-rimmed glasses, pleaded not guilty. He came prepared, carrying a black leather bag containing his toothbrush, toothpaste, and shaving gear. The Mafia boss was held without bail until the trial—confinement that would last the next five months, the most time Angiulo had ever spent locked up. Taken to the Charles Street Jail, the cantankerous Angiulo complained immediately about the food, rejecting the first

offering of fried bologna, stewed corn, and mashed po-
tatoes. The finicky steak man tried to pay guards to
fetch him a decent meal, and when he was rebuffed he
referred angrily to Barboza, shouting that the stool pigeon got to eat whatever he wanted. The next month,
Angiulo had to be moved from Charles Street to the
Plymouth County House of Corrections after he was
discovered making hand signals from the jail's top-floor
barber shop to girlfriend Barbara Lombard, who had
stationed herself at a Beacon Hill intersection overlooking the jail.

Shortly after the Patriarca indictment, which drew
front-page stories about a Mafia stool pigeon, an angry
Barboza tried to explain why he'd rolled over. He wrote
the Boston *Herald Traveler*: "All I want is to be left
alone. Leave my family alone." In mangled prose, he
told how he'd been duped into thinking the office would
take care of him, but instead he'd been used and spat
out. He had a warning for other would-be wiseguys:
"Younger inmates in Walpole and Concord would do
anything to get in with these people, figuring that they
would become big men. The office likes them to believe this because then they bleed every single favorable effort from these disillusioned kids and men—and
then throw them a crust of bread . . . and it goes on
and on in one complete cycle of evil and vicious-
ness while the office sits back, laughs and reaps the
harvest."

The Mafia made a final, feeble attempt to win back
Barboza. Not long after Patriarca was indicted, Henry
Tameleo, knowing his role in the Deegan murder was
under scrutiny, met with the attorney then representing Barboza, John Fitzgerald. The Deegan matter was
discussed. Other meetings followed. The Mafia was

willing to pay Barboza $25,000 to quit talking—he'd caused too much trouble already for Patriarca and Angiulo. Fitzgerald reported the offer to both the FBI and Barboza. Barboza actually showed some interest in the deal. The lawyer met again with Tameleo's associates, saying his client wanted $50,000. The Mafia agreed, but Barboza, after a huddle with his attorney and the FBI, held fast. There was no turning back now.

First up to bat was the silver-haired Angiulo.

In the January 1968 trial, the state's star witness, Barboza, testified for four days. During that time, the courthouse in Boston crawled with special armed guards and police dogs. To get through the testimony as quickly as possible, the judge scheduled long work days, including Saturdays. The only break came Sunday, January 14, when the sequestered jury was permitted to watch the Super Bowl.

Barboza described an elaborate murder scheme engineered by the mob leader from the North End. The motive was revenge—Angiulo had learned that DiSeglio was part of a foursome who'd been robbing lucrative dice games he controlled in Newton and Lowell. So Angiulo, as Barboza told it, summoned one of the other robbers, Benny Zinno, and gave him a choice: Either kill DiSeglio or be killed. The next week, Zinno and the other two defendants set up the victim at a bar in East Boston, luring DiSeglio to ride off with them and then shooting him three times in the back of the head. One bullet tore off part of DiSeglio's face, another went through his head and out an eye socket. The murderers drove to Topsfield and dumped the body.

Barboza told the jury he knew this because the accused killers Zinno and Richard "Vinnie the Pig" DeVincent told him so after the slaying. DeVincent bragged all about it. Barboza even went to see Angiulo at his office: "I told him that Benny Zinna and Vinnie DeVincent told me that he gave the order to whack out Rocky DiSeglio or he would whack them out. The reason I wanted to know was because DiSeglio was a friend of mine and to find out if he had done anything wrong on his part to be killed. I told Angiulo they were running at the mouth. That they came down and told me everything. Angiulo said he would talk to Zinna and that he didn't trust 'the Pig.' "

The jury listened, watching the menacing Barboza spew his words as he stood in court, his hands tightly clasped together, with tiny rings looking almost dainty on his pinkies. The man's head was huge and long, his jaw protruding. His shoulders were enormous, but his legs were undersized. His upper and lower halves didn't fit. It made him all the more disconcerting.

The Barboza testimony was the state's case. In less than two hours, the jury reached a verdict—not guilty. Angiulo clutched the dock rail and his body shook, the only defendant to show any emotion. He bit his lower lip and swallowed continuously. "I don't want to say anything right now," he said afterward to reporters. "I want to see my mother. She's 73, and this thing has been bothering her."

Despite efforts by reporters to coax jurors to explain their deliberations, none did. Twenty years later, however, jury foreman Kenneth Matthews said none of the sixteen jurors had found Barboza believable. "He didn't help the state at all," Matthews said. "He wasn't reliable. He was nothing as a witness. . . . Once you get into his background, you see he was a strong-arm man for loansharks who killed for practically nothing. He was an animal himself. How can you accept whatever he says? . . . Personally, I was glad when he was off the witness stand. When he was there I worried there would be trouble. In the courtroom somewhere. I'm not sure how. Just some kind of trouble. I was glad when that part was over." The problem with the state's case, Matthews recalled, was that it relied heavily on Barboza. "Everything was mostly his word," he said. "Maybe if he was used to corroborate other evidence, but as the only witness, it was a poor way to go about it."

Angiulo had beaten the rap. Barboza, singing solo, had not played well. But in the two sensational trials that remained, the results were far different. The government still showcased Barboza, but it buttressed his testimony with that of other witnesses and with physical evidence.

Two months after Angiulo's acquittal, Patriarca was convicted of conspiring to kill Marfeo. "I'm an old man," was the Mafia leader's reaction, as he leaned against the courtroom railing and gripped it with such force that his knuckles turned white.

During the trial, Barboza had taunted the aging Patriarca, striding to the defense table, staring at each of the three mobsters on trial, smirking at them, and then walking away. From the stand, he told how he had agreed to kill Marfeo for Patriarca for nothing, deciding it would be good business to ingratiate himself with the number one mafioso in New England. Marfeo was gunned down in Providence while making a call from a telephone booth.

The trials were coming down quickly—all three would

be staged within six months—but that didn't stop the Mafia from doing whatever it could to derail Barboza. Prior to the Patriarca trial, Barboza lawyer and adviser John Fitzgerald left his office in Everett after another day spent coping with his client's massive legal entanglements. He'd been driving a 1966 Olds belonging to Barboza, which was littered with papers, including a copy of Capote's *In Cold Blood* in the back seat. Fitzgerald opened the door, threw his briefcase inside, and stuck the key in the ignition. The explosion came the second he turned the key. Two sticks of dynamite had been used, each 15 inches long and weighing 6 pounds. The explosives had been inserted with a coil next to the fire wall behind the car's engine—a 30-second job. Fitzgerald survived, but his mangled right leg was amputated three inches below the knee. He was conscious after the 5:15 P.M. bombing, asking the local police at the scene to get him Paul Rico of the FBI. The lawyer later disclosed he'd received recent death threats because of his close relationship to Barboza and his self-annointed role as mediator between the Mafia and his client. In the aftermath of what newspaper editorials labeled the underworld's "brazen, terroristic act . . . a frontal assault on our system of justice," an outraged legal community rallied behind the maimed Fitzgerald, raising money for his family.

Knowing the Mafia was on the prowl, Barboza, under heavy guard, was moved around frequently—from Thatcher Island off Rockport, north of Boston, to Fort Devens, an army base west of the city. For a while, he was kept in protective custody in the junior officer's quarters at Fort Knox in Kentucky, where one of the young officers in the Army military police was a Kansan named John Morris. Within a few years, Morris would become an FBI agent bound for Boston. But, to the MP officer, the swarthy visitor meant little. Each owned a German shepherd and, on occasion, the two talked when they met walking their dogs.

The Mafia maneuverings to stop Barboza also included an attempt to convince an imprisoned convict to take one of the raps for them. The convict, already serving a life term for murder, was advised that the "office" wanted him to go down for the Deegan slaying—the next murder for which the top Mafia leaders would be in the dock. In return, the convict was promised $50,000, his kids would be cared for, and the office would try to work the parole board in his behalf. The convict had been approached about the deal by two mafiosi, one of whom was Ralph Lamattina—in jail as an accessory to the Nite Lite Café murders. But the convict didn't go for it; he went to the FBI and the bureau plugged another hole.

The Deegan trial was the longest of the three, beginning in late May 1968 and running for fifty days. The court record ran 7,555 pages and the cast of six defendants included Tameleo of Providence and Peter Limone, who was at that time Jerry Angiulo's most trusted underling.

Limone had hired Barboza to kill Deegan for having robbed some of his North End friends. Limone had met with Barboza on Prince Street, right near Angiulo's office, and offered the killer $7,500. Barboza had accepted, but sought out Tameleo at the Ebb Tide in Revere to confirm the killing was authorized. It was. Deegan had also caused trouble at the bar, which had become a favorite of Tameleo's ever since the Providence office became a part owner. Deegan had managed to become an annoyance to all. "He definitely goes,"

Tameleo told Barboza. "No punk like Deegan is going to push the office around."

Barboza enlisted the other four defendants in the murder plot. The group succeeded as far as Deegan was concerned, but bungled an attempt to whack out a Deegan compatriot who was with Deegan the night of the murder. The man escaped and became a witness to corroborate Barboza.

In the end, Barboza's scorecard was impressive—two out of three trials ended in guilty verdicts, sending four mobsters to death row, two to state prison for life, and New England Mafia leader Patriarca to the federal penitentiary in Atlanta.

For Angiulo, the Barboza broadside required some line-up changes. The loss of Limone led him to forge a stronger alliance with Larry Zannino, the brutal Capo de Regime who had already done a four-year state prison term for operating a "pay or die" loansharking ring. Zannino, born a year after Angiulo, was a favorite of Patriarca's. He rose to the top through sheer ferocity, not guile. Although he was born in the North End, like Angiulo, he moved at an early age to the heavily Italian town of Franklin, on the Rhode Island border. There his career took shape. Patriarca came to like Zannino's "can do" efficiency. The dirty jobs got done on time and there were never any excuses. The money was delivered or the legs were broken.

Zannino moved to the South End of Boston in the late 1930s, where his specialty was collecting loan-shark debts. Both he and Angiulo cut their teeth in the underworld at the same time, progressing in different career paths in the forties and fifties. While Jerry worked the numbers racket in the North End and South End, first as a clerk in Joe Lombardo's office and then as major-domo for Patriarca, Zannino ascended from street tough to dominant enforcer, extorting small businesses and banging heads all over town.

Had Angiulo not been such an impressive profit-maker, Zannino might have become the boss in Boston. But by the late 1960s the two were an item, and it was a pairing that worked. For fifteen years both men ruled the region, a formidable blend of brains and brawn.

In those years, one of the major pieces of business the Boston brass took up was the Barboza matter. Even though Angiulo had walked away a free man, and Zannino had never even been dragged into the mess, the two were the point men in the Mafia's patient pursuit of the turncoat.

Having testified in 1968 in three Mafia trials—all within six months—Barboza's legal problems eased. He pleaded guilty to conspiring to murder Teddy Deegan and, in return for cooperating with authorities, was given a one-year prison term to run concurrently with the year still remaining for possessing weapons. In March 1969, he was paroled on the provision he leave Massachusetts forever, an informant who had helped to initiate what is today a vast government witness protection program.

Barboza, however, could not lie low. The hitman was given a new identity and relocated in California, but within a year he'd killed an unemployed mechanic in a dispute over stolen securities. By late 1971, he was on trial in California for murder, amid reports that the Mafia had a $300,000 contract out for his life. Barboza pleaded guilty to second-degree murder and was sentenced to five years. It was at Folsom Prison that Barboza wrote the poems portraying the evils of the Mob and his own fearlessness. There was "Boston Gang War,"

"The Mafia Double Crosses," "A Cat's Lives," and "The Gang War Ends."

But Jerry Angiulo and the men of the Mafia never forget. Barboza, paroled in October 1975, moved into a $250-a-month apartment in San Francisco under the name Joe Donati. The mob was waiting. It knew Barboza's whereabouts, because a wiseguy from the Boston area named James Chalmas, alias Teddy Sharliss, had been living in California, visiting Barboza in prison and befriending the legendary hit man. Chalmas was even offered $25,000 to do the job himself, but declined.

Then, less than three months after he was paroled, on February 11, 1976, Barboza left Chalmas' apartment at midday and walked toward his car. Four shotgun blasts were fired from a white van that pulled up next to Barboza. Barboza was carrying a loaded .38-caliber revolver, but never had a chance. He was killed instantly.

"We clipped Barboza," Zannino would say five years later, unaware he was being taped secretly—tapes that the government would use to accuse Zannino and Angiulo of ordering the Barboza hit. Retelling the tale of the Barboza murder to his soldiers one night, Zannino described how much he admired the man—J. R. Russo of East Boston—who shot Barboza: "A very brilliant guy . . . who stepped right out with the fuckin' carbine. . . . I was with him every fuckin' day. Him and me discussed everything. Then he had to leave. He made snap decisions. There, he couldn't get in touch with nobody. And he accomplished the whole fuckin' pot, didn't he? Am I right?"

At the time, no one knew exactly who killed Joe Barboza, only that the Mafia had settled its score. The high-noon murder made for front-page headlines, but

Barboza's demise was not widely mourned. Said the Animal's sometime attorney F. Lee Bailey, "With all due respect to my former client, I don't think society has suffered a great loss."

For the FBI in 1969, Barboza's batting average of 2 for 3 was proof that informant cases could succeed. But for Dennis Condon and the other agents assigned to stalk Boston's mob leader, Angiulo's acquittal was a frustrating setback. The North End world was tough to crack and Angiulo was now cockier than ever.

Angiulo had dodged their best informant, Barboza, so the feds immediately followed with another. In October 1969, Angiulo was indicted in federal court as an accessory after the fact of an armored car stick-up that netted $68,000. The government's witness—one of the robbers—claimed Angiulo laundered his share of the stolen cash. For $15,000 of the hot cash, Angiulo gave the robber back $11,250.

The profit margin sounded like an Angiulo transaction, but once again the government had banked on a single informant. The case never even got to the jury, because the judge dismissed the charge after the informant testified. Angiulo, right from the start, seemed to sense an advantage. For the arraignment, he'd worn a custom-tailored charcoal suit, with fabric-covered buttons and black loafers. He acted bored, flipping through a copy of *Time* magazine while awaiting the bail hearing.

Angiulo's slippery reputation was enhanced by yet another courtroom victory. He had emerged unscathed from the sixties, and the FBI had exhausted the arsenal of mob informants paraded at a series of criminal trials.

Through his money, he had managed to tighten his grip on the region's independent bookies and loansharks, including dominant Irish gangsters who rose to prominence during the post-gangland war era out of a heap of dead bodies. To maintain a gambling and loansharking franchise based in Somerville but extending south to Cape Cod and north into New Hampshire, Howie Winter had to pay the North End and Providence $20,000 weekly. And, because of large gambling debts of his own, Winter wound up $250,000 in debt to Angiulo personally.

So the bureau shifted its focus to busting up these gambling and loan-shark operations that fed the Mafia leaders. The strategy was one the FBI adopted throughout the country during much of the 1970s—the idea being that by cutting off the Mafia's tentacles, the underworld organization would lose its life-support system. It was as if the FBI were following the unsolicited advice of Vinnie Teresa, the loudmouth mobster from Revere, Massachusetts, who in 1971 had testified before a congressional subcommittee. Teresa had counseled that "You've got to knock out the agents who are out on the streets. . . . Just remember the guy in the office can't operate without the phone ringing from the agent in the street. If you stop the agents and knock them out of business, the phones won't ring and . . . Jerry Angiulo can't operate."

In Boston, countless city, state, and federal gambling probes were launched. Bookies and loan sharks were busted, but Angiulo remained out of reach. The Mafia boss often got mentioned in FBI affidavits submitted in the gambling cases, but Angiulo himself was not accused. He drew constant attention from the press—articles that, in flat journalese, underscored the man's slipperiness. To explain the significance of the Prince Street office, one reporter noted, "The address generally is considered by Federal agents and Boston and state police as the headquarters of Jerry Angiulo and has been the object of numerous investigations for about 15 years."

During the summer of 1972, Angiulo was summoned to Washington, D.C., to testify at the latest round of congressional hearings probing organized crime. He refused to answer any questions, which included queries about his ties to Patriarca, about a horse track in western Massachusetts, and about a suspected acquaintance with Frank Sinatra.

Back home, Angiulo's name continued to surface during bugging or undercover operations. "Have you ever spoken with Jerry for any length of time?" bookmaker Mike Pellicci once asked a visitor at his Watertown car dealership, which was secretly bugged. "No, because he yells too much," replied the visitor. The tapes were littered with references to Angiulo, but contained nothing the feds could hang a case on. They got Pellicci, who ran the gambling and loan shark operations for Angiulo in the Watertown-Waltham-Newton area, but Angiulo slipped away again.

Right after the Pellicci case, the feds busted the man Angiulo assigned to take over Pellicci's region, William "Skinny" Kazonis. Kazonis was a favorite of Angiulo's and often drove the boss around. He was sent away after a loan-shark victim, wired with an FBI mike, snared Kazonis and a partner, Joseph "Joe Porter" Patrizzi, as they shook the victim down for his weekly interest payments of $75. Kazonis and Patrizzi got sentences of eight and five years, respectively.

Then the feds got two other Angiulo loan sharks,

including Richard "The Pig" DeVincent, who had been acquitted with Angiulo in the Rocco DiSeglio murder. The Pig was caught threatening to break the legs and use an ice pick on a borrower who'd lapsed in his $28-a-week payments.

But no one got Jerry Angiulo. He nimbly sidestepped the FBI's enhanced efforts to nail him, except for another one of those thirty-day jail stays. It took a couple of Coast Guard boatswains to accomplish what the federal agents couldn't—arrest Gennaro Angiulo and make it stick. Just as in the IRS assault case a decade earlier, this case played off Angiulo's temper. But while aggravating the mob boss, it hardly crippled him.

The incident occurred in the spring of 1972, when boaters in Dorchester Bay had complained to the Coast Guard about Angiulo's handling of his 45-foot yacht, *Tajaba*. Angiulo had a habit of ignoring the smaller boats and cruising the bay and Boston Harbor at speeds that caused huge wakes. On July 4, two guardsmen, Steven Brown and Steven Sacharczyk, spotted the Angiulo cabin cruiser in the inner harbor about 3 P.M., creating "excessive wake." They hailed the Angiulo boat, intending to stop her for a routine check, but Angiulo dismissed the young officers with a wave and sped off. The guardsmen gave chase, flipping on the emergency flashing lights on their 17-foot boat, and followed Angiulo for almost 3 miles to a marina in Dorchester.

Both boats tied up. Sacharczyk spoke first for the Coast Guard, informing Angiulo he'd caused too big a wake. "What are you, nuts?" Angiulo shouted in front of a small audience of friends who had been partying with him on his yacht. "That's the ocean out there."

The guardsman, ignoring the remark, told Angiulo

the large wake had caused havoc among the smaller boats.

"The other boats shouldn't be there then."

Sacharczyk and Brown, oblivious of Angiulo's status as Mafia underboss, began inspecting the yacht, which fanned the mobster's temper. "Who are you, the s.o.b. chief himself?" Angiulo shouted at Brown. Brown offered Angiulo his identification card, but Angiulo scoffed at it. "Who the hell are you to be promoting boat safety? If I had you in *my* Navy I'd teach you a few things."

Brown continued his inspection. "I've eaten up guys like you before," Angiulo screamed. Angiulo was at the officer's ear. "You do anything about this, I'll have your job. Your life will be miserable."

Three violations were written up: failure to stop, failure to carry the boat's registration, and continued harassment of the boarding officer. Brown handed Angiulo the citation and headed for his Coast Guard craft. Angiulo treated the citation as trash; he crumpled it and threw it aside.

Brown, having bent over to untie the stern line of his boat, stood up and found Angiulo facing him, no more than four inches away, his mouth yapping: "Walk around me, you son of a bitch. Don't you ever speak to me again, you son of a bitch. Take the violation and stick it." Angiulo then shoved the 29-year-old guardsman.

"You're under arrest for assaulting a federal officer," said Brown.

Angiulo howled in protest. From a second boat at the marina, jammed with about twenty of the mobster's friends, came a flurry of derisive comments. Brown, worried about the numerical disadvantage, called for help from the Registry of Motor Vehicle's harbor boat and the police. Brown and his mate then retreated from the marina, rendezvoused with the Registry boat, and returned to face Angiulo. Brown yanked out a Miranda card and began reading Angiulo his rights. The reading only triggered a fresh round of profanities. "Shut up and listen," Brown said.

After spending the night of July 4 in a police lockup, Angiulo was arraigned in federal court on the assault charge. The hearing drew a surprising number of federal agents—from the FBI, IRS, and the Justice and Treasury departments. They filled up several rows in the courtroom. "Brown had done what lawmen would give their handcuff tieclasps to accomplish," noted one reporter sardonically. "He'd arrested Gennaro Angiulo."

Angiulo missed the irony. "I listened to the sailor testify and 90 percent of the allegations are untrue, especially the suppositions of an assault," he complained after the arraignment, adding bitterly that the charge "was concocted on the 9th," a reference to the FBI office on the ninth floor of the John F. Kennedy Federal Building.

His organization took the matter seriously too. During jury selection, Salvatore Limone, brother of Peter Limone, summoned one juror to the back room of the bar the Limones owned in the fishing town of Gloucester, north of Boston. "We want you to vote not guilty," Limone advised the juror. "We thinks the guy is framed." Limone went on to explain that his brother Peter, who was serving a life sentence for the Deegan murder, was very close to Angiulo. "My brother would consider it a favor. I would consider it a favor."

But Limone got caught and convicted, as did Angiulo,

following a one-day trial on the assault charge on May 9, 1973. Just before Thanksgiving in 1974—after a retrial and a failed appeal—Angiulo surrendered to serve his thirty days. In many respects, the Coast Guard tangle had provided a kind of comic relief in the crusade against Angiulo, but it also highlighted how little ground the FBI had gained in its more than ten-year chase of the North End Mafia leader.

None of this was lost on FBI agent John Morris, the former Army MP who'd once chatted with a government witness named Barboza and was now part of the Boston bureau's organized crime squad. Morris and another agent, Jim Vaules, were among the younger guys on the squad. Morris had even inherited the ticket on the Angiulo case from the veteran Dennis Condon, who was preparing to retire from the FBI. Morris was troubled by the bureau's record, which had nibbled away at Angiulo, netting Pellicci, Kazonis, Peter Limone, and the Pig, but never landing the man himself, failing even with a snarling Joe Barboza. He saw a frustrating mindset among some of the other agents—agents who had tried a bunch of different ways to close in on Angiulo only to find themselves going around in circles. It was as if each failure provided yet another shred of proof to support the popular wisdom that Angiulo was simply too crafty and too well insulated in the North End to ever be apprehended. The FBI had had countless wiretaps and bugs on Angiulo operatives that were rich in hearsay and inside information but never yielded the direct, criminal link to the boss.

Morris and Vaules brainstormed constantly, meeting with informants and examining any possible openings they might exploit in the Angiulo fortress. One of those sessions occurred in 1975, the year Patriarca went home after spending six years behind bars. The conviction had been a big one, but everyone in law enforcement knew that the mafioso's outfit barely skipped a beat in his absence. Patriarca ran the family from prison, having provided for continuity in his underworld operations and for relaying messages when his word was required to resolve a particular problem.

To Morris, six years wasn't enough—they had to really put these guys away. But more to the point—meaning his target, Angiulo—Morris believed that if the FBI could get to Angiulo it could thoroughly disrupt his rackets. Angiulo was not a good administrator, not the way Patriarca was. Angiulo hadn't provided for any kind of continuity; he didn't trust anyone and demanded total control. It's what helped preserve him, but, if the FBI could ever catch him, it would also create permanent havoc in Boston. With this going on in their minds, Morris, Vaules, and one of the squad's best informants considered once again the major hurdle they faced—Angiulo's insulation. Few in the underworld had access to the Mafia boss, and those who did, saw him at the impenetrable Prince Street office.

The two FBI agents left that meeting frustrated, knowing they'd been spinning their wheels, unable to come up with any fresh insights. But Morris began rethinking what the informant kept stressing—that Angiulo conducted his criminal affairs at his Prince Street office. Mulling this fact, Morris realized the informant was telling them something—oh, not directly, not even intentionally. The fact of Angiulo's modus operandi was old hat. Everyone knew about the office and how secretive and careful Angiulo was. Still, the truth was there, as it had been for some time. To get Angiulo someone had to challenge the conventional wisdom about the Angiulo fortress and attempt to do the seemingly impossible.

Turning to Vaules and stressing every word, Morris said, "We have to put a mike in that place."

5

THE WAVE

For the next two years, there wasn't much John Morris could do about the extravagant idea to bug Jerry Angiulo's headquarters. He was reassigned to a squad that was trying to solve a series of truck hijackings. But he had plenty of time to consider all the crosscurrents underlying that moment of illumination he and Vaules had shared when the prescription for nailing the Boston Mafia revealed itself in the simplest of terms: Get Jerry Angiulo to indict himself in his own words. If only the FBI could record those words.

It had become painfully clear to Morris that the strategies to fight the local Mafia during the 1970s had had minor success at best. He and his colleagues had spent years tailing bookies and busting Angiulo's agents, but the raids and gambling probes only disrupted business. They did not significantly alter it. In the end, taking down the agents on the street had amounted to a small bother to Angiulo. Working for the Mafia was still the big leagues for many Italian street kids who were just waiting for their chance—just as Angiulo had waited for his. So, there were always plenty of substitutes to fill in for those sent away to jail.

Even when the FBI did succeed in making a major gambling case against an Angiulo associate, Morris watched in dismay as the courts imposed light sentences. Gambling simply was not the kind of crime that carried hard time. By late 1977, when Morris took over the organized crime squad, the Barboza era had also been closed out. It had been a year since the Animal was shot down in the streets of San Francisco. Barboza may have failed to wound Angiulo, but he delivered some major blows to Providence. He was one in a million. Morris could not count on finding another Joe.

What all of this trial-and-error experience meant to Morris was that the bureau had to go after the Mafia as an organization, to show the public that it was a blood-thirsty outfit and not simply made up of gruff bookies who took bets on Celtics games. He wanted to take that organization to court to show that it savagely assassinated people in order to expand and control its rackets.

The stratagem to get the entire enterprise brought him back full circle to Jerry Angiulo, for Morris long ago had come to realize that, in Boston, the Mafia enterprise and Jerry Angiulo were one and the same. Angiulo was the epicenter. You could not get at the enterprise without getting at Jerry, and if you got to Jerry, you hit the organization in the bull's-eye.

The reason for this was that Angiulo had spent years

insulating himself not only from law enforcement, but also from his own. Morris had learned this firsthand from some of the better informants he'd had a chance to listen to over the years.

In the many gambling cases, he'd found that even those few mafiosi whom the FBI had coaxed into talking knew little about the inner workings of the Angiulo enterprise. Such ignorance made them useless to an FBI struggling to develop a case or corroborate the crumbs of evidence they might have been able to gather elsewhere.

The informants then told Morris repeatedly how Angiulo would explode into a rage at one of his brothers if the Mafia boss decided that too much about "the business" was being discussed in the presence of a non-family member, even if the person was a member of the Mafia. Angiulo never even liked to discuss the business in the presence of the city's second most powerful mafioso, Larry Zannino.

So Angiulo was wrapped within a couple of heavy layers of insulation—the Mafia's and his own family's. The reason for the second layer, Morris would eventually learn, was mainly greed. Working in obsessive secrecy, Angiulo managed to keep some of his enterprise outside the stream of Mafia commerce, so that it was all his own. There would be no 50–50 split on this money with Patriarca in Providence. But the reason for the furtiveness didn't matter. The net effect was that a second layer served as further protection against the FBI agents assigned to stalk him. "If there is such a thing as an evil genius, Jerry was an evil genius," a federal prosecutor who dogged Angiulo for years once said. "Jerry got to the top because of that ability."

The invulnerability of Gennaro Angiulo all came down

to something Nick Angiulo once said of another grand jury probe of his reigning brother. "Jerry Angiulo for what? The guy don't meet nobody. He don't do nothin' with nobody." Which was why Morris knew he had to bug Angiulo at 98 Prince Street—the nerve center where Angiulo did talk incessantly to his brothers and the few others he trusted.

Toward the end of his first year as chief of the organized crime squad, Morris raised these thoughts at a meeting with the agent in charge of the Boston office, Dick Bates. It was a meeting between an older, seasoned supervisor serving his final office before retirement and a young, aggressive squad chief trying to make a name for himself. Bates, with a gentle smile, was skeptical. Morris pressed his case, noting that thousands of man-hours had been spent on bookmaking cases and on developing informants who knew little or nothing firsthand about Angiulo's criminal behavior.

He played off frustration felt throughout the bureau regarding an investigation against Zannino. The strong-arm man from the South End had begun to exploit a defense strategy that would keep him from facing new charges on bookmaking and loansharking for years to come. Zannino, by now in his late fifties, began convincing judges that his physical infirmities were severe enough to keep him from standing trial. It was a tactic that worked—trial delay upon trial delay was granted. And the legal maneuvering kept Zannino on the street, where, Morris knew all too well, he was apparently fit enough to meet regularly with Jerry Angiulo, or attend card games where he gambled and drank late into the night.

Morris stressed the major factor working in their

favor—Angiulo's irrepressible ego. The ego was their money in the bank. It represented a virtual guarantee that if they could set up electronic surveillance it would capture the sort of incriminating braggadocio of which conspiracy cases are made. Morris explained that his squad fully expected to capture blunt talk of crime and punishment that Angiulo indulged in only when he was comfortably behind his office door—including vintage Angiulo proclamations that he was boss of Boston; that he was an intimate of Vito Genovese and Raymond Patriarca; and that whatever he did—be it bookmaking, taking layoff, loansharking, or ordering a hit—he did it the best. Every other word would be *I*. Angiulo would brag about his crimes and expound on his plans.

Bates, without giving a flat-out commitment, permitted Morris to run with the idea. If Morris wanted to take that kind of chance, then he'd back him. This sent Morris to the offices of the New England Organized Crime Strike Force, about ten blocks away in the federal district courthouse building. The strike force consisted of the federal prosecutors who would have to take care of the FBI's legal flank—first assembling the mounds of legal paperwork to seek a judge's approval for the electronic surveillance and, once they got the Angiulos on tape, presenting the evidence at trial.

Morris began by going over the inventory of organized crime cases—where they stood, what the problems were. Then he launched into how the FBI would like to do things differently. It was routine fare, until Morris explained to the strike force chief, Gerry McDowell, what *differently* meant: "Gerry, what we're going to do is we're going to put a microphone in Jerry Angiulo's office."

Morris could tell that McDowell regarded the proposal as half-baked, but he also knew that the strike force would sign on. Morris was no neophyte in bureaucratic circuitry. The high-risk proposal was no sweat off the strike force's back. The FBI absorbed all the risk for installing a bug. It would be Morris's neck on the line, not a prosecutor's.

So Morris was not at all surprised when the strike force offered its full endorsement for the bugging plan. He and McDowell jointly agreed it was an opportunity to "depict them as the organization that they are." But for any federal prosecutor in late 1978, the idea of attacking the Mafia as an organization hit a relatively new set of legal chords. Morris's plan to take on Angiulo as an organization meant drawing upon on a statute known as the Racketeering Influenced and Corrupt Organizations Act, called RICO for short.

Even though RICO had been passed in 1970, the powerful crime-fighting weapon had mostly gathered dust. In part, this was due to the complexity of the statute. Mostly, it was due to prosecutorial shyness. The law had not really created any new crimes. What it did was combine existing criminal behavior into a new offense that carried far stiffer punishment. RICO covered eight state and twenty-four federal crimes. If a prosecutor could prove a mobster committed any two of the crimes, he'd succeed in showing a pattern of racketeering and the RICO sanctions kicked into action. Finally, federal agents frustrated by meager sentences resulting from gambling and loansharking convictions could combine the results and, bingo, nail a wiseguy for operating a racket and win some big jail time—at least twenty years.

By the time Morris conferred with the head of the

New England Strike Force in late 1977, RICO had only just begun to be used sparingly around the country. In New England, the feds had broken RICO ground only two years earlier, in Hartford, and the effort netted two minor crime figures. In Boston, RICO cases were launched against an Irish gang leader and another minor mobster, but any attempt to use RICO to go after the entire Angiulo crime family would be, by far, the most ambitious case in the country.

McDowell told Morris the plan was terrific if the FBI could pull it off. Let me know when you're getting close to the affidavit, he said, referring to the first round of legal papers Morris would need to convince a judge that Jerry Angiulo warranted the FBI's secret surveillance.

Easier said than done. Morris immediately began assembling a team of agents, but nearly two years later not a single one had set foot inside Jerry's place. During that time the FBI suffered a series of agonizing setbacks that kept Morris jittery and the mission in jeopardy.

The first disappointment came six months later, in June of 1979. Agent Mike Buckley was working the graveyard shift monitoring a secret video camera hidden in the North End. The camera, mounted on a rooftop, was trained on a dark alleyway behind 98 Prince Street where Angiulo parked his cars.

The FBI had had the video running for several weeks. The idea was to record the comings and goings of Jerry Angiulo and his associates from the Mafia office. It was all part of the methodical and laborious first step if the FBI wanted a judge's permission to bug Jerry. To win court approval, they first had to establish that the office was where Jerry Angiulo and other mafiosi hung out.

So far, at least as far as Morris was concerned, things had gone pretty well, if slowly. He'd gotten most of the people he had wanted for the mission, particularly his first choice for case agent, Ed Quinn. Quinn was steady and even-keeled. He had the calm determination to keep a long-term operation on track. He was the perfect counterpoint to a sometimes frenetic and intense squad chief. Morris had happily handed Quinn the ticket on Operation Bostar.

With Quinn, Morris had then spent the early months of 1978 choosing the other players. It was like naming a starting lineup for opening day. He grabbed a bunch of veterans. Nick Gianturco was selected for his street smarts and undercover work, Jack Cloherty because he had prepared bugging affidavits before. Tom Donlan, Joe Kelly, and Pete Kennedy had worked organized crime for years. And finally John Connolly, like Quinn, was a Boston native, from Southie, who'd returned home in 1973 from New York, where he'd busted one of the guys wanted for blowing off the leg of Joe Barboza's attorney, John Fitzgerald. Connolly worked the streets too, an agent who stroked informants well, though he had his share of run-ins with the North End's first family. He was a dapper dresser who wore a ring with a symbol of Galway, Ireland, where his parents were born.

Connolly and Angiulo had gone nose to nose in the middle of Prince Street one night in 1976 when Connolly and a couple of other agents arrived to search Jerry and his office as part of a gambling probe. Angiulo was livid, screaming about how he was going to sue Connolly and how Connolly would wish he'd never set eyes on Jerry Angiulo. The very next morning Connolly was back in the North End cruising down Prince Street.

Jerry stood on the corner, spotted Connolly, and pointed to him. Connolly stopped his car and threw it in reverse. Angiulo raced into the street to meet him for round two.

"You got a lot of balls," he yelled at the agent, "being down here by yourself after what you pulled last night." Looking out of the car, Connolly calmly said, "Jerry, listen: Yes, I got balls, and are you trying to tell me there may be someone down here who might want to commit an assault on a federal officer, knowing that brings a mandatory prison sentence and a large fine? I mean are you tipping me off to that? You want to be in the witness protection program, or what? Because I can arrange that, you can be a witness." Angiulo shook his head and left, smiling derisively. From then on, he often greeted the agent mockingly, wailing "*Connnnnnly. We meet agaaaaain.*" Angiulo loved verbal jousting, as long as it was on his turf.

So Morris grabbed Connolly and the other veterans and added relative newcomers Bill Regii and Mike Buckley. The starting nine had seven Irishmen and two Italians, shades of the ethnic breakdown of Boston a century before. Quinn began interviewing women agents for roles as decoys, and the team started trying to snap photos of Jerry at Prince Street. Right off, they discovered nothing would come easy.

For the photos, Morris turned to Bill Schopperle, the cowboy of cameras. Known as Shaky, the mustachioed video expert with sharp Germanic features hardly looked the part of the typical buttoned-down federal agent. He once described himself as an 18-year-old trapped in a 51-year-old body. The man kept odd hours, often going without sleep for days on end. He was the first to admit he was a bit hyper about his work. He preferred boots, flannel shirts, and blue jeans to suits and ties. His gut protruded and he kept his service revolver tucked into his belt. But Shaky Schopperle was as determined as he was eccentric. He almost always got his pictures— one way or another.

The North End posed a special challenge. You couldn't just go down there, set up a camera, and start firing away. Angiulo's people would be all over you in a second. So Schopperle actually began by taking an elevator to the roof of the FBI building. Using a lens that was nearly 6 feet long, he tried to focus in on the corner of Prince and Thatcher streets where Angiulo and his brothers often lingered. It was only a dozen or so blocks away, but too many other buildings blocked the view. Moreover, the pictures he did take, once they were blown up, lost most of their resolution. So he tried riding by in a car, hoping for an opportunity to catch an Angiulo arriving or departing at 98 Prince Street. But that didn't work either. Too hit or miss.

Schopperle then grabbed a green truck and had another agent drive it down into the North End and onto sunless Prince Street, which snaked through the neighborhood. The agent pulled the truck up onto a sidewalk across the narrow street from the office, locked the vehicle, and left for a while. Schopperle hid inside, snapping photos. Within minutes a large garbage truck rumbled up behind him and couldn't get by. The driver leaned on his horn, which drew dozens of onlookers onto the street, including the Angiulos. The truck driver actually began breaking into his truck when the second agent finally returned to get a sweating Schopperle the hell out of there.

Schopperle concluded that a cameraman simply could not stake out the office. He would have to come up with a remote system. If only they had some petty cash to buy a place on Prince Street, he joked to Morris. Morris, of course, couldn't swing that, but he did have Jack Cloherty study property and rental lists to see if the FBI might approach someone about using his or her apartment. He found no openings, no one they could trust enough so that word about the FBI movements would never get back to Angiulo.

By May, Schopperle settled on the video camera installed behind the office, overlooking the darkly lit Lombard Place. He succeeded in hooking it up to an electrical line and aiming it on Jerry's back side. For nearly a month, the FBI camera was rolling, until one night in June on Buckley's shift.

Buckley, sitting alone in the FBI office, sat bolt upright when he saw Angiulo enter the moonlit picture. It was about 1:30 A.M. and the Mafia boss was calling it a night. Buckley flicked on the tape to capture the image of Angiulo as he stepped across the alley to his AMC Pacer.

But then something Angiulo did made the young agent's stomach turn. Jerry's hand went up and he seemed to wave at the camera concealed in a container that Schopperle had built to look like a utility box. "Wait until the guys see this," moaned Buckley.

The next morning, as they did every morning, agents assembled to review the tapes from the night before. But this time Buckley fast-forwarded the reel to the moment that quickly became known as The Wave. Schopperle's first reaction was to deny to his crestfallen colleagues that his camera had been made. He studied The Wave and said, "Maybe we're OK. Maybe he's waving to someone in the window?"

"At 1:30 A.M.?" someone else asked.

Another agent noted there was no apartment back there. Morris watched the replay of The Wave over and over, the way a football coach might dwell upon a key interception that cost his team the game. He felt sick as his mind reviewed the months of work it had taken merely to get a single video camera going.

Without having to be told, Schopperle went down to the North End, climbed the building to the rooftop, and ripped out the camera. It was a lot easier taking them out than putting them in, although you had to put up with strutting wiseguys eager to let you know they had won that hand.

During the next several days, while Quinn and Morris struggled to figure out how they'd lost the camera, the resilient Schopperle quickly installed a second one right on Prince Street itself. He put it inside an air conditioner, which was in the window of a utility company building less than a block from Angiulo's office. Schopperle angled the camera so it focused on Jerry's front door.

This one lasted only two days. The video showed Jerry Angiulo rounding the corner of Thatcher Street and pausing in front of his office. He turned to the camera, looked straight up into the lens, and slowly raised his left hand to his neck for what seemed like an eternity to the monitoring agents. There was no mistake about it: He was giving the FBI the choke sign.

Even before Schopperle could go down and haul this one back in, the FBI watched Frankie Angiulo point out the camera to a group of schoolgirls dressed in matching dark skirts and white blouses. Frankie had the girls wave. Then he had a young punk climb a ladder and poke around the air conditioner. This netted the FBI a vivid close-up of a hand and an eyeball.

Quinn and Morris never did figure out how the rear camera was discovered, but there was little mystery about the air conditioner camera: it was made by the vigilant neighborhood network. Their mistake had been to alter, ever so slightly, the exterior landscape that surrounded Jerry Angiulo's domain. Stunned, Morris and his squad were frozen in their tracks.

Drop back and punt, thought the indomitable Schopperle, who set out to devise new camera techniques. But leaders Quinn and Morris and the other agents became increasingly wary about Angiulo's ability to pick up every move they made. Sure, they had gotten a solid start in gathering the photos and intelligence to go to court for a bug, but the photographic surveillance simply could not end at this early stage. If they ever did succeed in setting up a secret microphone to record conversations, they would also have to have ongoing picture-taking so they could match voices with wiseguys. You could not have a blind microphone and get the kind of precise identification of speakers needed to stand up in court.

Maybe, some of the agents began wondering, you really couldn't overcome the mythic moat that surrounded the 98 Prince Street address. Maybe the idea of bugging Jerry Angiulo was too tall an order?

Slowly, painfully, Morris and Quinn began drawing strength from these early failures, regarding them ultimately as a challenge that grew into a fierce determination to crack the North End. For inspiration, all they had to do was conjure up the image of the defiant Angiulo rubbing his neck in the choke signal for the air conditioner camera. Or there was the unforgettable wave that Buckley first witnessed. All Morris had to picture was that "look on his face, you know, kind of arrogantly waving at us."

To preserve morale and restore energy, Quinn had his agents back off for a while, not wanting the FBI to err too soon on the heels of the camera debacles. Angiulo obviously knew the FBI was up to something, and some breathing space—or lull—was in order. But a few months later, they resumed the often tedious process of gathering all the information they could about the North End, from the layouts of streets and utility lines to details about the people who lived there. If they were going to develop a bugging plan, they needed to know the North End completely—what the patterns and rhythms of everyday life were.

It was an intelligence-gathering process that moved inch by inch, and it wasn't until a year later, the spring of 1980, that the squad thought it was ready to make another formal sortie into the North End. They were putting the finishing touches on a plan to bug the office, using a "hardwire"—a microphone hooked up to a telephone company line that provided a clean and continuous signal.

This meant the time had come to tap the strike force for some legal prep work. McDowell was gone, replaced by an ambitious and prickly prosecutor named Jeremiah T. O'Sullivan. He assigned the newly hired, first female attorney in the Boston office of the strike force to perform the legal grunt work on the so-called T-3 application for a court-approved bug.

For the next two years, Wendy Collins would spend more time with FBI agents than she would with fellow prosecutors. She actually ended up preferring it that way, finding the teamwork among agents who are likely to spend their entire careers with the FBI more real than the jockeying among federal prosecutors looking to hit and run the government—grab some experience fast and then cash it in for some high-paying position with a highbrow law firm.

But Collins had no idea that this would be the case when she reported to work for the first time on March 11, 1980. She left her parents' house in Fitchburg, telling her mother she expected to spend the day filing forms and that she would probably be home early. She was dead wrong. She was immediately briefed on the heady plan to bug the headquarters of the Boston Mafia and told she would serve as the legal link between the strike force and the FBI.

She began researching both the RICO statute and the legal requirements for showing probable cause for a bug. Shortly after she started, an FBI agent took her to the North End to show her the lay of the land. They parked a bureau car on North Washington Street, one of the streets that define the neighborhood's boundaries. In the back seat was her briefcase jammed with legal research and articles about electronic surveillance law that had taken her hours to assemble in a law library. When they returned from their tour they found the car had been broken into. The briefcase was gone. The car radio was still there, but also stolen was a box of bullets agents are required to carry in their glove compartments. And this was the outskirts of Angiulo territory.

Luckily, there was nothing in the briefcase that revealed anything about the plan to bug the Angiulos, but Collins was forced to retrace her steps in the law library. Then she was introduced to Ed Quinn and the other agents, prompting a brief reevaluation of what she was undertaking and why. Here she was, a graduate of Clark University—not the most right-wing school around—who wrote her thesis on the FBI's harassment of the radical Berrigan brothers. She was fresh from a job with a U.S. House of Representatives subcommittee that was probing the FBI's undistinguished role in investigating the assassination of Martin Luther King, Jr. And here was case agent Ed Quinn, who while in New York had been part of a team assigned to stake out a church to arrest Daniel Berrigan. Quinn was the company man in a company that Collins had strong misgivings about.

But two things happened quickly to put to rest any of her opening suspicions. Quinn impressed Collins quickly with his integrity, his even temper, and his low-key style. He never let up and he rarely lost his cool. Then Collins realized there was a common ground for them in the bugging project. This wasn't the Vietnam War or political activism. This was the Mafia. Collins had no problem seeing eye to eye with Quinn on the evils of the mob.

Quinn began shoveling raw information about Jerry Angiulo and his outfit to Collins so that she could sort through it and fashion the T-3 affidavit. The law, drafted to prevent the FBI's abuses in the 1960s, when the bureau had initiated countless illegal bugging operations to gather intelligence rather than evidence, required strict court supervision. She studied other T-3 packages the Justice Department had assembled in other cases and watched her own grow in thickness, from 20 to 30 to 40 pages.

But it was all for naught. The hardwire plan died on the vine, stymied again by Angiulo's security network. While Collins was working up the legal documents, Morris and Quinn had been ironing out the remaining wrinkles in the bugging plan. They needed the telephone company's cooperation in order to pull off a hardwire, and Morris had been having trouble securing a lease, or open, line that the FBI could tap into. There just weren't any telephone lines left in the thickly populated neighborhood, and the Angiulos would surely ask plenty of questions if they saw work crews stringing up new ones.

Still, it was a snafu Morris was determined to work out, except that solving the problem became moot one day in the late spring of 1980 after a meeting with an informant. "Jerry knows," the informant told the FBI. "He knows all about it."

"About what? Whaddya talking about? He knows what?"

The informant explained that Jerry was heard telling an associate he had learned the FBI was going to try to put a bug in.

Morris was stunned, dejected, outraged. The hardwire plan collapsed instantly and Collins's 40-page application for a secret bug was never forwarded to Washington. Once again, Jerry's stature grew. He had his own network of informants everywhere.

In two years, the FBI had been knocked out of the box twice. Two stunning setbacks that affected the two principal pieces of any secret surveillance—first the video camera and then the listening device. But Quinn and Morris realized each carried a lesson for them, and in both instances the lesson was the same. To power their cameras and their mikes they could not rely on any sources but their own. No cameras from a rooftop someone else owned, hooked up to power lines someone else controlled; no cameras inside air conditioners jutting from a building belonging to outsiders; no microphones tied into telephone lines that the FBI did not control absolutely. Just as Jerry Angiulo eschewed outsiders for his protection, so too would the FBI. *Self-reliance* became a word to live by on both sides of the fence. They began working from the premise that everything would stay within the bureau. Their first major break came from Shaky Schopperle. In the late summer, he came up with a way to supply continuous photographic surveillance on the entrance to Boston's underworld. He wanted to plant a camera in the front grille of a car, powered by batteries that he would hide under the back seat and in the trunk. He'd been tinkering around and figured he'd need ten car batteries strung together to keep the camera going all day and into the night, until that car could be replaced with a second equipped with a camera and a fresh string of batteries. He studied Prince Street and saw that a car parked at the corner of Prince and Thatcher could maintain a constant eye on Jerry's door.

Quinn and Morris liked the idea. They also realized that Schopperle would have to come up with an elaborate plan to first secure the parking spot and then choreograph the nightly switches of a dying camera car with a charged one. They knew they could not just plunk one car down on Prince Street for several months. Sooner or later such a car would stick out. The Angiulos would wonder why the same car was always in the same place. Wiseguys would begin poking around. The tires would get slashed. The video car would get made. No, an elaborate procedure had to be developed to rotate the cars, so that their car looked just like any other that came and went in the North End. Eventually, Shaky found he needed a tag team of six agents to maintain the fleet of video cars, recharging batteries and driving the vehicles in and out of the two parking spaces—one on the corner and one two spaces back—that he ended up securing exclusively for the FBI.

It took him three months that fall to round up the cars. The first—a 1974 maroon Nova—he got from the bureau's own lot. It had been used in an earlier undercover operation. The rest he bought. He got the cash from Quinn and began checking out the classified ads. He'd meet people trying to unload an old used car and confuse them with his reaction. No this won't do, he'd say, unable to explain to the puzzled seller that he had certain space requirements and it wasn't enough that the car ran. He couldn't use a car with a V-8 engine—not enough room up front for the camera. It turned out that the junkier the car, the more adaptable it was to carve out the space for all the batteries.

His hunt took him to Beverly and countless other suburban towns. He bought one car on the South Shore from a plant worker during the guy's lunch break—met the guy in the parking lot and paid cash right then and there. He even paid the asking price, though it seemed that the $400 price tag was negotiable. The worker probably raced back to his buddies and bragged how he snookered some idiot. In addition to the Nova, Schopperle picked up a 1965 gray Rambler, a 1970 gray Impala, and a rust-colored 1972 Dodge van.

Schopperle registered all of the cars to fictitious people—names he made up off the top of his head so a license-plate check by the Angiulos would never be traceable to the bureau. He picked one name and said the guy lived on Lowell Avenue in Peabody, north of Boston. He picked another and gave a Lawrence address in a housing project. He picked a Framingham condo complex. The last one was registered to a Jamaica Plain address in Boston, at an apartment house with a lot of turnover. He purposely chose large housing sites so a mobster trying to trace a car would not get suspicious if neighbors had no idea who the person was.

With Schopperle making significant headway, Morris, Quinn, and the others spent weeks brainstorming and consulting with technical people about various bugging options. The watchword was still self-reliance—there would be no more leaks because they would do everything themselves. They would use FBI bugging equipment powered not by any telephone or utility line, but by their own batteries. The techies warned that the best they could give them was a month's worth of power from the log-size battery packs. This meant that if Quinn and Morris wanted the bug to last more than four weeks they would have to replace the drained power packs with new ones.

But Quinn and Morris went for it. Even if they had to break *back* into 98 Prince Street following an initial installation, they preferred to hold the fate of the mission in their own hands rather than risk exposure by tapping into any outside power sources. They'd had too much trouble already. They had also realized that summer was the worst time to break in, even if their hard-wire idea had not died. Too many people stayed on the streets late into the night to have a team of agents skulk around and slip into 98 Prince Street undetected.

They began aiming for a wintertime entry—smack in the midst of a cold snap, hopefully, that would keep anyone in their right mind indoors. For months, Morris had been putting up with the inevitable office jabs about whether his crew was planning on pulling anything off this century. It had been more than two years. But the squad leader finally began to feel a little momentum building in their favor, and, in his view, the mistakes had been necessary in order to fine tune a plan with a prayer of working.

Starting in early autumn, Morris dispatched teams of agents to comb the North End. The movements of the Angiulos and associates like Richie Gambale and James "Fat Peter" Limone, who hung out near Salem Street, were recorded. The Salem Street corner was a favorite with the many Angiulo disciples trying to impress the Mafia boss by keeping an eye out for intruders. When the "law" did cruise by in an unmarked car, as it regularly did, the vehicle was quickly identified by its license number. The Angiulos were notified. Prince Street was theirs.

Morris's men kept tabs on this corner and monitored the pulse of the entire North End—who lived where, when Prince Street was busy, at what hour it got quiet. They noticed that when the neighborhood did shut down, it shut down abruptly. One moment people were walking around, the next the street was deserted. Agents talked about being able to feel it happening, this sudden closure, almost like a curtain being drawn quickly. "We're going in," Morris promised at one of the many squad meetings, to ensure morale wouldn't sag.

They'd decided to try a second bug as well, in the North Margin Street hangout of Angiulo's number two man, Larry Zannino. Zannino conducted a late-night card game at the club, after which he often lingered and drank with the soldiers who worked in his regime. Morris viewed the two bugs as offering the best possible coverage of the Angiulo enterprise, for there was a symbiotic connection between the two sites, located a mere two blocks apart.

The FBI knew that 98 Prince Street was a place where Jerry often issued orders to Larry Zannino, and that Zannino, on at least two nights a week, then returned to his North Margin Street gambling hall to discuss how to execute his boss's commands. Morris assigned agent Shaun Rafferty to run the North Margin Street angle. Operation Bostar was expanding in both manpower and ambitiousness.

The entire pace of the mission picked up. On the legal front, Collins's workload doubled. She single-handedly drafted two court applications for electronic surveillance—for Angiulo and Zannino. She'd basically had to start from scratch after the hardwire failure, because the informant and other information she put together earlier in the year had grown stale by the fall. The courts required fresh inside intelligence. The trick was drafting the applications so that any one reading it, including Jerry Angiulo some day, could never decipher the identities of the various informants the FBI relied upon. The possibility of burning an informant gave her nightmares. She began working late into the night and throughout the weekend. At some point in the late fall, she realized, all she cared about was the mission, and all she wanted for Christmas was for the FBI to install their microphones with no one getting hurt.

In the courts, there'd been an appellate decision that worried the strike force attorneys, but it was not enough to throw the operation off track or even into a slow-down. It was just something that had to be watched carefully.

The case involved RICO and the conviction of a two-bit thug named Novia Turkette, Jr., who had been convicted in federal court in Massachusetts under RICO for operating a drug ring and other illegal enterprises. He'd gotten twenty years in prison, but then appealed to the First Circuit Court of Appeals in Boston by attacking the legality of RICO.

The issue was whether the term *enterprise* in the RICO statute was intended to encompass both legitimate and illegitimate activities. Turkette argued the law was meant solely to protect legitimate business enterprises from infiltration by racketeers. He claimed that the law did not apply to an outfit that performed only illegal acts, like his drug trafficking business. So he couldn't be convicted for merely participating in a criminal racket, especially since he'd not tried to take over any legitimate businesses. In other words, RICO didn't apply to the mob or any racket until the outfit tried to muscle in on bona fide business.

The appellate court adopted Turkette's line of reasoning. It overturned his RICO conviction. The government immediately appealed the ruling to the U.S. Supreme Court, and the high court agreed to hear the case that winter. The local circuit's point of view was at odds with circuit court rulings around the country, which had rejected similar attempts to limit the scope of RICO. Nevertheless, the Turkette decision, at least for the time being, offered mobsters everywhere a ray of hope. For Quinn and Morris, it meant that if the decision stood, they might never be able to go after Angiulo for operating a Mafia enterprise that engaged in ongoing criminal activities. But they could still go after the Mafia family for any specific crimes of conspiracy, gambling, loansharking, and accessory to murder they might uncover through their secret bugs.

So the two FBI leaders chose to let the attorneys worry about the intricacies of pending RICO litigation.

They kept their attention on cracking the North End. Lengthy "work-ups" were prepared on each of the Angiulo brothers, chronicling their daily patterns and habits. Mike Buckley and Bill Regii took turns walking the streets during the day, up Thatcher Street, past Pizzeria Regina, right onto Prince Street, and up to Salem Street. Jack Cloherty and John Connolly did the same, hanging out, soaking up the atmosphere, noting a car registration or any other tidbit into the tiny tape recorders most of them carried. It got to the point where they could pick a time during the day and accurately guess where each of the Angiulos would be. Where was Mikey Angiulo? Usually standing outside on the corner, greeting women as they strolled by. Up on another corner, at Salem, outside a bakery, another lookout was always leaning back in his chair, smoking a cigar.

Certain faces began to emerge from the crowds on the busy side streets—faces belonging to the foot soldiers of Jerry Angiulo. To avoid detection, the agents varied their own appearances. Regii, who probably did the most footwork, grew a beard. One day he'd carry a tool box, the next a gym bag. He'd wear a vest, then an army jacket, then maybe an overcoat. The FBI had never known where Frankie Angiulo lived, but this daylong surveillance seemed to yield an answer. Each morning at about nine, Frankie would emerge from 95 Prince Street—the building that housed the old office—and walk across the street to open up 98 Prince Street.

Late in the fall, Jack Cloherty and Mike Buckley spent their nights in a van, to count heads after a third agent drove the van in, parked it, and walked away from an ostensibly empty vehicle. The pair then tracked each of the Angiulos leaving the office for the night.

Their first stab at the surveillance was a bust. They'd been parked only a few minutes when a curious teenager began eyeing the van. The two agents, hiding inside, could only watch helplessly, using the rearview mirrors. "This kid is going to steal the van," Buckley whispered to Cloherty. Then they saw the kid reach into his pocket, which got the agents guessing. What's this, a gun, a knife? Out came a switchblade. The kid knelt and stabbed one tire, then moved and stabbed a second. They radioed for help, which came instantly. The van was towed away.

By December, Collins was completing the thick mound of paperwork for the two bugs. The surveillance teams had confirmed that the quietest time was Sunday night, so Quinn and Morris, who'd been fine-tuning a plan in a conference room at FBI headquarters, designated Sunday nights for primary entry. From the daily FBI surveillance they'd also come to realize that the last Angiulo to leave the office each night always seemed to pull down the front shade, so a drawn shade came to mean the shop was closed. The pieces were falling into place.

Most of them, at least. Nobody at the bureau knew whether anyone stayed over to guard the office. The information was obviously critical, but informants were never at Prince Street that late. Not surprisingly, this gap in the intelligence worried Quinn the most. He was the one leading two teams of agents into the Mafia's office. All their legwork certainly supported the premise that Angiulo left the office empty overnight. That would have to do, because Quinn knew they were getting close. Nearing Christmas, Quinn reassigned Regii to a four-to-midnight run, to see that no one, at least on a regular basis, came by to check in. No one did.

But in trying to check and recheck their intelligence the squad hit another last-minute snag that once again upset the sense of surefootedness that had taken three months to regain. It was an afterthought almost, because by this time Quinn's confidence had peaked. Maybe it was instinct, he'd never know. But Quinn corralled two female agents in the office and asked them to do him a favor. "I want you to pose as nurses," he told them, "and drive a car up to 98 Prince Street tomorrow at dawn and knock on the door. If any one answers, your story is this: You're looking for Mary Romano, another nurse, and you're on your way to work at Mass General. I'm 99 percent certain nobody is going to answer."

But somebody did.

Later, Quinn could not tell who was more shocked, the female agents or himself. "What the hell are you trying to do to us?" they yelled when they got back. The nurses had barely got the first knock off when some guy swung open Jerry Angiulo's door. The worst part for Quinn was that the agents, not experienced in Mafia matters, could not tell him who the doorman was. He had them look at the photograph book, but they just couldn't make a positive ID. They'd been too shocked. Maybe it was someone from one of the apartments upstairs in the four-story building the Angiulos owned? Quinn asked. No way, one of the women said. "I knocked once and the door opened immediately. The guy had been right there."

The man had to have been in the Mafia office. Quinn, perplexed, considered the possibilities. He was unwilling to accept that all along, throughout their months of surveillance, someone stayed inside. Maybe it was someone who came back after Quinn's agents had

counted everyone out. Possibly he had stayed over just
for that night. Maybe others were there, and an early
meeting was already under way. It had to be an aber-
ration. If only Quinn knew who it was—then he could
have the guy tailed to see if being at the office at that
hour was routine.

Quinn concluded that somehow the man had slipped
through a seam in the FBI's surveillance. He sent in
more agents. He stepped up the nighttime lookout. On
New Year's Day, he called Regii and told him to switch
to a midnight-to-eight shift. Everyone was now working seven days a week. Quinn had the office covered
twenty-four hours a day. The mysterious appearance
became a nagging worry, but the FBI never figured
it out.

Then, on January 9, Morris called him to tell him
the bugging operation had been approved by U.S. District Judge W. Arthur Garrity. There was no more time
to plan. No more time to worry. Not about his nurses,
not about this unidentified guy, not about what they
might find inside. Quinn put his team on alert. The
roller coaster was under way, and it was too late to
get off.

6

FAILURE

John Morris motioned the driver, agent Pete Kennedy, to pull over to the snow-crusted curb of Hull Street, running along the dark backside of a sprawling parking garage. It was a familiar spot by now, one they had used two nights ago, and two nights before that.

Since Judge Garrity had secretly authorized the FBI's bugging plan a week earlier, Morris's crew had tried twice to break into Jerry Angiulo's office, and twice they'd failed. The court order gave them thirty days to install their bugs; they'd now used up seven.

"The clock is ticking," the agents had bantered in a light vein the Sunday night they had first assembled to take the opening stab at getting inside the 98 Prince Street office. But now the ticking clock was nothing to take lightly.

With the car engine still running, Morris received word from the lookouts stationed at key points throughout the North End that Prince Street was empty; that there was no activity on the surrounding streets; and that Ed Quinn, agent Debbie Richard, and their locksmith could now make their way toward the Angiulos'. Morris leaned over the back seat and signaled to Quinn and the others to make their move.

The squad leader, staring at the backs of the trio of agents as they climbed the icy hill, sensed his own mounting anxiety. Kennedy pulled the car away from the drop-off site and the two agents began the first of their many slow circles around the North End—Kennedy keeping his eye on the road and Morris working the radio to juggle all the different pieces that had to be synchronized if they were ever going to pull this off.

The effort to infiltrate Angiulo's office had overtaken every one of their lives, leaving little time for the Christmas holidays and New Year's celebrations. But the agents also knew these kinds of distractions worked in their favor. A Jerry Angiulo planning his annual New Year's Eve bash at Tony C's nightclub in Nahant was a Mafia boss less likely to be looking over his shoulder.

One of the most seasoned members of Operation Bostar, Kennedy was an agent who appreciated the slightest advantage. As a member of the organized crime squad, he had tracked Angiulo for nearly nine years— but with little success.

In 1974, he participated in a gambling probe intended to plug the steady stream of bettors' dollars flowing from throughout the region into Angiulo's hands. Investigators traced phone calls from one betting office to the satellite offices in the North End, studied telephone company records, and then got warrants to search the addresses the phones were listed to. But, as Kennedy would never forget, when they raided eight of the North End addresses, they only made the grade at two. The other places were empty: no gambling slips, no adding machines, no money, no soldiers, nothing. It wasn't that the Mafia had been tipped off. Rather, the apartments and rooms they searched were not being used as gambling offices.

The mobsters had taken the telephone line that was billed to each location and "backstrapped," or run, the line out of that location—going underground, along a rooftop, through walls, whatever route worked—to a second and secret location. It turned the North End into a maze. And it was exactly that sort of moment —standing in an empty room in a North End walk-up with a meaningless warrant—when the impenetrability of the North End really hit home.

So Kennedy was among those who had reacted with some skepticism to Morris's plan. He and some of the others had shaken their heads and tried to explain to the eager Morris that they didn't think you could bug Jerry Angiulo in his office. But nothing else had worked, and Kennedy began to respect Morris's willingness to challenge the conventional wisdom that you could never take down Angiulo in the North End. In Morris he came to see a singleminded motivator who kicked the squad in the butt and got the high-risk venture rolling.

But contrary to appearances, Morris, who had picked Kennedy as his partner because of his experience investigating illegal gambling, was harboring his own doubts. He didn't have much to say to Kennedy as they rode away from the drop-off site for the third time that week. He didn't reveal any of his feelings either. That was not the FBI way. Yet, inside, he was consumed by the intricacies of the entry plan he, Quinn, and the other agents had fashioned. Oh, in recent weeks, he had taken superficial notice of what the rest of the world was talking about: Young kids had been getting murdered in Atlanta with frightening regularity for the past eighteen months; John Lennon, gunned down in New York City in early December, was still being mourned; the newly elected president, Ronald Reagan, was almost finished choosing his Cabinet. But Morris was too preoccupied to really take any of this in; his only concern about the Reagan presidency was practical: Would someone in the new Justice Department be ready to authorize the FBI's secret bugs when the time came?

What increasingly worried Morris was time—from the running court order to each passing minute since Quinn and the other two agents had left his car. Morris heard from Quinn just as the agents reached the intersection of Hull and Snow Hill streets, a crest from which you could scan the North End rooftops or look north across the harbor to the rising slope of Charlestown, where other agents were stationed inside an apartment wired to monitor the bugged conversations. Receiving his approval, the agents began their descent down Snow Hill onto Prince and the final 40 yards to the Angiulo headquarters.

This blueprint they were following to break into the Angiulos' had been worked and reworked, with agents having had opportunities to practice their parts during months of surveillance work in the North End. Now that they had received court approval to break into the Mafia headquarters, it was finally time to put the pieces together. But their first attempts had collapsed, resulting in an agonizing week of trial-and-error.

. . .

The agents' first break-in attempt, on Sunday, had been quickly aborted. The trio had not even made it down Snow Hill Street when they were startled by three men walking ahead of them. They were young guys and they all wore leather jackets—the styled, waist-length jacket popular among the strutting young mafiosi.

If it had been early in the afternoon instead of early in the morning, Quinn would have expected to see these men on the corner of Prince and Salem, a hot spot for wiseguys dressed in dark slacks, dark shoes, and open shirts—even in January. Going around with open shirts in winter was all part of their machismo image. The same dress code called for the light leather jackets after sunset—a look that put Quinn on alert. The guys walked ahead of them down Snow Hill, staying 15 to 20 yards in front.

The agents hoped they would keep on walking—onto Prince, past the Angiulo office, and out of sight into the night. But they had stopped smack at the corner of Prince, where they stood talking, rocking from one foot to another. Quinn couldn't hear them; he could only see the vapor their breath made in the frigid night air. This had forced Quinn, Richard, and the locksmith to stop. "What are they doing in this cold?" Quinn complained, knowing the guys near Prince Street could ask the same question of them. Quinn radioed Morris about the stumbling block, and the squad leader instructed the trio to hold tight for awhile.

The game had begun, with each group sizing up the other.

To send a signal that they were just midnight ramblers, Debbie Richard snuggled into Quinn, giggled, and joked with the locksmith. She rolled back her head, her curly blond hair dancing from underneath her hat, and led the others off Snow Hill onto a narrow side street, Cleveland Place. The trio huddled against the cold.

Of the three, Debbie Richard was the youngest, 31, but she was also the most experienced at undercover work, having worked the beat for ten years. She'd been one of the first women hired by the police department in Huntington Beach, California. Good female cops were hard to find, and, always the tomboy as a kid, Richard had had the drive and self-assurance to mix it up with the men and win their acceptance. In her role-playing, she'd done the prostitute bit, the girlfriend, the secretary, and the career woman, and had learned very early on that you had to be fast on your feet to survive the unexpected. Her uninhibited personality would become a matter of lore in the bureau. At one seminar on undercover work and ethics, the question posed to a large group of mostly male agents had been what to do when solicited for sex. After a long pause, Richard brought the house down with a crack from the back of the room. Leaving the possibility of an active sex life open, she demurred: "I'd say you never take a hit for the company."

One time in California, she had posed as a model trying to get hired at a sleazy joint where models doubled as whores. She wore a hidden microphone to the interview. The old guy sizing her up suddenly grabbed her for a hug and inadvertently hit the secret recorder. What gives? he challenged her. What the hell is that? Richard quickly concocted a story that she wore a pacemaker, that she had heart problems even at her age. The guy bought it. Richard had not only kept up her cover, but, more important, got out of there without getting hurt.

So she knew they had to do something when they spotted the three guys at the foot of the hill, something that would keep the agents in character and make it seem they belonged there in the middle of the night. She tugged at Quinn and began playing up her role as girlfriend out on the town. Quinn immediately played off of her lead, and laughed as if reacting to a private joke.

She'd liked Quinn right from the start, ever since he and another agent had picked her up at Logan Airport after she was summoned to Boston two years before. Morris had just begun assembling his team for Operation Bostar. He'd had Quinn and some others studying the files of the female agents around the country to see who had the experience required for the role they had in mind in the Angiulo break-in. The bureau hadn't had many women to choose from, although by 1979 Richard had already logged five years as an FBI agent, mostly in Las Vegas. Only since J. Edgar Hoover's death, in 1972, had the bureau begun hiring women as agents.

It seemed like Richard was always being sized up. The Boston crew wanted to know if she'd be interested in the grueling investigation, but mainly they wanted to scrutinize her in person and gauge whether she could handle the assignment. When Quinn and the second agent, Jack Cloherty, described what the office was planning to do, Richard was immediately drawn to the high-stakes venture. But she never forgot how secretive the two agents were. They never even took her to the FBI office. "We gotta keep you under wraps," explained Cloherty in his hyperactive patter. "No one knows you're here."

The concern, as always, was the Angiulo family; it knew most of the FBI agents working in the city. Morris didn't want them to get to know Debbie Richard. And he didn't want to have to cope with the following scenario, no matter how small the possibility: One of the Angiulo brothers is seated in a coffee shop and one of his agents, whom the Angiulos know, is also there; Debbie Richard happens to walk in and the agent inadvertently greets her. This would be guilt by association; Richard would be made, and Morris would have to hunt up another woman decoy.

In the end, Morris decided the best way to eliminate the possibility entirely was to keep Debbie away from the other agents. Until just a few months before they actually began trying to crack the Mafia headquarters, Morris had had her working out of the FBI office in Portsmouth, New Hampshire, rather than Boston.

The obsession with identification didn't end with her. The locksmith and technical personnel who were needed to install the bugs had been flown in from Washington for each entry attempt. Even Quinn, the leader of the break-in crews, had tried to stay out of the North End.

For Richard, the only drawback in all the beguiling talk about this mission of a lifetime was the Boston weather. She hated the cold and cursed repeatedly as she stood in the cold side street with Quinn and the locksmith, trying to outlast the guys lingering on the corner of Prince on the night of the first try. "I shoulda worn my woolie undies," she cracked.

Quinn smiled, appreciating Richard's spunk. Then he led the others out of the alley, but the three guys were stuck on the corner. "Hey, guys," Richard called down the street. "Where's the party? I think we got the wrong address." All that came back was some hoarse chuckling. The agents retreated up Snow Hill, acting as if they were calling it a night. Once out of sight, Quinn contacted Morris by radio.

The crew chief had been waiting anxiously in his car with Kennedy; and more than fifteen other agents, scattered around in cars, lookout vans, and on foot, had all been on hold. Quinn told his boss the bad news—too much foot traffic at the bottom of Snow Hill. There were three guys who gave Quinn a bad feeling. Morris checked his watch, talked with Quinn, and after a few more minutes, the trio tried again. Again, they were stymied. The face-off went on for an hour before the tired agents, wary of an approaching dawn, called it a night.

So the first break-in attempt had ended in a stalemate. It was a setback that took a little bit of punch out of the usually steady squad leader. But their second try a few days later had been even worse than the first—because the screw-up was the FBI's own fault. It was beginning to seem that, for each step forward, Morris and his squad took two steps backward.

In the second attempt, Quinn's team did not even make it out of the drop-off car. Morris had made his final round of radio checks before sending Quinn off, to ensure that everyone was in position. But he had heard nothing back from one pair of agents. He tried again. Still nothing.

The marching orders he'd given for the mission had been to stay off the radios as much as possible. Again, the concern was security. The FBI knew the Angiulos kept a police scanner on constantly in their Prince Street office. There was always the chance some mobster would pick up the FBI talk.

Morris worried about this possibility even though his agents talked in code. Jerry Angiulo, for example, who was originally dubbed "Captain," was now known as the "Maitre d'." Morris ordered the change because he worried the first nickname was actually a tip off, since Jerry was so fond of boating. The other code names were nautical—Nick was "XO," short for executive officer; Danny was "First Mate"; Frank was "Spotter"; Mikey was "Seaman"; and Jerry's son Jason was "Disco." They renamed all of the key streets in the North End, calling Prince Street "Broadway."

The problem was being overheard at all—the Mafia eavesdropper may not understand what was being discussed, but he would know something was up. Morris had always stressed: Stay off the air. But unable to raise the two agents in a routine check, Morris called the agents traveling the other streets surrounding the North End, such as Commercial Street, known as "Sponsor," or North Washington Street, known as "President's Way." Has anybody seen them? he asked. Anybody heard from them?

No, was the answer.

He and Kennedy exchanged looks, but neither mentioned any of the thoughts that began racing through both their minds.

Listening to a distant police siren wailing in the night, Kennedy feared the agents had been mugged or stabbed, knowing from his years of stalking the North End that the agents' lookout spot, Snow Hill, was not in the safest section of the neighborhood. There had been a rash of muggings on that isolated and dark part of the hill, where drug deals were also known to go down.

Morris's first fear was carbon monoxide. All of his men had been out in their cars for hours in the frigid night. To stay warm, the agents had probably kept their engine running, and they could have been breathing poisonous fumes all this time. Even worse, Morris worried in a brief capitulation to paranoia, was the possibility that Jerry Angiulo, having somehow acquired an inside track on the FBI's movements, had ordered his soldiers to kidnap the agents.

Morris put everything on hold. No movement toward the Angiulo office until all the agents could be accounted for. He radioed Jack Cloherty and John Connolly, who patrolled the North End periphery in another "roving" car. Their assignment was to be ready to distract any unexpected visitors to the 98 Prince Street area such as a milkman, maybe a city cop, even one of the Angiulos. The way Cloherty saw it, he and Connolly were to put on dancing shoes and use whatever ruse necessary to grab the person and get him or her out of the way. But it was a role that, in theory, was only to be played to protect Quinn and the other agents once they were actually inside the Mafia headquarters installing the bugs. No one had ever really contemplated the possibility that two of their agents would suddenly disappear.

"Drive by," Morris ordered.

They did. The car wasn't there.

Cloherty and Connolly scanned up and down Snow Hill.

No agents.

They saw cars jammed into spaces all along the snowy street. Not one belonged to the FBI.

No agents, no car.

Christ, Morris thought. He cursed himself for ever having put the two agents together. The idea was to have them appear as lovers parked in a car, but both were young and inexperienced. He should never have matched the two neophytes. The mistake was his. "Find them," he said, deciding right then to call off the entry attempt altogether. Other agents left the positions they'd taken for a break-in and joined the search.

Ninety minutes later, Cloherty and Connolly met Morris at the corner of Hanover and Commercial, not far from a Dunkin' Donuts. "I'm going to give them another 20 minutes," Morris said. After that, he explained, he'd have to call and tell the special agent in charge of Boston about the problem, a step that could have led to a decision to end the mission as too dangerous.

Cloherty and Connolly headed back down Commercial to the beginning of Prince Street. Cloherty was not optimistic. He could not come up with any plausible explanation. Even though the agents were young, they were conscientious. They were FBI. They would never just take off without telling someone.

"Where the hell is this car?" Cloherty asked his partner as they approached Prince Street. It was not on Snow Hill, they reasoned. It was not on Prince. Nor was it on any of the other streets they and other agents had inspected.

Then Connolly stopped in front of the large and empty parking garage at the corner of Prince and Commercial streets. The two agents got out and walked into the mostly abandoned building.

They drew their guns and began using their hands to signal one another. They walked and walked, up the first-floor ramp, onto the second, and finally all the way to the rooftop level of the garage.

That's where Cloherty spotted the vehicle. Down the

other end of the rooftop overlooking Snow Hill. The motor was running.

Cloherty and Connolly walked toward the vehicle, and each spotted the backs of two heads, slumped in the front seat. Both had the same thought: carbon monoxide.

Cloherty reached the car first and ripped open the door on the driver's side.

"What's the problem?" one groggy agent asked.

"What's the problem!" Cloherty shouted back.

In a matter of seconds, the story tumbled out.

The two lookouts had been sitting in their car on Snow Hill doing their job, which was to make sure the street was empty so that Quinn and his team could use the route. But then they had seen someone watching them suspiciously from an apartment window across the street. They became nervous, worrying they'd been made. Not wanting to jeopardize everything, they had decided they'd better move. So they had driven away from their location on Snow Hill Street and circled around until they found the abandoned garage. They drove to the roof and discovered a spot that gave them a commanding view of the street below.

Perfect, they had thought, and called Morris on the radio.

This was the moment in the tale when Cloherty grasped the only explanation for the massive screw-up. He took the agents' radio from the car seat and tried it.

It didn't work.

The young agents sank farther in their car seats.

All along, they had thought Morris knew their whereabouts. They had figured Morris never radioed back because of the squad leader's strict orders about keeping radio silence. They had figured they never heard any of the other agents conversing on the radio with Morris because, like them, everyone else was also obeying the rule against radio communications.

Morris was immensely relieved to hear the agents were safe, that the snag had been a radio malfunction. But he still didn't let himself off the hook. Only two inexperienced agents would ever display such radio discipline. Only virtual rookies would ever take so literally his instructions.

The Snow Hill lookouts went home after that second fiasco feeling like damn fools, only slightly buoyed by Morris's "forget about it" sign off. In the office, the episode became known as "Car 54, Where Are You?." Morris, however, couldn't appreciate the joke. Instead, he fought back a feeling that perhaps this mission was doomed. First, bum luck—bumping into those guys the way they did. Then, radio foul-ups—lousy FBI equipment. He played what had happened over in his mind, shifting through the two abortive attempts in search of a pattern, something to adjust. But all he found was bad luck.

On the third attempt, after Morris okayed the Quinn teams' descent down Snow Hill Street, he refused to put too much stock in how smoothly things were going. He sat in the car with Kennedy, tracking Quinn's progress, waiting for another shoe to drop. Throughout the day there'd been no surprises. The opening move went off without a hitch. It involved agents Cloherty and Buckley. Starting in the late afternoon, they'd taken up their position in the back of a lookout van parked on Prince Street a half block from Angiulo's office. From there, they watched the office for the departure of each of the Angiulos. The monitoring took hours, with brothers sometimes departing only to return shortly afterward, but nothing else could begin until the lookouts sent word that Angiulo and his minions had left for the night.

Morris heard from the lookouts around midnight, which wasn't too bad. By the agents' head count, the office was empty. He then dispatched other teams of agents to scour the streets, including a pair to relieve Cloherty and Buckley from the van, which got colder and colder as the night wore on. The new pair would monitor the street while Quinn was inside. Cloherty and Buckley split up and joined new partners in two of the roving FBI vehicles.

In little more than an hour, everyone was in place. Quinn, Richard, and the locksmith had left Morris's car and easily made their way to the foot of Snow Hill and Prince. The Quinn team was about ready to make its final crossing, past the lookout van and to the front door of 98 Prince Street. Encouraged, Morris, for the first time during any of the attempts, ordered his three electronics specialists to stand by. The techies were going to follow Quinn in, once Quinn's team was safely inside the office. The chief's radio crackled with reports from lookouts that the street remained quiet.

Morris listened as Quinn, in a hushed voice, described his team's slow progress. Even though the FBI had carefully counted heads, every member of the break-in operation knew that this wasn't an absolute guarantee the office would be empty.

There was no guarantee, because even their best informants could not provide such critical information as whether someone was assigned to sleep in the office. In all the surveillance and intelligence work they'd done to prepare for the bugging, the FBI still did not know exactly what went on in the office from midnight until dawn.

Morris and Quinn had struggled with this gap, and, hard as they tried, could come up with only one idea. They could have an informant secretly drop a tiny microphone behind a couch during a daytime visit to the Angiulo headquarters. That way the FBI could determine whether anyone was inside the office late at night. But what if the mike made a noise when it hit the floor? What if it rolled out from under the couch? If the Angiulos caught their man, he would surely be killed and the bugging plan would have to be abandoned. They concluded the plan was too risky.

The FBI also didn't even know whether the office was equipped with an alarm, because no agent had ever gotten close enough to check for one. If Quinn, Richard, and the locksmith ran into an alarm triggered by a key at the door, well, no problem. They could disarm it. But there wasn't much they could do if the office had a silent "motion" alarm that rang elsewhere.

So the best the Quinn team had going for it was the scorecard that Cloherty and Buckley kept. As they looked across Prince the office certainly seemed abandoned; lights were on in other buildings, but 98 Prince Street was black.

Receiving word from the two agents in the van that the street was empty, Quinn hurried across Prince Street to the alcove of 98. Richard was at his side, and the locksmith a foot or two behind them. They found the lock on the outer door was frozen solid, leaving the agents momentarily stuck in limbo, exposed in the open street while the locksmith rubbed his thumb and breathed on the lock to defrost it. But in less than a minute, the outer door was open and they were on their way.

Having finally gotten inside the building, they confronted the one thing no one had expected but everyone had feared. They heard voices inside the office in what sounded like low, steady conversation. Instead of trying the second door, Quinn backpedaled quickly and led a hasty retreat, his mind spinning with confusion.

Hearing over his radio what was unfolding, Morris slapped the dashboard. In their own cars, Cloherty and Buckley were in shock. Both knew immediately that fingers would be shaken at them. They were the ones on early surveillance who had cleared the office. Had they miscounted? Had they blown it for Quinn? Even though they'd never been absolutely certain, all the surveillance work the FBI had done supported a premise that no one lived in the apartment. Were they all wrong? Or, Morris wondered, was this another round of bum luck—the night they pick to break in is the night some wiseguys happen to stay over?

In his car with Kennedy, Morris searched his mind for an explanation. The two previous failures had been frustrating, but this was becoming a bad joke. He could see Kennedy was about to say something, probably going to put into words the frustration that agents had so far refrained from expressing: Maybe they were not going to be able to pull this off. Morris knew he had to take control, had to quell the dismay. Quinn and his cohorts were fleeing the office, while agents in cars and on foot were shaking their heads in bewilderment. "Hey, look, we're never going to know," he told Kennedy with unwavering calm, insisting they had to keep trying and promising a fourth attempt. "Let's do it."

And three nights later, they did.

7

BREAK-IN

The same month—January 1981—that FBI agents in Boston were struggling to install a secret bug inside the headquarters of the city's Mafia boss, authorities in New York City bugged a reputed rising star in the Gambino crime family, John Gotti.

Gotti, an imposing figure with piercing, dark eyes, coiffured hair, and custom-made suits, was a capo de regime who was intimately familiar with the machinations of the Gambino family. In the 1981 bugging of his club in Queens, however, authorities quickly found that Gotti was tight-lipped when it came to his alleged Mafia business. Instead, when serious matters arose, he conversed while walking up and down 101st Avenue in Queens. So the secret tapes were weak, and in 1986 Gotti beat a federal rap charging him with illegal gambling, loansharking, armed hijackings, and at least two murders over an eighteen-year period. Today he's considered the new Godfather, the most powerful mobster in the country.

In Boston, John Morris and Ed Quinn did not worry about just getting small talk from inside Jerry Angiulo's office at 98 Prince Street. Based on intelligence secretly provided by a network of informants, the federal agents knew that Angiulo conducted nearly all of his business affairs in his North End headquarters. It was where he felt insulated, where he had worked uninterrupted for nearly three decades. The problem was getting inside to install their own secret bugging devices.

They'd had three failures in seven days.

Battle weary, the squad at least had the solace of making the fourth attempt on the optimal day— Sunday. It was the only night the neighborhood turned in early. Quinn, Richard, and the locksmith once again sat in the back of Morris's car. Pete Kennedy, the driver, had the engine running and the heater blasting at its maximum. Boston had suffered through a string of days with subfreezing temperatures—so cold that schools had closed early on Friday to conserve natural gas supplies. Maybe it was the anticipation of being out in the frigid night, strolling the North End streets, but Debbie Richard shivered, even as she sat in the car with its windows fogged from the heater. She'd worn a thick wool sweater and heavy slacks and wrapped her hair in a scarf. She hated New England winters.

In the front seat, Kennedy was worrying about the last failure. To him, the voices the Quinn team unexpectedly encountered meant only one thing—that the Angiulos kept someone on the premises overnight to guard the place. Kennedy and other members of the squad hadn't come down too hard on the two agents who watched the office to make sure the Angiulos had left, but, still, it left him feeling uneasy about a fourth try. It meant being vigilant and ready to sweep in to back up Quinn at the first sign of trouble.

Morris, sitting next to Kennedy, worried about the voices too, but he had not reached any conclusion. During the months of surveillance in the autumn, he thought his squad had gotten the Angiulos' routines down pretty well. The findings suggested that no one stayed overnight at the office, but there had been the incident of the agents posing as nurses, whose knock on the Prince Street door had been answered. That surprise, however, seemed the exception rather than the rule. In fact, the premise that the office was empty had been reinforced just a few nights earlier, the night of the first attempted break-in, when Quinn had to bail out because of the wiseguys loitering on the street. That night, everyone had gone home except the two lookouts on Prince Street. Morris, always looking for fresh information, had them remain in their van until dawn to monitor the office. The agents had seen nothing.

So Morris went back and forth on this vital matter: Was the office empty or not? Now the latest crisis— the voices—had thrown his squad into a tailspin. The only conclusion Morris had reached was that no matter how much they prepared, the break-in was going to be a hit-or-miss proposition. The only way to find out for sure was to do it.

Morris became increasingly exacting in monitoring the progress of his agents, particularly the periodic reports that came in earlier in the evening from Cloherty and Buckley about who was departing from the Mafia office and when. Morris had the agents account for each of the major players—first the various Angiulo brothers and then key soldiers such as James "Fat Peter" Limone. The mobsters had been picked up as they left the office, either in a car or on foot, and then followed until they left the North End altogether. Angiulo had been followed home and "put to bed" by an agent hours ago at his estate on the North Shore. Now Morris had everyone just sit, to make sure neither Limone nor any other associates made a U-turn and returned to 98 Prince Street.

Nearing 2 A.M., the reports coming in were encouraging. Prince Street was quiet. Meanwhile, as Morris kept tabs on the big picture, Quinn, waiting in back for the final go-ahead, was preoccupied with a much narrower focus. He saw things in terms of the route he had to take to reach the Angiulo office. It covered the length of a football field, and the first 75 to 80 yards—up Hull and onto Snow Hill—were relatively safe. At that hour, they could expect to find the dark and narrow streets empty; and they still hadn't reached the immediate vicinity of the Angiulo office, so that even if someone did spot them it shouldn't be cause for any special concern. They were just three people who happened to be walking down the street. But once they reached Prince Street and the final 20 or 25 yards—that's when they had to worry. That's where they'd seen the wiseguys. And where anything appearing only slightly out of the ordinary was expected to register with the Angiulo neighborhood network. For Quinn to cover this stretch and make it inside, the neighborhood's back must be momentarily turned.

Of course, Quinn retained a residual concern about the voices from the other night, but, like Morris, he couldn't let this deter him. They were going in. However, the voices did remind him of the moments he most hated, and was most apprehensive about, in his sixteen years as an FBI agent—going through a locked door. You never knew if somebody was going to be on the other side with a club or gun. Working armed robberies in New York City, Quinn had done some door-bashing. He'd busted into apartments and ratty hotel rooms knowing an armed robber was on the other side. It was the worst a perilous business had to offer, knowing you were going to face a gun on the other side. One time, he broke down a hotel door, crouched, and aimed his Smith and Wesson at a robber lying on a bed just as the robber's hand was reaching beneath a pillow for a pistol. It was a moment his memory had seized forever, a photograph in his mind's eye.

But, for the most part, Quinn was feeling ready, having prepared for this fourth attempt in the calm, businesslike manner he was known for. In the afternoon, he'd watched the Celtics beat the Lakers on television. The Lakers, playing to a packed house at the Garden, had led most of the game, but the Celtics pulled it out 98-96. Larry Bird was off, hitting a miserable 4 of 13. Robert Parish was strong, scoring 22.

At six o'clock, Quinn drove from his home on the South Shore to the FBI office. He dressed neatly, but casually. He wore a long overcoat. He took off his large Boston College class ring, but kept his wedding band and wrist watch. Morris was already at the office, and the two went over the game plan. Cloherty and Buckley were in their white van on the early shift monitoring the office. By about ten, the other agents straggled in.

For the entire squad, the three failed break-in attempts meant, on the one hand, that they'd all had a chance to practice and polish their roles in the bugging plan. But, on the other hand, with a thirty-day deadline, the pressure was mounting. It was day ten, and this time, Larry Sarhart, the agent in charge of the Boston office, was participating in the mission, a new development that many of the field agents weren't certain how to interpret.

The agents drank coffee, sat around on top of their desks, and waited for the night to wear on. The large, open squad room on the ninth floor, with desks lined up facing north, resembled a big classroom, and the wisecracking among the agents was not unlike the ribbing heard in any high school homeroom. Periodically, Morris dispatched a team of agents. After midnight, he was on the road himself, with Quinn and his team in the back seat.

The prolonged waiting game ended shortly after two. Quinn, Richard, and the locksmith climbed out. Quinn pulled up his collar against a stiff breeze. The ice on the street crunched beneath his feet. Richard shook from the night air and her nerves. "Let's speed this up, I'm cold," she complained.

The three were just beginning their hike up Hull Street, everyone feeling tense, when Richard slipped. She almost caught herself, but her foot slid out from under her on a slab of ice. She began laughing, and the others joined in. Here she was supposed to be acting so cool and she'd gone down like a clown in the first few steps. Quinn helped her to her feet.

The fall actually cut some of the tension. The trio joked and began acting more like the partygoers they

Jerry Angiulo's office was equipped with an impressive kitchen including a large commercial stove that had a double oven. (*Justice Department Photo*)

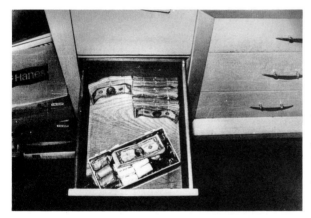

One of Frankie Angiulo's drawers, containing gambling money, at his apartment on the third floor at 95 Prince Street. (*Justice Department Photo*)

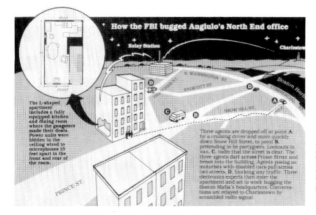

How the FBI bugged Angiulo's North End office. (*The Boston Globe*)

The intersection of Prince and Thatcher Streets in the North End, where each day the FBI parked the cars containing the hidden video cameras. *(The Boston Globe)*

Five of the six Angiulo brothers in 1964 at the Suffolk County Courthouse where they appeared before a special Grand Jury probing organized crime. The brothers are, from left to right, Antonio, Michele, Nicolo, Gennaro, and Donato. *(UPI/Bettmann News Photos)*

Jerry Angiulo's photograph from the 1936 Boston English High School yearbook. *(The Boston Globe)*

JENNARO J. ANGIULO, "Jerry"
One touch of nature makes the whole world kin.
Ambition: Criminal lawyer
Suffolk Law School

Ilario Zannino at 51 North Margin Street during a raid by federal agents in 1981. (*Justice Department Photo*)

Jason Angiulo and John Cincotti watch as jurors march into 98 Prince Street during the 1986 trial. (*The Boston Globe*)

New England organized crime boss Raymond L. S. Patriarca leaves U.S. district court in Providence after being arraigned in 1981 on labor racketeering charges brought by a Miami grand jury. (*Providence Journal-Bulletin Photo*)

Jerry Angiulo as he enters a state court in Massachusetts for an arraignment on the Patrizzi murder charge in 1987. (*The Boston Globe*)

Jerry Angiulo inside the Salem, Massachusetts, courtroom. (*The Boston Globe*)

The three Angiulo brothers, from left to right, Francesco, Michele, and Donato, outside their Prince Street office. (*The Boston Globe*)

Mafia chief Joe Lombardi.

FBI agents Edward Quinn (left) and Peter Kennedy (not shown) escort Jerry Angiulo from the Boston police station after his 1983 arrest. (*The Boston Globe*)

FBI agent Edward Quinn ran the Angiulo bugging operation. (*The Boston Globe*)

FBI agent John Morris conceived the Angiulo bugging operation. (*The Boston Globe*)

Wendy Collins, the Strike Force prosecuting lawyer assigned to the Angiulo case. (*Toby Talbot Photo*)

Jerry Angiulo sits handcuffed in a car as he is transported from federal court in Boston after a jury found him guilty of several racketeering charges. (*The Boston Globe*)

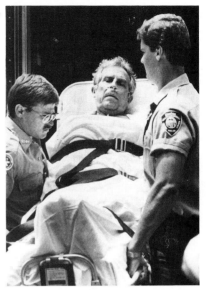

Ilario Zannino, who claims a history of heart problems, was carried from U.S. district court in 1985 after he slumped to the floor during opening arguments in his racketeering trial. (*The Boston Globe*)

Filippo (Phil) Buccola, former head of the New England Mafia. (*The Boston Globe*)

Attorney William Cintolo at the Federal courthouse in Boston. (*The Boston Globe*)

Jerry Angiulo lived in this spacious oceanfront home in Nahant, Massachusetts. (*The Boston Globe*)

Deborah Richard is the FBI undercover agent who played a key role in breaking into 98 Prince Street in order to plant the listening bugs. (*AP Photo*)

were supposed to be playing. They paused at Snow Hill to await word from Morris that they could descend onto Prince. Quinn could see that the street below was empty.

He preferred the early Monday morning slot for attempting an entry. All of their footwork showed this was the quietest time in the North End. On other nights at 2 A.M., cars were triple parked outside places like the Café Pompeii up on Hanover Street, which the Angiulos owned. On a night like this, they still could encounter people who went to work before dawn, but they didn't have to deal with the wiseguy element. If ever there was a night the wiseguys stayed home, it was the Sunday to Monday swing.

Surveying the area, Quinn could see lights on in the buildings that hugged the narrow streets, but they lit mostly entryways. Few apartment lights were on. The popular pizza parlor a block behind the Angiulo headquarters, Pizzeria Regina, had been closed for hours. Chairs were stacked atop tables and only a night light shone. The North End was as still as it ever gets.

The first phase of the entry went off without a hitch, the kind of smooth action that delights a movie director who is shooting a scene and gets it right in a single take. Had there been a camera rolling, it would have captured this seven-minute scene:

Three revelers share a bottle of Scotch and small jokes as they meander down Snow Hill looking for an after-hours party.

They pause briefly at an alley, where the woman nuzzles up against the men, and talk quietly.

When they reach the corner of Prince Street, deserted

in the early morning shadows, the three suddenly step briskly across the intersection to a doorway faintly framed by a streetlight.

With the camera zooming in for a close-up, it's clear the trio in search of a party is not dressed for one. Bulletproof vests are beneath their overcoats and .38-caliber revolvers hang from their belts.

After climbing the five steps, two of them huddle as the third kneels and picks the lock.

In a matter of seconds, the FBI is standing at the Mafia's inner door.

Behind the scenes other agents made myriad movements prior to that seven-minute stroll—all of them choreographed by Morris from his car.

Morris kept Quinn from walking down the ice-capped hill into the tight confines of the old neighborhood until he received final word from his two agents in the lookout van that Prince Street was empty.

Nick Gianturco and Shaun Rafferty, having relieved Cloherty and Buckley around midnight, were seated on milk crates in the back of the van. For hours they had been alternating between binoculars to see out the van's front window and peepholes to peer through the sides.

Even though they thought they'd learned their lesson after the first screwed-up effort at breaking in, they still froze their butts. That first night, when Morris had had them stay in the van after the break-in was called off, to see whether anyone came or left Jerry Angiulo's place, they had been there for almost nine hours. Rafferty had worn only his wingtips, and his toes all but froze. He'd never been so cold in his life. Ever since, the agents had come prepared, or at least tried to. Rafferty found a pair a thickly lined boots with heavy soles issued by the U.S. Air Force—called Moon Boots. He climbed into them, a pair of long underwear, two pairs of pants, and a couple of sweaters. His partner, Gianturco, had a pair of battery-operated, heated socks, but the damn things stopped working. He wore long johns, several sweaters, a hat, and a couple of pairs of gloves. Gianturco also brought along some munchies—eggplant sandwiches to bug Rafferty, who didn't like them. Rafferty munched on candy bars. Eating helped break the monotony of watching and waiting.

The van was parked strategically on Prince Street, in the second of two spaces that Shaky Schopperle had acquired squatter's rights to by parking his cars there for the past several weeks. Inside the van, Rafferty and Gianturco didn't have much room to move around, and even when they did they worried someone would spot the vehicle stirring. They threw blankets over their shoulders, were forced to urinate into a can, and kept wiping the fogged-up windows, taking care that no one saw them.

Rafferty's toes still went numb, but he and Gianturco always managed to keep Angiulo's place in sight.

They were Quinn's eyes.

As the penultimate step, Morris signaled Bill Regii. From the foot of Prince Street, where it intersected Commercial, Regii began walking down Prince. He walked past the west side of the abandoned parking garage and toward the back end of the lookout van.

He scanned the entryways and alleys, making sure no one was hiding in either.

Rats scurried along the curb amid the rubbish.

By radio, he reported back to Morris that the lights in the Angiulo office were off and the shades were drawn. Months before, they had learned drawn shades meant no one was home—most of the time, anyway.

After looking left to check for lights in the building where Frank Angiulo lived, Regii continued past 98 Prince Street to the intersection of Salem Street, where some Angiulo soldiers and associates lived.

All was clear.

Morris then gave the go-ahead to Quinn, Richard, and the locksmith. He quickly made another radio call and, in code, issued a car-blocking order. Suddenly, two vehicles pulled out to clog the two streets leading to 98 Prince. Buckley, with Regii back at his side, steered a Chevy Impala across the opening of Prince Street at Commercial Street on the harbor side of the North End.

Tom Donlan maneuvered his navy blue Buick to block Thatcher Street at Endicott. Riding with Donlan was Larry Sarhart, the top man in the Boston office.

Though blocks apart from one another, the agents' actions were identical. Sarhart and Buckley climbed out of their cars, popped the hoods and, until receiving word that Quinn was safely inside Angiulo's office, acted like motorists whose cars had conked out on them in the bitter cold. For the next seven minutes, no cars were going to get past them and drive down Prince Street.

Overall, the plan had been designed to ensure that the neighborhood's back was indeed turned for the few seconds it took Quinn and the others to cover the final 20 yards.

For, Quinn, Richard, and the locksmith, standing motionless in the foyer of 98 Prince Street, it was pretty much now or never. But once again they were thrown by the sound of muted voices coming from inside. Instead of retreating quickly, they hung on. The thirty-day clock on the court order was running and they'd already suffered three failed break-ins. So they stayed, and after several seconds they began to detect an odd cadence in the steady talk. Fighting off anxiety, they listened long enough at the door to realize the noise might be radio voices.

The locksmith went to work on the office door, but the lock wouldn't release right away. Richard was standing to one side, waiting, squeezing the neck on a bottle of Cutty Sark.

Using the Scotch as a prop had been her idea. The brand was actually Quinn's, but he'd only sipped it to put the odor of booze on his breath. Suddenly, Richard heard a noise up on the second-floor landing. She reacted instinctively, thinking: Christ, somebody hears us. It sounds like they're coming. We might as well make some noise and sound like we belong.

"Hey, Frankie, really," she blurted, slurring her words as festively as she could. "Is this where the party's supposed to be?"

The question hung in the air.

Frankie, one of Jerry's four brothers, lived on the second-floor across the street, and if any of the Angiulos was guarding the office, Frankie was the most likely candidate.

Fortunately, no one answered.

The agents looked at one another, relieved they did not have to draw upon a threadbare ruse of having the wrong address for a party. For even though Richard was improvising, they all knew that if their cover got blown Quinn would have to shout, "FBI." Guns would be drawn. With luck, no shots would be fired.

The locksmith worked the lock free, and Quinn signaled to him to go ahead and open the door that led from the hallway into the office. Quinn took a deep breath. He wasn't scared, but he was apprehensive—if some wiseguy was behind the door waiting for them, his only hope was that the guy wouldn't shoot.

Quinn went in first. He crouched at one side of the door; Richard quickly crouched at the other. They were consumed in the apartment's darkness, except for the low light of the radio. They stood perfectly still, their eyes straining to see. Richard took over, again relying on instincts developed in years of undercover work. "Hey, Frankie, I'm heah. Where's the pahty?" It was not a line the team had rehearsed, but Quinn understood immediately. If an underworld figure were hiding in one of the dark corners and heard a woman call out for Frankie, he would be puzzled long enough for Quinn to react.

Richard offered more greetings and stepped around the office, which was L-shaped, about 30 feet long and 12 feet wide. The quarters came into focus—the kitchen in back, a table in the middle, a bathroom off to the side of the kitchen, a television up front near the two windows facing the street. The smell of garlic was overpowering.

The only sounds came from the radio. The agents immediately realized what had thrown them before: The Angiulos had left the radio turned to WEEI, the city's all-news station, as a precaution. There was nobody here, just radio voices.

Over his two-way radio, Quinn told Morris that the break-in had come off cleanly. Morris stiffened in his car cruising around the parameters of the North End. He ordered the second team of agents, the techies, to stand by.

Neither he nor Quinn thought they were home free. They'd overcome one hurdle, making it inside, only to face another. The next ten minutes would be the most tense. Had someone seen the three agents enter and notified one of the Angiulo soldiers living in the neighborhood? Had a silent alarm sounded? If someone came running down the street, this was when Gianturco would quickly notify Morris. Morris and all the other agents would then descend upon the office. Quinn could only hope they would intercept the runner before he reached them. Morris had all routes to the office covered, and his theory was to overwhelm any unwanted visitor with FBI bodies, using surprise and, if necessary, firepower. No one was to reach 98 Prince Street.

Inside, even the irrepressible Richard let the ten minutes pass in silence. It didn't take long for them to begin sweating in the overheated and stale apartment air. But nothing stirred and no alarms went off, something Quinn and the other veteran agents of the organized crime squad would later shake their heads about back at the office. The Angiulos had foolishly relied exclusively on their neighborhood network to protect their domain. It was part of the hubris that would bring them all down in the end.

From his van, Rafferty told Morris the street remained quiet. Rafferty's voice was actually changing, Morris thought, thinning in the subfreezing chill. Morris signaled the second group.

Unlike the Quinn team, this trio—all electronics specialists—hustled down Snow Hill Street, sending rats scurrying for cover. The agents lugged satchels of equipment. This was the most nervous Morris had ever felt. There was no attempt to play partygoers with the techies. They were dressed in their work clothes, carrying heavy equipment. They clearly did not belong in the North End, but rather resembled three paratroopers who'd hit the ground running. If they were spotted on Prince Street, Morris thought, that would have been it—the mission would be a guaranteed wash.

Quinn met them at the outer door and ushered them into the apartment. With six now inside, the tiny office was suddenly overcrowded. Everyone stood still for at least another five minutes. Nobody talked. They listened, but heard nothing, except for one another breathing. The FBI radios crackled in their earplug receivers with reports that the street remained empty.

In their car, Morris and Kennedy slapped one another on the back. Kennedy was ecstatic he was proved wrong—no one was inside the office. Morris was elated. After their third failure, he had privately begun to worry the break-in was doomed. Snags were to be expected, but three misses? And he, along with veterans like Kennedy, knew the stakes—if the Angiulos caught them breaking into their headquarters it would knock the FBI out of the box for the next ten years. Their gloating target, Jerry Angiulo, would construct a new maze of defense measures that would take agents years to decipher.

But now, on a day when the rest of the city and country was preoccupied with the pending release of 52 Americans who'd been held hostage in Iran for 444 days, and when Ronald Reagan was just hours away from assuming the presidency, Morris had six agents in the geographical center of the Angiulo operation, a place few people, never mind federal agents, had ever seen before.

Inside, Quinn motioned each agent to an area of the apartment. Using penlights, they inspected their turf. When they were done they had to leave the room as they'd found it.

Looking around, Richard was disappointed. She had expected elegant touches from the mob leader. These guys had so much money, she figured they'd use some of it to make their workplace comfortable. But this was pure tacky—worn, crummy-looking white vinyl chairs; beat-up unpadded carpeting; walls covered with cheap panels of fake wood and dotted with Mediterranean prints that looked like $10.99 specials from a flea market. The only impressive feature was the huge stove in the kitchen, the commercial model found in restaurants, with its four burners and double ovens.

The bugging specialists unloaded their satchels and went to work. They kept their flashlights under a black cloth to avoid the possibility of someone outside spotting a flash of light. Quinn and Richard stayed in constant contact with Morris and watched as the installers scanned the seam between the ceiling and wall to find spots to implant two tiny microphones. So he could reach the ceiling comfortably, one of the agents grabbed a ladder he'd found leaning against the wall. It became an inside joke at the FBI: To install the bugs they'd used a ladder the Angiulos had thoughtfully left behind.

Richard decided to sit in one of the vinyl chairs. "What happens if we have to use the bathroom?" she whispered. "Do we flush the toilet or just leave it?" The others snickered. There were jokes about cooking up a feast on the Angiulo stove.

The work went in spurts. They were careful to stay away from the front windows, knowing that if they got too close someone outside could see their silhouettes, even though the window shades were drawn. But every ten minutes or so word came across the FBI radios to stop—someone was approaching on foot. Or a car was driving down Prince Street toward them.

Quinn and the others would duck and freeze. Each time their hearts pumped faster, worrying that someone would enter 98 Prince, or the car would pull up out front. Each time Morris held his breath, wondering if their cover was blown and he'd have to send for the dozen agents roaming the neighborhood's boundaries on foot or in cars, to rescue them.

The agonizing waiting game was easier when the alert was prompted by an approaching car; it would pass quickly. But the passers-by on foot seemed to take forever to make their way down Prince Street. To deal with some of the late-night pedestrians, Morris sent Regii up Prince Street several times, usually when the unknown person appeared from the direction of Salem Street, the area popular with Angiulo soldiers. Regii did his thing, casually checking to see if the person was Mafia.

But each time proved to be a false alarm. The agents resumed placing two bugs about 15 feet apart, one up front near the television and the other halfway down the room, close to a large table where the Angiulos ate. Based on their informant intelligence, they were hiding the mikes as closely as possible to where Jerry Angiulo usually held forth.

In the near darkness, Quinn didn't see the wrench when it fell from the hand of the agent standing on the ladder. But he heard the tool when it hit the floor.

Several agents swore. Quinn's body tensed. Oh my God, he thought, if anybody was in the building he or she would have heard that ringing noise. Even taking into account that his senses were magnified in the situation, Quinn was convinced the office was like an echo chamber and the noise had awakened the entire street.

No one moved. The agents waited a few minutes, but nothing stirred.

Resuming work, the installers strung wires from the microphones to power cells the size of fireplace logs. In this case, there would not be any hookup to a telephone or electrical line, not after the Angiulos caught wind of their past attempts to use the two utility companies to supply power for a bug and camera. The risk of having to reenter the apartment every thirty days to install new power units was determined to be lower than the risk of a leak from outsiders.

To make an opening, the installers pushed aside several of the tiles that formed the dropped ceiling. Quinn and Richard watched as they carefully placed the huge power units on parts of the framing that supported the tiles. They made sure the heavy units were safely in place. The concern was that the ceiling might collapse under the weight, with the units crashing down into Angiulo's lap.

The installers then began stuffing mounds of insulation around the power units. Quinn couldn't see everything the men pulled from the satchel to conceal the batteries, but installers were known to bring along rat turds to scatter around a secret installation. The idea was to make it as difficult and unpleasant as possible for anyone to find the three power packs.

"How much longer?" Morris asked Quinn over the radio.

The installation was actually going smoothly. They'd gotten the bugs in place in about an hour. To test them, Quinn and the installers began talking in low tones. Richard listened from her seat; if she had been doing the talking, she probably would have pulled a Neil Armstrong: "This is one small step for the FBI," something like that. But Quinn was all business: "Testing, one, two, three. Testing, one, two, three."

It was a system with several parts. The transmitter in the ceiling would scramble the agents' words and send the signal to a booster located five blocks away atop a North Washington Street building. They used a scrambled signal to safeguard against people in the neighborhood bumping into the bugged conversations on their own scanners.

The booster then sent the signal across Boston Harbor to a monitoring site in Charlestown equipped with tape recorders. By the time the signal reached the agents stationed in Charlestown, it was unscrambled and understandable.

On his radio, Quinn contacted agent Joe Kelly, who was at the Charlestown apartment listening to the bugs through earphones. Kelly quickly radioed Quinn the good news: He could hear their chatter. More successful tests were conducted. But suddenly the transmission failed. One microphone worked, but the second didn't. The installers began poking around. They cursed the equipment. The microphones were top quality, but the supporting equipment was older. This was one of the prices they'd paid for staying inside the agency. They'd had to take what was available off the FBI shelves in Washington.

"How much longer?" Morris asked for at least the tenth time.

Quinn and the others had been in there for more than ninety minutes and still the system was down. Morris was worried. Quinn had gained entry at 2:00 A.M. They'd all hoped the installers would be out by 3:30, or 4:00 at the latest. Hitting a snag, Quinn and Morris kept postponing the last possible departure time.

"How much longer?" Morris asked again over the radio.

"Give us thirty more," Quinn said. He couldn't imagine getting this far and then having to leave without a working bug.

They moved their deadline to 4:00 A.M., then to 4:30.

Richard could see that the installers were acting more and more nervous. She couldn't believe the equipment foul-ups or understand how they ended up with this stuff, given the amount of money the agency had to work with. "When the hell is daylight?" one of the agents asked rhetorically over the radio. Morris ordered someone to find out. An agent drove to a pay phone and dialed the weather service number. Daylight, he reported back to Morris, was at 7:08, but already Morris could detect a lightening in the sky. He also knew that activity on Prince Street began even before 5:00 A.M. People left home to go to their jobs in hotels and factories. The bakery on the corner of Salem Street had already opened. A few trucks had even made some deliveries to North End restaurants and stores. Quinn had to be out of there soon—or all was lost.

In their van, the semifrozen Gianturco and Rafferty kept track of both the increasing light and foot traffic. Inside, the agents, especially Quinn and Richard in their bulletproof vests, were soaked in sweat. Where's James Bond when you need him? Debbie Richard thought to herself. But she made no more jokes. Nerves were frayed. Richard was hungry and actually did have to go to the bathroom. She worried that they had gotten so close and now the bugs were never going to work properly.

"Let's get this equipment going and get out of here," she said aloud.

"How much longer?" Morris asked yet again. He turned to Kennedy, "My God, are they ever going to get this to work?"

Quinn held on. Suddenly Kelly was on the radio reporting that the bugs were up: Both worked.

There was a rush of elation and relief, a kind of soothing electricity that flashed around the darkened office. The agents began their housecleaning assignments, sweeping up any material that fell from the ceiling and making sure they left every item in the office just as they found it. They remained another ten minutes to make sure the connection stuck and nothing was amiss in the room. The installers packed up their tools and put the ladder back where they'd found it.

Quinn asked for clearance. Morris gave him the go-ahead. The three installers left first. They turned left and hustled down Thatcher to a car waiting for them at North Washington Street. The locksmith, Richard, and Quinn left the apartment. Quinn took a last look behind him. Everything appeared to be in place.

It was 5 A.M. The city sky was brighter than Quinn had expected. He could smell the bread in the ovens of the bakery up the block. He and the others made their way past the lookout van, hurried down Prince Street, and climbed into Morris's car, parked on Commercial Street.

Morris reached back and shook Quinn's hand firmly. There was quiet jubilation—victory grins, but not much talk.

"We'll find out in the morning," Quinn said laconically. The FBI would be listening when Frank Angiulo opened up at nine.

8

INSIDE
98 PRINCE STREET

When the bug was first planted it was a handful of weary-eyed agents who gathered the morning after the installation to find out whether their predawn mission had achieved what had always seemed so impossible —getting the Angiulos where they lived.

Ed Quinn, sleepless, had remained guarded, even after leading Debbie Richard and the others safely out of 98 Prince Street with the morning light brooding over the neighborhood. Still in his mind was the possibility that somebody had watched them from a window the whole time they were inside. There was the chance that the mobsters, upon entering their domain, would begin singing nursery rhymes. Or someone might start praising J. Edgar Hoover as the second coming of Christ. Or there would be this loud, back-slapping talk about how wonderful the Angiulo family was for all the charitable contributions they made to the church.

This was Quinn's fear. It wouldn't be the first time mobsters had talked nonsense into a bug to signal the monitoring agents that what was supposed to be the FBI's secret had become the Mafia's morning laugh. So, when his agents, eavesdropping inside a cramped apartment in Charlestown, reported, "We have a go," Quinn experienced his most rewarding moment during three years of fretting, planning, and setbacks.

Morris, too, breathed a sigh of relief. Right up until the moment Frank Angiulo arrived to open the shop at nine o'clock, the crew of FBI agents had continued to go about their business in a very mechanical way. There was still so much to do, particularly at the monitoring site. It was like an operating room, Morris thought. Not a lot of emotion because of all the work remaining to complete the surgery. But once Frankie Angiulo arrived and began talking with a visitor about bookmaking accounts, it was as if the surgical team had closed up the patient, knowing he would survive.

Word spread quickly among the crew. This was the heartbeat of La Cosa Nostra in Boston, they realized, and they were right where they should be. But the satisfaction of not having been made was quickly overcome by another concern. As Pete Kennedy listened to Frank's first words, his heart sank. Sure, you could catch Frankie Angiulo talking, but it wasn't easy. Frankie's voice was competing with an obfuscating din caused by the police scanner, the radio, and the television he'd switched on. Kennedy was not alone in his dismay. Tom Donlan, listening to Frankie's conversation, thought, I'll never learn those voices. I don't know what the hell they're saying.

The clash of sounds became a major concern to Morris and Quinn. For use in any courtroom, they had to capture the words clearly. Maybe they would have to break back into the office to wreck the radio? But Jerry Angiulo would only get a new one. Technical agents went to work figuring out ways to separate the conversation from the other noise in order to enhance the mob talk. But eventually the static proved not to be as bad a problem as it first seemed. In the end, the agents just got used to the background noise and grew accustomed to the halting dialogue, the half-sentences, the mangled syntax, and the sudden shifts in thoughts that came from Jerry Angiulo and his men. Besides, Angiulo tended to shout, not talk, making his voice easier for monitoring agents to follow.

John Connolly, for one, felt euphoric. By day's end, the FBI was eavesdropping on Jerry himself. It was a melodious voice, as Connolly would joke later, that he'd heard many times out on the street, including the run-ins he'd had with the Mafia boss. But Connolly felt great, listening to the voice this way, on tape—a voice engaged in what were casual conversations to the Angiulos but criminal conversations to the rest of society. Connolly knew they'd gotten right next to the mob's jugular. It was only a matter of time.

For the next 105 days of secret surveillance, agents got heavy doses of Boston's leading Mafia family. There was their daily bookmaking, gambling, and loan-shark businesses to care for; talk of murders to commit, one as a favor to a New York family; and Jerry's growing preoccupation with the feds and his constant concern about the threat of the powerful RICO law.

Leading the chorus throughout was Jerry Angiulo, the tireless braggart who often indulged in a politician's penchant for dropping names and defining turf. He couldn't hold his tongue. Much later, Quinn remem-

bered that during the break-in of the Mafia office he'd
noticed a motto posted above a desk that Jerry Angiulo
was going to wish he'd followed. "It is better to remain
quiet and be thought a fool, than to speak and remove
all doubt."

"What the fuck is this?" Jerry Angiulo complained to
Larry Zannino, his second-in-command, one night when
the two were going over the card game Zannino managed. Angiulo was angry about the other owners being
slow to cough up their stake to sponsor the game, a
shortfall Angiulo was not about to make up himself.
"Remember, I didn't give anybody anything out of the
goodness of my fuckin' heart."

It was a line from the Book of Angiulo, part of a rubric
reflecting Angiulo's basic belief: Everybody owed him
something because he owned a piece of everybody. The
sermons included Angiulo's bloodless view on the loyalty due the people who carried out his enterprises.
Following a gambling raid, he once told Zannino and
two of his brothers, "We find that one of these indi-
viduals that we use becomes intolerable, we kill the
fuckin' motherfucker and that's the end. We'll go find
another one."

The bugged conversations also confirmed what the
FBI had always suspected. Angiulo had legions of lookouts. Frequently, Quinn's men listened as young wiseguys rushed into 98 Prince to tell Frankie Angiulo that
"the law" was on Salem, Hanover, or some other North
End street. They'd taken the license plate number and
it wasn't long before the Angiulos knew whether it
was city, state, or federal.

In the first days of the bugging, however, the Angiulos' network did not pick up any federal cars around Prince Street. Agents like John Connolly, who for years had openly hung out in the North End, were now tied up at the monitoring site. This, Quinn quickly realized, was a terrible mistake. It was the kind of alteration in the daily rituals of the North End that Angiulo would soon detect. He'd get suspicious and start asking, Where's Connolly? He'd start wondering whether the FBI was up to something. That was the last thing Quinn wanted. Nothing should appear different. He yanked the earphones off Connolly and had him resume his North End routine. It was a move Connolly didn't mind—he much preferred the streets to a tape recorder.

But most of the agents had never had any direct dealings with Angiulo. For months, they'd secretly stalked the North End, trying to piece together the lives of the Mafia's men from the outside. They'd done workups on all the brothers, again, from the outside working in.

Now, from Charlestown, they were picking up life inside. Over the years, the 62-year-old Jerry had been the family spokesman in public. During a gambling raid, or at a courthouse, Jerry was the chatterbox. Now, from Charlestown, the FBI heard them all—Nicolo, Frankie, Mike, and Danny Angiulo, as well as the eminently quotable Larry Zannino.

Within a few weeks, the agents came to know the Boston Mafia's daily routines. A typical day began almost exactly at 9 A.M., when, like clockwork, Frankie emerged from his apartment across the street and opened up. Agents heard the 60-year-old Angiulo brother, a heavy smoker, cough, spit in the sink, and put on the coffee.

Later, James "Jimmy Jones" Angiulo, a nephew who ran a bookmaking office a few doors down at 126 Prince

Street, showed up, followed by Mike. The youngest brother at 53, Mike was not a made member of the Mafia; he was the cook and errand runner, the one sent to bring the car around or fetch another bottle from the wine cellar. But he was also the handyman who could rewire, or backstrap, telephone lines in and out of different apartments and across rooftops to confuse investigators.

When he was feeling well enough, the eldest brother, Nicolo, who was 64, would join them to read the newspaper. As consigliere, his job was to arbitrate disputes among mafiosi. Zannino, needing counsel, once said to him, "You're my attorney, Nicky, let me ask you a question here."

The fourth brother, Danny, did not frequent 98 Prince Street. Danny, 57, conducted his loansharking and other businesses from the back of the Café Pompeii. He was a capo regime, a lieutenant, who chafed under the control of his older brother. Putting Jerry and Danny together was like striking two stones to get sparks, especially when the talk turned to money.

During daylight, Frankie Angiulo was the boss. His time was spent settling up with the bookmakers and loan-shark customers. The problem for the FBI was that during the often routine gambling transactions few inminating words were spoken. Collecting as much as $45,000 gross a day from the family's illegal ventures, Frank might grunt a greeting or exchange a few words in the code of the trade, but often that was it.

What the hidden microphones did pick up was the steady shuffle of cash being counted. Eventually, the FBI conducted a lightning-quick gambling raid on Prince Street to kick the hornet's nest, but in the first few weeks of bugging, the only time Frankie's vocal cords got a workout was when the gambling figures were off or loan payments were late.

"When are you gonna start giving me the $1,545 you owe Peter, never mind the thousand you owe me?" he demanded one day of a delinquent customer. "What are you doing here?"

"I, I, I . . ."

"You owe me a thousand right here. I lent you."

"Right."

"And you owe Peter $1,545. When are you gonna start paying this?"

"I'm starting right now, I'm getting . . ."

"You ain't starting nothing. You been telling me this for a month. What are you doing?"

"I'm just starting to get on my feet."

"You been telling me this for a month."

"I, I'm, I'm telling you the truth. I didn't make nothing on horses. I'm just starting to make something on, ahh, on dogs, and I'm, ahh, working hard."

"Get some money."

"And I'm not drinking. I'm not drinking."

"You better not."

"I don't smoke. I don't go out. I do nothing but trying to get even and make some money for myself."

"That's what got you in debt to start with."

"The drinking did. I, I, I did it. I'm not blaming anybody else. Give me a little opportunity, pal, and you'll be paid completely and we'll be friends for life."

Frankie cuffed the customer, intimidating him further, and then let him scram with another extension.

What the FBI couldn't figure out about the family accountant was why he chose to live across the street at 95 Prince Street. The third-floor apartment was shabby and barely furnished. At the end of the day, Jerry Angiulo drove twenty miles north to his oceanside mansion in Nahant, Nick returned to Revere, and Mike and Danny headed to Medford, but Frankie, not needing a coat even in the dead of winter, hustled across the street to his hole in the wall. He never seemed to go anywhere except back and forth between 95 and 98. He never even ventured the few blocks to the bustling Faneuil Hall market. His world began and ended in the old neighborhood. He was an easy tail for the FBI.

Each day the beat changed around 4:00 P.M., the time Jerry Angiulo pulled up in his red and silver AMC Pacer (he usually left his baby blue Cadillac at home). With his entrance, the tenor of the office went from casual to deferential. He asked the questions and set the agenda as he sat in the big chair at the front of the office.

He talked about food and business and money and murder until 7:30 P.M., when the "Wild, Wild World of Animals" came on on Channel 2. Then he demanded quiet as he watched intensely, commenting on the strength or cunning of the animals featured on the show.

Sometimes the group watched the Celtics. Because most of Boston's fans bet on the hometown club, a Celtics win meant more bets to pay, and a smaller profit margin for the bookies. Self-interest dictated that the Angiulos root against Larry Bird and his teammates, so they did.

Often, Mikey Angiulo cooked dinner—lamb or veal, maybe linguine with clam sauce, or they would adjourn to Francesca's restaurant, where several nights a week they ate at a table in back. Larry Zannino was often around, as was Jerry's longtime favorite, Skinny Kazonis.

There was much business to discuss, such as fixing gambling cases pending in Roxbury District Court against one soldier who managed a family's numbers office. "I straightened out that pinch," Frankie bragged to Jerry one night in March. "That pinch is all over with. Sixty-one hundred dollars, the whole fucking shooting match."

"What happened the last time when you went for close to $100,000?" Jerry shot back, never forgetting figures and rarely, if ever, complimenting someone on his work.

Or they would trade stories about collecting debts. "How much trouble did I have with this mother?" a boastful Zannino asked Jerry rhetorically another night while explaining how he'd received most of a $59,000 gambling debt. "I threatened his fucking father, his fucking brothers. You fucking cocksucker, you'll pay this fucking . . ."

The outcome of Zannino's scare tactics? "They're down to $15,000," Zannino disclosed proudly.

"And our fuckin'—wait, wait a minute," Angiulo pontificated on yet another occasion, interrupting others, as he usually did, in order to stroke his own ego. "And our fuckin' claim to fame is accounting."

On this score he was spewing truths that had long been self-evident, for Angiulo rose to the top on his knack with numbers and operating illegal lotteries that for more than a decade were considered the biggest and most profitable Mafia games in the country. "You take Jerry Angiulo," mobster Vinnie Teresa told congressional investigators in 1971. "You couldn't count his money if it took you three days, with a whole firm full of accountants." More than a decade later, authorities estimated Angiulo's ill-gotten wealth at up to $10 million.

Angiulo was so powerful financially that he was every

bookmaker's backup—the guy who would take their layoff when too much of the betting money was wagered on one number. For handsome fees, Angiulo would assume some of the bookies' risk. It was a form of insurance, and it made Angiulo's outfit the Lloyd's of London in the gambling circuit. These fees, of course, were in addition to the share of the profits that bookies regularly paid Angiulo just to do business.

The mob boss kept dozens of accounts in a handful of Boston banks, and for years he had had a special arrangement with the Bank of Boston that helped him launder his money and circumvent federal banking laws. Beginning in 1970, under the Bank Secrecy Act, banks were required to notify the Internal Revenue Service about any cash transactions with customers involving more than $10,000. The law was seen as one way to get a handle on all the illicit cash that mobsters and drug dealers dumped into the banking system to launder. The feds might at least hope to get a tax fraud case out of it.

But within a few years, Jerry Angiulo, always the manipulator, managed to place his two real-estate companies on an exemption list kept by the Bank of Boston's branch office a few blocks from his 98 Prince Street headquarters. It was a move guaranteeing that all the hard cash he and his associates brought in shopping bags to the tellers was never reported to the government. The setup worked smoothly until 1983, when a government probe of the bank's general reporting failings stumbled upon Angiulo's involvement.

For the FBI, it was yet another example of Angiulo's business acumen. The self-educated financier made his money where he could, with vast sums pouring in from his own bookmaking operation that employed two hundred in offices scattered throughout greater Boston. He also siphoned proceeds from lucrative Las Vegas nights (jazzed-up versions of Bingo nights, featuring roulette wheels that were staged allegedly in the name of charity). There were at least five gambling businesses, including poker, craps, and the Greek dice game called *barbooth*. Some of the games floated, meaning players met in an alley near Cross and Salem streets in the North End to be escorted either by foot or in a car to the secret location of that night's gathering. The barbooth games were in the North End or Lowell, a city north of Boston. The loansharking was managed out of 98 Prince Street.

From the day the bug went in, January 19, 1981, Angiulo had been preoccupied with the federal RICO statute and a test case pending before the U.S. Supreme Court. He read newspaper articles about the case out loud to Frankie and Jason. "Now the most important part is the last part of the whole fuckin' law," he told them in late January. Scanning the newspaper, he read: "The pattern of racketeering activity is defined elsewhere in the act as the commission of any two of thirty-two specific state and federal crimes within a ten-year period." Angiulo stopped reading and turned to the others. "Now we're fuckin' idiots we never looked up the thirty-two specific crimes." Seconds later, he added, "In other words, if you break one of those crimes this year and within the next ten years you break the other one too, they will take your fuckin' head off."

On several other occasions, he and Zannino debated whether a Mafia soldier by the name of J. R. Russo would be able to return safely to Boston after five years of hiding. Russo was a leading suspect in the murder of Joe "The Animal" Barboza in San Francisco in 1976, but had never been indicted as far as they could tell. The five-year statute of limitations on a possible federal civil rights charge had expired, meaning a favored soldier of Zannino's might now be home free.

"There's always that 10 percent chance they might have that indictment," a worried Angiulo cautioned Zannino.

"Secret indictment," added Zannino.

Angiulo then framed the issue. "Do we tell this man to come back? Do we leave him where he is because we have no facilities, right now, for finding out whether the indictment exists or not, and we do not feel that from the questions we have asked various people that the facilities will be made available in time? Do we call him and tell him, 'If you feel like it, come back, because all we can find out is the statute's run out?' "

In the end, they agreed to consult Patriarca.

Throughout the bugging, Angiulo was concerned with the turf lines of the illegal marketplace and was particularly concerned about his image—among other mafiosi and even law enforcement officials.

He was quick to defend Joseph Palladino of Saugus, who was a partner in several Worcester porn shops, when two wiseguys opened up a competing shop in that city with the blessing of New York's Gambino crime family. Angiulo, livid at the intrusion into his turf, told Palladino that he would immediately intervene on his behalf.

Angiulo's main point to Palladino, however, involved an issue that was probably way over the porn shop–owner's head. Angiulo launched into a discourse on image, namely the tough image he sought to preserve with the various law enforcement agencies that tracked his activities. Image, to him, was another line

of defense—the more menacing it was, the more likely
the authorities would move with caution. Any sign of
weakness and the authorities might pounce.

"You know the most important part of this conversation?" he asked Palladino. "The law over there knows
exactly what we are. If we would allow a different group
to come in and they run roughshod over everybody,
the law would lose respect for us. You don't mind los-
ing the respect of that section, but then you lose it in
every other section. What am I supposed to do? The
law in that section tells the other law, say, 'Hey, these
fuckin' motherfuckers got no balls here. They backed
away from . . .' "

But the very same Palladino suddenly became just
another expendable associate in a matter closer to Angiulo's heart—money. Palladino had borrowed $200,000,
with interest running at $2,000 a week. In his impe-
rious manner, Angiulo warned that although he didn't
need the two grand a week for any special reason, the
porn shop owner had better pay up, on time.

"You ain't never gonna cry baby, and you're never
gonna miss a week. I'm gonna tell you the kinda fucking people we are."

The flip side to this cavalier attitude about money
he showed to the likes of Palladino was the downright
cheapness he revealed in the presence of family only.
Trying to work out a strategy to hide his property, he
dismissed his son's proposal to transfer ownership of
their yachts to a straw. How would that work? he demanded of Jason. The straw would get a loan, Jason
explained, and it would appear as if the straw was the
owner of record while Jerry Angiulo would remain the
owner in reality. Forget it, Angiulo responded. To win
the straw's participation in the scam, Angiulo would

at least have to pay the interest on the straw's loan. "Cost me 18 percent a year," he said, citing prevailing interest rates for loans obtainable through legal channels. "To you, 18 percent is shit. To me, it's a lot of fuckin' money."

But then, Angiulo was rarely impressed with anything his son suggested. By 1981, Jason was managing several of the illegal businesses, including the heartless Las Vegas night scams the family pulled on different charity groups. The elder Angiulo made a habit of using his son as a whipping boy.

In March, the two were reviewing a Las Vegas night Jason had managed at the Studio Four in Lynn, Massachusetts, allegedly to raise funds for the North Shore Association for Retarded Citizens, but in fact to fatten their pockets. When told old dice were used in the crap game, Angiulo exploded.

"How much do you really think you know about dice that are used in a crap game?" he demanded. "Now watch how you answer me."

But Jason didn't want to answer. Trying to bob away from his father, he mentioned a crisis at the blackjack table that he did handle—how he came down hard on a dealer named Vardie who was permitting bets above the house limit.

The old man persisted. "Tell me why that table in that fucking Studio Four had old dice."

Jason tried to weave. "I was gonna fucking choke him," he said about the dealer. "He's letting people bet $300 on my fucking table with a $25 limit."

"Hey, keep quiet. We're talking craps now."

"We're talking about Mister Vardie—"

"We're talking about craps."

"Mister Vardie is my—"

"Fucking, motherfucking, big mouth cocksucker. Shut up."

One last time, Jason tried. "You gonna listen to me?"

"No, you motherfucker. Now shut up. Let me tell you something. I've been in the crap business when you were—weren't—born, you cocksucker that you are. Don't you ever, ever have a pair of dice go more than one and a half or two hours without replacing it with a brand-new set, and that set goes in your fucking pocket and they're thrown down the fucking sewer. Do you understand that? That's a fucking order because you're a fucking idiot. Now just shut up."

"Yeah, let me tell you."

"You talk and I'll hit you with a fucking bottle. You go to a Vegas night, you figure to last six hours, you have three sets of dice, and no set of dice will ever stay on that table more than two hours. Why, you cocksucker, I got a thousand sets of dice for a Sunday game. Thousand dice by the set. Not one you got 'em, you cocksucker, fucking what the motherfuckin' cunt. . . . How about playing cards? How many new decks you got every time you use them? You use used cards, you dirty mother. You hear this motherfucker?"

Jason tried to say something.

"Shut up," Angiulo interrupted. "Just shut up. You ever put a deck of used cards in the blackjack game in any fucking Vegas night or anywhere else again, I'll kick you the fuck out of here. That's an order, too. Why you fucking idiot you. If I was at your Vegas night the week before, I'd know every fucking card in that fucking deck, you motherfucker."

"There was only five decks of cards cause we ran out

of fucking cards cause some asshole spilled fucking shit on the bar. Then we dropped them on the fucking floor . . ."

"Who?"

"Some idiot playing at the fucking table."

For a moment, Jason had distracted his father. Angiulo wondered if ruining the cards was deliberate. "Think about it. Did you think about it?" But within minutes, Angiulo became bored by the idea that a cheater had preyed upon the game.

Winding up the tirade, Angiulo first threatened to replace his son as manager of the Vegas nights with another soldier, but then concluded with a warning: "Remember what I told you. You ever let a crap table go more than two hours with the same set of dice, and they ain't brand-new every fucking time, you better run out of here."

But there were calmer moments as well, usually later in the evening, after the meal and a few bottles of wine. Often Larry Zannino was present, the true mafioso who revered the rules of the secret fraternity that newer members increasingly winked at. Zannino relished going over past crimes, expressing nostalgia for the gangland killing era. Over the years, Zannino had done it all and, with all due respect to Jerry Angiulo, he, too, was something of an expert on the more brutal aspects of the underworld.

On the very first day of the FBI's secret bugging, agents listened to the city's leading capo advise Angiulo on the art of killing. "If you're clipping people, I always say, make sure if you clip people, you clip the people around him first. But get them together, cause everybody's got a friend, Jerry. He could be the dirtiest motherfucker in the world, but someone, someone likes that guy, that's the guy that sneaks you, you don't even know it."

They heard the consummate Mafia martinet harshly instruct his soldiers on the ways of Mafia life. "Who the fuck are you to make a decision?" Zannino once accused a soldier in a diatribe on the privileges of rank. "You'll make no fuckin' decisions. You know when you make a decision? When they put fucking stripes on you."

Other times, Zannino would simply profess his love for mob life, outlining its differences from normal life. "That's the one thing we got going for us. No one can hide. But we can. In other words, no one can hide from us, but we can hide from everybody. You understand?"

He gave the FBI an earful. "This Thing comes first," he once reminded another soldier, John Cincotti. "Johnny, This Thing we got here is beautiful. You understand? This Thing is so beautiful that if someone slapped Debbie in the mouth tonight, your girl, we would kill. . . . Don't underrate it."

For the FBI, Zannino's sentimental line about Debbie was good enough to become the "Quote of the Day." Soon after the bugging started, agents began posting the best quote to come from a mafioso mouth. It was a daily contest that helped overcome the monitoring grind.

The agents called the tiny Charlestown apartment where the monitoring equipment was set up "the plant." They worked in shifts, with one agent logging the content of the conversations and another, seated in the jump seat, simply listening in. They were required by law to shut off the tape recorder when the talk was not criminal, forcing agents to dance among the dials because of Angiulo's sudden shifts from talking about the weather to ordering a slaying.

Some nights it was dead. The mobsters assembled around the television set and watched movies such as *The Good, the Bad, and the Ugly,* with Clint Eastwood. Nothing happened. Sheer ennui. Other days agents scrambled to keep up with all the criminal dialogue. Mondays were crazy because that was the day many bookies came in to square their accounts with Frankie Angiulo.

Quinn served as a kind of director, keeping track of the different plot lines that were developing and advising the new shift on what to listen for. It was the worst pressure in his career, staying on top of the recordings, working every day, reviewing the tapes from the day before. In the beginning, it was so hard to make out the voices the tapes had to be played back at the FBI office a dozen times.

Quinn put on weight, and he wasn't the only one. The agents sat with the earphones on and nothing was happening, so they ate. Donuts. Steak and cheese subs. You couldn't wait for lunch, so lunch came at 10 A.M. Then you ate again at 2. The agents working in Charlestown were like school kids who couldn't wait for recess to get the hell out of there.

But they kept at it—all twenty-five of them, maintaining the video cars, secretly tailing people out of the office to identify voices on the tape. Guys like Joe Kelly, a gruff veteran on the squad, set the tone. He had to have surgery to relieve a painful elbow, so he had the operation after the end of one shift, then showed up the next day with a couple of pillows to prop up the wounded arm. He never missed a shift, never took any medication that might affect his concentration. He had to listen.

The quality of the tapes kept driving Morris whacky, but as squad leader he never had to do any actual monitoring. The others kept reassuring him that you just had to get used to the voices. Besides, the techies thought they had found ways to enhance the conversations to improve their clarity.

There were countless housekeeping chores to attend to—most important maintaining the mikes and the video cars, their ears and eyes on Prince Street. The battery-powered microphones lasted thirty days, meaning that in the almost four months of secret surveillance Quinn's team reentered the office three times.

For the most part, the reentries went off smoothly. The FBI even had a key to Angiulo's office; the locksmith made one up after the first break-in. With the bugs in place, they also eliminated what had been the major fear during the first break-in—that any of the Angiulos or some other wiseguys were inside. With agents listening to their bugs, Quinn was assured the place was empty each time he led the others down Snow Hill and across Prince Street to the office.

In no reentry did Quinn harbor doubts about getting in and out cleanly. The agents were practiced at the plan and, basically, they followed the same format each time. Why fuss with what worked? They got it so they were done and out of there within sixty minutes. For the last reentry, Quinn didn't even go in himself but sent a single team of technical agents to replace the batteries.

There were times when agents in lookout vans had their tires slashed, or watched as punks hacked at the tires of some fancy car parked nearby, but nothing ever happened to threaten their mission seriously. The Mafia stayed asleep.

The only scare came not from the Mob but from the Boston police. During the first reentry, in February, John Connolly was in the back of a van that another agent had driven into the North End and parked behind Prince Street. From his position, Connolly was to watch the back side of the office and the streets that led to Francesca's restaurant, where the Angiulos often ate.

The problem was that with the snow piled up on the street, and with so many other cars jammed together, the FBI driver parked the van awkwardly. The driver, who then took off, left the vehicle jutting out into the street so that it actually blocked traffic. Connolly, inside and moving from window to peephole, wasn't aware of this at the time. But it wasn't long before he spotted a police cruiser and then heard the crackle of a police radio.

Someone had called the police to complain about the blocked street. The next thing Connolly knew was that his van was shaking. Keeping low, but using a side mirror, he watched two cops trying to get the door open. Connolly cursed under his breath, and his mind raced. If the Angiulos ever found out that Connolly was inside, dressed in black, at two o'clock in the morning, alarm bells would sound all over the North End.

If they get the door open, Connolly figured, he would blow past the cops and take off into the night. He'd gone to high school in the North End and knew all the alleyways. He didn't doubt he could shake them. And the van was registered to a bogus company, so no trace to the FBI was possible. He only hoped that in the confusion the cops wouldn't open fire.

Connolly couldn't even use his radio to notify Morris, for fear the cops outside would overhear him. In his earphone, he could hear Morris trying to reach him as part of the final round of checks before sending Quinn in. But there was no way he could respond.

Morris began asking other lookouts about him— What's with Connolly? Then Connolly heard another agent tell Morris, "He's got a black and white on him, hold on."

This had always been one of Morris's many worries—that other cops would stumble upon them and, not having a clue it was the FBI, start shooting at his people. Morris didn't want to tell the Boston police, or send agents to intervene with the cops at the van, because there was always the chance that Connolly's presence there would get back to the Angiulos through their police sources.

Connolly's other hope was that the cops would call a tow truck. Then he'd jump out once the van had been towed out of the neighborhood. He'd be able to radio the others and have them ready to pick him up after he fled.

But as suddenly as the cops came, they simply left. Connolly radioed Morris and briefed him, and the squad leader quickly gave Quinn the go-ahead. Connolly and the others kept watch for the cops or a tow truck, but Quinn was finished, probably in record time, before either showed up. The van's driver returned, and on their way out Connolly gave him a lecture on parking.

And that was it, the only tense moment during the three reentries of February, March, and April.

After the successful bugging of the office, keeping the secret cameras operating so the FBI could match faces with voices on the tape was the trickiest job during all of Operation Bostar. It belonged to Shaky Schopperle, whose day began at midnight when he went to the garage he'd rented in Woburn to store his fleet of four video cars. Schopperle began by charging the ten batteries needed to run the cameras. Eventually he favored two cars, the 1974 Nova and the 1970 Impala, so that he was usually replacing one with the other. Then, about 3 A.M., came the nightly car shuffle. Schopperle, or one of his assistants, strolled down Prince Street and climbed into the battered car parked at Thatcher and Prince, just down from Jerry Angiulo's entranceway. He sat and waited for the arrival of the replacement car.

Schopperle had kept a log on what was going on at 3 A.M., so after a while he knew what to expect on the street at that hour. There was always a light on in a third-floor apartment in a building overlooking the corner, but he soon discovered it was somebody getting up to go to work at a nearby laundry. There were two older guys, in their fifties maybe, who often walked down Prince Street, also on their way to work. Two other people waited at another corner to get picked up. He even noticed a little cat outside 30 Prince Street sleeping in a box or eating from a bowl.

Using the rearview mirror, Schopperle watched the stretch of street behind him, waiting for a car with a broken front parking light. That was the telltale signal. Schopperle then started the engine of his car and pulled out just in time to let the second car, with ten fresh batteries hooked up to the camera hidden behind the front grille, take the precious parking space with a view of 98 Prince Street.

The driver of the second car ran a check on the camera to make sure it was working properly. The camera was equipped with a light-intensifying system designed for nighttime photographing. With it, streetlights provided enough illumination to get video pictures. The driver then locked the car and left the North End.

Morning after cold morning, Schopperle directed his team of six, with only a couple of near disasters. A fistfight almost broke out one morning when an FBI driver pulled out too soon, having thought he'd spotted the car with the broken parking light approaching. But it wasn't an FBI replacement car, just some guy looking to dump his car and call it a night. The parking light wasn't even broken. The agent hit the brakes and wouldn't budge. The other driver beeped. Schopperle, who that night had been driving the replacement car, was stuck behind the unknown driver. He beeped. There was some shouting, but finally the man sped off angrily. Schopperle quickly slipped into the spot.

The FBI almost lost Schopperle when a car battery actually exploded in his hands. But he bandaged his damaged hands and stayed on the job, although he finally heeded John Morris's nagging about wearing safety glasses.

There were distractions, like the night the tires were slashed, which delayed the rotation until Schopperle commandeered a tow truck, or the days neighborhood kids sat on the front fenders or trunks of the video cars, causing the camera to bounce up and down. Sometimes during the day the sunlight hit the camera almost directly, creating a blind spot that was frustrating. This problem cleared up, however, as the winter wore on and the sun's angle changed.

The Angiulos and their associates, who prided themselves on noticing any change in their neighborhood, apparently found nothing suspicious about the "new" cars on the street—most often the 1974 Nova and 1970

Impala, but sometimes the 1972 Dodge or the 1965 Rambler. Instead, the cameras rolled almost twenty-four hours a day for nearly four months, providing pictures to go with Jerry Angiulo's free-flowing monologues. The camera showed Jerry coming, Jerry going. It showed Zannino, all the brothers, countless bookies, wiseguys, and hit men. Not once did it show Jerry waving, or giving the camera the choke sign—images from the video-camera failures of 1979 that still haunted Morris and Quinn.

The only time that Quinn actually worried the video cars might have been made came when an Angiulo lookout peered directly into the grille, producing a close-up picture of an eyeball. Quinn anxiously waited for more trouble, but it never came.

9

AN ATTEMPTED
MURDER

Within days of the successful entry into the Boston
Mafia's inner sanctum, the FBI, having survived para-
chuting behind enemy lines and literally working its
way into the woodwork of 98 Prince Street, found itself
with the general on a holiday.

Without warning, Jerry Angiulo had gone to Florida
in February of 1981 to bomb around the Ft. Lauderdale
coast in his new toy, the yacht named *St. Gennaro*,
putting his brother Frank in charge of running the office. Every day, nine to five, eavesdropping agents were
recording the profane, peculiar argot of the numbers
racket while they listened to the staccato slashing sound
of money being counted and stashed. But was it enough?
Was this banal business going to be all there was to
such a daring and successful sortie?

No. It would not do. Gennaro Angiulo was what they
were after, the vain and bombastic prime mover who

had run the mob with monomaniacal drive for close to three decades. They needed Angiulo back from Florida to get the type of case they wanted, one that could bring down the whole hierarchy. Only Angiulo set major plans in action or approved them, and only Angiulo conjured the conspiracies that are the cornerstone of a racketeering case, the kind that allow confiscation of property and produce prison sentences in the decades.

What to do?

One possibility emerged as the FBI's Ed Quinn and novice prosecutor Wendy Collins reviewed the first few frantic weeks of gathering evidence. Besides the humdrum of numbers betting, one of the first things through the door was the case of two loan-shark customers from Boston's adult entertainment center, the Combat Zone. Louis Venios was a rotund man who wore wide-brimmed soft hats and ran a strip joint, the Mouse Trap. Walter LaFreniere, a dark-haired man in his thirties, was Venios's son-in-law and bartender. He was also in debt to Angiulo.

The FBI and prosecutors decided to dangle the pair as bait to lure Angiulo back from Florida. Authorities promptly called Venios and LaFreniere before a grand jury—the sole spontaneous tactic in four years of meticulous planning, which also created a perilous house of cards that could collapse at any second and leave them with a bloody murder on their hands.

In all the endless talk of gambling at 98 Prince Street, the grand jury subpoenas became the highest stake game of all. After word of the debtors's upcoming court appearances filtered back to the Angiulos, Jerry raced back to town. In a stunning display of self-immolation, he demanded to know everything that had happened with the debtors—which amounted to a group confession of extortion from his brothers, a recitation carried on secret microphones to the FBI's spinning tape five miles away. The compulsive Angiulo had to constantly talk out his countermoves as well, which handed the FBI vivid accounts of a criminal conspiracy to obstruct justice. He wound up giving the feds what he had devoted his criminal career to avoiding: His direct participation in a crime. No witnesses were necessary, just his own raspy, cocksure voice.

The first crack in the once impregnable Angiulo empire began innocuously one night in the winter of 1980 when Venios brought LaFreniere to Jason Angiulo's North End dice game known as barbooth.

LaFreniere, a denizen of the Zone as a Mouse Trap bartender, had credentials to be at the game: He took money on the shark from Danny Angiulo and hung out with some minor-league wiseguys. That night, his troubles began when he thought they were over. The dice table had gone cold for him and he had to go to the house for credit to continue playing. The worst thing that ever happened to him was that he got it. In a transaction that would later drive Jerry Angiulo to distraction, Venios, who went back decades with the Angiulos, spoke directly to Jason Angiulo and got LaFreniere a fast $2,000 right there at the table. The mob leader's son handled the deal himself. None of the expendable buffers were used as intermediaries.

It became a sore Angiulo loved to rub, this unpardonable breach of security. In just one of the rebukes of his son, Angiulo told him: "Frank and I made you the boss, but you were the only boss with insulation.

Skinny, Johnny O, and Candy. How did you allow your-self to sit at the table with Louis Venios's son-in-law that he could ask you right at the table for the fucking two thousand?" The three underlings were sentries walking the camp's periphery for the generals and they weren't used. Shame.

But what was merely a long-running tirade directed at Jason became a lethal matter for the blasé LaFreniere, who, without even knowing it, had been sucked into the violent vortex on Prince Street. Within weeks of the game, LaFreniere was a hapless pawn in the deadly game of chance between the FBI and the head of the Boston underworld.

In March 1981 his future was as precarious as a death-row prisoner's in Florida. Walter had emerged as bait on the very first night the secret microphones were in place in January when Angiulo welcomed FBI inter-lopers with a classic harangue. Venios was late with the two grand a week he owed in loan-shark interest payments, known as "vig," for operating his strip joint and porno store on Mafia turf. No matter that Venios had just been released from Beth Israel hospital, a se-riously ill man who would be dead in a year. He was two weeks late and no one keeps Jerry Angiulo away from his money that long. "Get me my fucking money" were about the first words investigators heard out of Angiulo's mouth.

As the first of 540 FBI tapes rolled five miles away on the top floor of a row house in Charlestown, Angiulo reiterated his views on laggards to henchmen in a ma-fioso's Magna Carta. "Louie didn't bring the fuckin' money. You understand? When Louie comes out, if he ain't got two thousand, you go get the fucking' money. 'I gave it to you.' Just like that. Got that, friend. . . . I don't know nothing about Louie. Okay pal. Bring me my money. That's it. All of it."

It was vintage Angiulo: merciless about money while putting someone else up to the nasty job of getting it from a moribund debtor. Cold heart, clean hands. Only later, when the operation was clearly in trouble, did he modulate his "past due" speech, realizing anew that extortion came down to "the same old story. It's how you ask for your money." You should be tough, but don't threaten. But on January 19, 1981, after decades of beating the feds at their own game and an invincible neighborhood "watch" in place, who was worried about Louie Venios?

As the slashing soliloquy continued, Angiulo unwittingly set the LaFreniere trap in motion. He had been over some figures and didn't like what he saw coming out of his son's twice-weekly dice game: There were some new players and they'd better not be more deadbeats who had a way of showing up every eight or nine months. Who needs deadbeats? "You're all fuckin' idiots in my opinion," he told those running the game. "Remember what I tell ya," he said to sentry Johnny Orlandella. "A man takes money on a Tuesday, he don't bring it on a Friday. Stop right then and there. Cashin' him. 'C'mere, don't tell me a fuckin' story. Go get my fuckin' money. . . . I'm not interested.' Got that straight?"

Getting that debt straight with Walter LaFreniere would put them all in jail, but only after a dizzying series of moves in a Machiavellian game within a game.

On one track, the FBI would put Venios, LaFreniere, and even Jason Angiulo before the grand jury. On the other, Jerry would debrief the witnesses, brainstorm with his lawyer, and badger and belittle his brothers

— 199 —

in his office, plotting obstruction of justice, suborning perjury, and detailing extortion as the FBI listened in. When the day's hearing ended, Angiulo's lawyer, William Cintolo of Revere, would rush down to the North End to recapitulate the questions the prosecutors had asked so that Angiulo could get a fix on where the feds were heading. At the same time, Wendy Collins, the prosecutor running the grand jury, would go about the same distance from the courthouse to FBI headquarters, somewhat dazzled by the strange, titillating knowledge she had about the other side's intentions. She listened to key portions of tapes, just as obsessed in her own way by the case as Angiulo. A member of the Organized Crime Strike Force less than a year, she was now working a hundred hours a week and loving it and hating it, entranced and repelled by the vain, vile little man who called her a dirty mother and a cunt and rued *"che la puttana 1'ha nato* [that the whore was born.]"

After Angiulo's marching orders to get the Venios payment and screen barbooth players, his brothers went into action, chasing down both Venios and LaFreniere. After a fatuous series of telephone calls, they finally pinned down LaFreniere, who agreed to bring the money to Prince Street—and then failed to show up.

Venios had already been visited and chastised in the hospital by Mike Angiulo, the youngest brother, and still nothing happened. Not that Mike didn't do his best. He found Venios in intensive care. "He looked up at me," Mike told his brothers. " 'You fuckin' guys come right in the hospital, huh?' " "Louie," Mike said, "my brother wants to know, are you alive?"

Finally, LaFreniere agreed to come the next day to square the Venios debt with Frank, the operation's accountant and the closest thing Jerry had to a confidant.

Frank counted out loud the $2,607 that was handed over to him by LaFreniere and then issued a harsh demand note for two more weeks. "You tell me you're going to be here, be here. Don't let me come up the joint looking for you. Okay. What's the matter with you . . . you just don't give a fuck. By the way, you owe a thousand at the game, don't you? . . . and tell the other guy I'm lookin' for him. What's his name, Walter?"

"I'm Walter," LaFreniere said.

Frank finally got it straight and adjusted his books. "Yours ain't a G-note," he told LaFreniere. "Yours is more than that." The loan was put at $2,000.

The who's-on-first colloquy was a key tape for the FBI as it sorted through the evidence to get Jerry Angiulo back from Florida. Louie Venios and Walter LaFreniere and extortion? Why not stir the pot with those ingredients and see what happened?

Venios went before the grand jury in February, about a month and a half after he got out of the hospital, taking the Fifth to all questions. LaFreniere did the same about two weeks later, in mid-March.

Jerry Angiulo scrambled home to Boston the day Walter LaFreniere got his summons on March 9 and never regained his footing on turf that had been his for a generation. He knew Venios was an old pro who would walk the plank, but this kid Walter LaFreniere, could he trust him to stand up?

Angiulo went into geostationary orbit over the family's foolhardy direct contact with a dicey stranger— and stayed there for a full week, pacing and fuming about how to foil the feds. He gyrated daily between smug fatalism and panicky pessimism. One minute it was the cocksure Jerry who had seen it all before and beat the feds at every turn, including acquittals on murder and money-laundering charges. The kid's okay, he said of LaFreniere, "he knows the score and he'll keep his mouth shut." Almost in the same breath, he turned murderously morose. No, the kid's a rat who's gonna sink us all—he has to go.

By March 12, about two months after the secret FBI entry and the day LaFreniere took the Fifth before the grand jury, the Angiulo brothers were struggling to figure out what the story was with this nobody bartender. How much did he know and what was he saying to a federal grand jury?

Later that night, Jerry learned that the grand jury was asking LaFreniere about all the Angiulos and loansharking. "Oh, my fuckin' life," he moaned. "Now you got me a problem. . . . Fuck what Louie thinks. I knew all of sudden, this was something very fuckin' new."

Angiulo was apoplectic that a fringe crap player had direct dealings with two of his brothers and his son. His worst-case scenario: LaFreniere testifies that Jason gave him a usurious loan of $2,000 in a barbooth game controlled by Gennaro Angiulo himself, all of which violated federal extortion and gambling laws. Together, it could add up to a racketeering conspiracy charge, a family affair covered by the dreaded RICO law. In a stunning set piece, Angiulo outlined the case against himself with all the crisp flair of a prosecuting attorney, pulling all the elements of the crimes together, handing investigators a road map to his own demise.

He summed up the case for his brother Danny: "Remember, they're not saying this or that. They're saying Angiulo. Angiulo. . . . It could be me, you, him, him, and him too. Nobody knows. Under RICO, no matter who the fuck we are, if we're together, they'll get every fuckin' one of us. . . . We've been sleepin'. I've been jerkin' off in Florida for three weeks. . . . Why, I don't even know where the fuck we're at now."

Jerry was especially fearful of the confiscatory leverage of a RICO conviction because not only do the feds put you in jail, they take what you've made in ill-gotten gains—or the bulk of Angiulo's estate. "They take every fuckin' motherfuckin' cocksucker thing every fuckin' one of us owns, including your fuckin' eyeballs."

His fears, however, were not fully shared by the most steady hand in the house, that of the oldest brother, Nicolo, the consigliere for the Boston Mafia family. An experienced if crude arbiter, he had settled some disputes without violence and had occasionally worked out jurisdictional disputes with Providence. On the LaFreniere grand jury matter, Nick thought Jerry was overreacting. How could Jerry be in jeopardy, given his fanatical insularity. "Jerry Angiulo for what?" he asked rhetorically. "Their ass. The guy don't meet nobody."

Nick just didn't see the situation as that big a deal. He figured Venios and LaFreniere would be asked if they had dealings with the Angiulos and they'd say no—whether they did or not. Case dismissed. If things had been as they appeared, Nick would have been right. But the omniscient bugs overhead and the spinning tape changed everything. Without the recordings, nothing would have come of the LaFreniere caper. But, as the grand jury pressure grew, Angiulo looked for a new scapegoat every day. On an afternoon in mid-March, he turned on his brother Danny, who was also known by the misnomer Smiley. Danny was an infrequent visitor to 98 Prince Street, preferring to do business from the back of Café Pompeii. He was a capo de regime, a lieutenant, who chafed under the control of his egocentric older brother. He was also the most independent and vicious of the brothers, the one said to have "earned his bones," killed men to become a made member of the Mafia.

There was a history of bad blood between Danny and Jerry Angiulo, with shrill shouting matches over money and property and even over who was loved more by their domineering mother. Jerry thought Danny was stupid and Danny thought Jerry lacked guts.

On this day in March, Jerry Angiulo's badgering had a point to it beyond bad blood. He wanted a culprit in the screw-up, forgetting the brothers were just doing what he had told them to do. "Who called LaFreniere first?" Jerry asked Danny. "Did you ever have a conversation? . . . You're all mixed up again . . . a dummy anyway. Why'd you call for him in the first place? . . . Hey, Smiley, this kid's a rat. Let's get it straight." Recriminations over, at least for the moment, the brothers speculated that Venios had waddled into their lives because the feds had someone undercover at the Mouse Trap and had been following its managers around, including their visits to the North End on payment deliveries.

As usual, Jerry saw the problem most clearly of the brothers. The vig payments only mattered if someone said they happened. Louie wouldn't squeal, no matter what. Walter probably wouldn't but there was a chance with him. Plus, Walter wasn't so smart and didn't know the ropes of grand juries and testimony. Angiulo fretted that the feds would get LaFreniere for perjury if he denied all, producing some witness that LaFreniere talked to about paying the Angiulos. That would mean LaFreniere would face three years in jail for borrowing $2,000 from a family that had done nothing but abuse him.

Angiulo didn't like it, not a bit. He began to lean toward the simple and sinister, talking for the first time, at least out loud, about eliminating what he had been told was a pill-popping, dope-smoking wild card. He said he would tell Venios, "Get rid of that fuckin' kid. It's your son-in-law. Get rid of that fuckin' motherfucker. That cocksucker will put us all in jail one of these days. All junkies do." Angiulo had always avoided the drug end of the business, not because of any moral reservations, but because he saw it as the rat's nest of the underworld, suffused with informants who all held something back to trade up when they were in a jam. No stand-up guys there.

Normally a clearheaded thinker, Angiulo had become convinced LaFreniere came to 98 Prince Street as part of a setup, forgetting that LaFreniere was only summoned there after Angiulo himself lambasted his brothers for laxity. They had simply followed his instructions to chase Venios wherever it led to get the money. It had led to LaFreniere and now it was all their fault.

Angiulo's growing paranoia was fueled by a tip the family received from Station One of the Boston police department, which Angiulo had cultivated going back to at least the early 1960s. He was told the feds were following his son Jason around. The proposition, he said, was getting down to basic arithmetic, which Angiulo reduced to yet another Mafia malapropism. Figuring out Walter LaFreniere was now as simple as adding three plus three. LaFreniere, he concluded, had been followed by the feds.

"Put three and three in your fuckin' mind," he told

his attorney, William Cintolo, during a review of the case. "He's at the fuckin' games. . . . *Ce la cornata pui' cornutu di christo* [It's Christ's worst kind of fucking]. Do you understand it now? . . . I hit it right on the head. *Mannaggia la cornata* [damn the fucking]."

Cintolo then unwittingly delivered what amounted to Walter LaFreniere's death sentence when he told Angiulo that prosecutors were going to seek immunity for LaFreniere, meaning he couldn't take the Fifth any more and would likely face a year and a half in jail for contempt if he refused to answer the government's questions. To Angiulo, that simply meant eighteen months for LaFreniere to change his mind and cut a deal to get out of jail.

Cintolo told Angiulo: "They ask him . . . 'you know Danny?' 'Yeah.' 'You ever take any money from Danny or ever been down to 95 Prince Street?' 'Ever give Mike Angiulo something?' He takes the Fifth to every one of them. She [Wendy Collins] asked him to leave the room. . . . Five minutes later, she comes back out and she says 'The grand jury doesn't accept your answer. We will be in touch with you, ah, in order to make you answer the questions the grand jury wants to know. . . . Get yourself a . . .' "

Angiulo interrupted. "Get yourself a lawyer. Just like that. Okay. Well, he can't have a better lawyer than you. Do you want to represent him?"

"Hey, we don't mind," was the fast, fateful decision of the lawyer who would face charges of obstruction of justice himself. By the end of the legal postmortem, Angiulo was harboring thoughts that presaged murder. "I got a decision to make," he said ominously.

Three more days of brooding ended abruptly at 8:04 on the night of March 19, 1981. Jerry succumbed to his darkest impulse, the one that puts two bullets behind the ear of a man in a stolen car. He had talked it out for days and it was time to stop the dancing in the dark with Walter LaFreniere. "Get me Richie," he snapped at Mike Angiulo, "I want to see him." Richie Gambale and another enforcer, James "Fat Peter" Limone, arrived at Prince Street at 9:29 P.M.

At that very minute, in Charlestown, FBI agents had just put on a fresh tape, not knowing it would be the most important one of the case. The FBI listened as Angiulo greeted the two wiseguys at the door and pulled them aside immediately, huddling with them at the front of the L-shaped room by the blaring television. Jerry then did something that immediately caught the attention of the monitoring FBI agent: He lowered his voice.

Quinn had repeatedly warned the agents to be vigilant about danger to the vulnerable LaFreniere. Sinister whispering with a thug named Richie was enough to produce a fire station scramble at the FBI monitoring site. Fighting the media din of Angiulo's office—a television blared most of the night along with the radio—the supervising agent of the four-to-midnight shift handed a headset to one of the bureau's veteran Mafia hands. Nick Gianturco took the "jump seat." He picked up the conversation when it was half over, listening intently to the hushed voices speaking just below a microphone planted in a ceiling seam. The voices sounded like ship-to-shore conversations heard over a fuzzy short-wave radio. It was not exactly easy listening, but it would prove lethal in court nonetheless.

Getting down to basics, Angiulo assaulted Gambale with bad news. "Did I tell you that a certain guy might get called back to the grand jury?"

"Yeah."

"Did I tell you what could happen if he got called back?"

"Yeah."

"What is your opinion," Angiulo said, keeping up the pressure. "I want to hear it . . . will he or won't he stand up?"

"I got to see him tonight."

"You gotta see him tonight?"

"Yeah, I told ya that."

Even as the conversation neared its climax, Angiulo was instantly diverted by the testy tone of Gambale's "told ya" response. "Sh, sh, sh, sh. Never say a word. You don't have to make the decisions. That's why I'm the boss . . ."

Then Angiulo got back on track: "Let me put it to you this way. If you had this kid in the Mouse Trap and you are takin' three or four thousand a week . . . then if he goes to the grand jury, you're gonna get indicted . . . if you don't worry about it, why should I worry the fuck about it? What the fuck, I don't even know him, except through you. Motherfucker. Motherfucker."

Gambale risked an opinion. "I think he'll stand up."

This was not the answer Angiulo was looking for. He found himself in a debate with the 39-year-old Gambale, a reluctant killer who was missing the point. "Your answer is no . . . strangle him. And get rid of him. Hit him in the fucking head. . . . Let me tell you why, okay? Make you feel better."

By now, agent Gianturco was on line and Quinn had been called at his South Shore home.

Angiulo's rationale continued. "In the last six weeks the feds have had Jason Brian Angiulo and Skinny Kazonis. Mean anything to you? Has to be a spy in the game. Who do you think's been in the game, owes two thousand. Huh? . . . You see what we're doing here? Huh?"

Gambale continued to resist the execution order, citing the lack of a stolen car as one reason why LaFreniere could not be killed that quickly.

"You ain't got a hot car," lamented Angiulo. "You ain't got nothin'. You think I need tough guys. I need intelligent tough guys. Huh? You're not gonna get him? You're gonna hafta. . . . I feel that my son might be in jeopardy. I feel that Skinny might be in jeopardy. . . . Well, what do you want me to say? Do you want me to say to you do it right or don't do it? . . . Richie, you want to be careful because you can be killed. Because the only guy he's gonna bury is you and . . ."

Suddenly, Angiulo abandoned the entreaty and, with mounting frustration, told Gambale to just do it. "While you strangle him. While you strangle him . . . you get him where you want him, don't ever tell me that something happened and we had to pass. Because you will be in more fuckin' trouble than you were to start with. You understand? Even if you gotta snatch him off the fuckin' street. You understand that? . . . Because I'm gonna tell ya how I feel about it. . . . Tell him to take a ride, okay? . . . Get out of the car and you stomp him. Bing! You hit him in the fuckin' head and leave him right in the fuckin' spot. Do you understand?"

Shortly after Angiulo told Gambale to track down LaFreniere at the Mouse Trap, two agents brought the tape to the FBI's Boston headquarters for a final review. They had to be sure it was a hit because taking action would surely jeopardize the bugging mission. The crafty Angiulo would suspect a bugged office when a contract could not be executed because the feds broke it up the night it was supposed to take place. But the FBI had unintentionally set LaFreniere up and they would have to save him—even if the price were electronic surveillance equipment strewn all over Prince Street the next day.

Angiulo shut down the office for the night with a final exhortation: "Meet him tonight. I hope it's tonight. . . . Just hit him in the fuckin' head and stab him, okay? The jeopardy is just a little too much for me. You understand American? Okay let's go."

The mild threat had become a fatal obsession. It was 9:54 P.M.

An hour later, after a review of the tape at FBI headquarters, Gianturco talked again to Quinn at home to confirm a planned hit and to tell him it could happen that night. Quinn told Gianturco and Jack Cloherty, the night shift supervisor, to meet him at the Mouse Trap in Park Square. The mission: Save LaFreniere first, and flip him as a witness against Angiulo second.

They got to the lounge around midnight. Cloherty talked to the doorman, Gianturco to a waitress. Quinn, who was the only one who knew what LaFreniere looked like, having handed him a summons ten days earlier, cruised the periphery. They were absurdly transparent among the late-night crowd nursing drinks and ogling strippers and half-naked waitresses, three feds in suit coats asking for Walter. They could almost feel the room contract in suspicion. Someone asked them to not stand around, to order a drink or sit down. Finally, a waitress told Cloherty that LaFreniere had been in earlier but had gone.

The agents conferred briefly and left, satisfied LaFreniere was not there. They went across the street to the Park Plaza Hotel to call him at home in Woburn. By the time they got to the hotel, the Mouse Trap bartender had called LaFreniere to warn him cops were skulking the place looking for him.

Quinn went to a lobby pay phone and reached LaFreniere's wife.

"Is Walter there, please?"

"Who's calling?"

"Ed Quinn."

"Wait a minute [long pause] . . . no, he's not here."

Knowing it didn't take LaFreniere's wife thirty seconds to realize her husband was not home at midnight, Quinn breathed a sigh of relief that Walter was home and alive. He sent Cloherty home and headed to Woburn with Gianturco, arriving at a supermarket parking lot near LaFreniere's house about 1:30 in the morning. Quinn called from another pay phone and LaFreniere answered the phone himself.

"I have nothing to say to you," he told Quinn.

"Fine," said Quinn. "I don't want you to say anything to me. I just want you to listen. It's a matter of life and death, specifically yours. You don't have to believe me. But just hear me out. We're just around the corner at the Purity Supreme."

Walter agreed to come talk.

After twenty minutes went by with no sign of La-Freniere, the agents headed off to the house but made a U-turn when they saw him pull out of his street. They all drove into the supermarket lot together. LaFreniere got out and clambered into the back seat of Quinn's 1979 blue Ford Fairlane. It was now 2 A.M. Quinn introduced Gianturco and got down to business: An informant had told the FBI that there was a North End contract out on him. No supposition, all fact. It could happen as soon as today and definitely before the next grand jury appearance. Quinn looked him in the eye the whole time and knew LaFreniere believed him, his face frozen by the dilemma: the FBI or the mob? Who do you trust?

Quinn outlined options: Go into the federal witness protection program that night, taking his family with him into hiding; disappear for a month until the danger blew over; or, in the vernacular of the trade, "reach out" to the North End and see what happened. But Quinn, a decent as well as determined agent, gave LaFreniere the cold comfort of sincere advice: No matter what you decide, Walter, if you don't want to come with us, don't meet with them alone in a car. If you have to talk with them, do it on the phone or in a crowded place.

Nonplussed, LaFreniere struggled silently with the fact Gambale had called him that night at 11:30 and asked to have a few drinks with him the next day. He then mentioned part of this to Quinn—that he'd already gotten a call.

Quinn immediately asked who made the call.

No answer.

Where were you supposed to meet?

"I'm confused about this," replied LaFreniere. "I need to think."

LaFreniere then promised to call Quinn the next morning but never did. Instead, he called his father-in-law Venios, who put him in touch with Danny Angiulo, who quickly passed him on to the family lawyer Cintolo. Cintolo eventually advised LaFreniere not to talk to the grand jury and dutifully relayed all prosecutor questions to Angiulo—a liaison that would later net him a prison term for conspiring to obstruct justice.

By the late afternoon of March 20, Angiulo had been briefed on Gambale's abortive attempt to rendezvous with LaFreniere and carry out the murder pact. Angiulo was now in full retreat. Like LaFreniere, he too needed time to think. One decision had been made for him: You can't execute a witness who knew what was up and, worse, was being watched by the FBI. Maybe in Sicily, but not in Boston.

As astute as Angiulo was in assessing all the chess moves swirling around him, he remained obtusely and fatally oblivious of the two microphones in his midst. The closest he got to the mark was concluding that Gambale's car had a hidden microphone. "His car is bugged, you know it," he said. "There's a fucking bug or beep on it. . . . Next thing you know, they'll be coming from the parachutes. . . . The Mouse Trap is gotta be bugged . . ." He began seeing bugs every place except over his head.

Try as he might, Angiulo simply could not get to the obvious. His hubris precluded any breach in the neighborhood network that had protected his turf for decades. His office didn't even have a burglar alarm, for who in their right mind would rob the Angiulos in the North End? No, there was some undercover work going on here but it was someone at the Mouse Trap.

Angiulo's worst fear was that the feds would flip LaFreniere and that he would land on his son Jason, who was then 23 years old but treated as a bumbling child by his father in alternatingly comical and poignant encounters. With the LaFreniere execution blown, Angiulo's focus shifted to the grand jury on the nineteenth floor of the federal courthouse in Post Office Square.

Angiulo's plan was to have Jason tough it out at the

grand jury, to lie about running the floating barbooth game, knowing that LaFreniere and Venios would not contradict him. The dice game cut close, though, because Angiulo was behind it, sharing in the meager proceeds—probably a thousand dollars on a good night—from a passé gambling racket that was no longer the big money-maker that it had been in the 1950s and 1960s. Nevertheless, it was easy money that had become a criminal exposure for Angiulo. And that was something never far from his mind.

While Angiulo continued to detest the very idea of having to trust LaFreniere, his preoccupation with him receded as he got constant reassurances out of the Combat Zone. As the LaFreniere crisis faded, Angiulo turned his obsessive energy to the next step: prepping his protected son for grand jury pressure, something Angiulo himself had been through. While he knew his stuff, his impatience with the unfocused Jason made the tutoring sessions excruciating for both.

With great pedantry, Angiulo instructed his son to always say, "to the best of my recollection," instead of, "I don't remember," because the latter implied he once knew the answer. It becomes a semantical jumble, with Jerry's rapid-fire instructions leaving Jason confused rather than confident. Frustration turned to abuse.

On March 25, the day before Jason Angiulo was first scheduled to testify, Angiulo lashed out, ostensibly to toughen him up, but the sarcasm was loaded with disappointment. When Jason arrived carrying a basket of flowers a friend had given him, Angiulo greeted his son: "There's a kid that's worried to death he might go to jail tomorrow morning."

"Fuck you, Dad."

"Look at him, goes around with fucking roses. . . .

Why is that basket shaking like that? You got the willies or something?"

But the moment of truth before a grand jury was deferred when Jason's appearance was postponed for a week because prosecutors planned to oppose Cintolo's representation of both Jason Angiulo and LaFreniere.

Assured of LaFreniere's fidelity, Angiulo grew positively jaunty the closer his son got to his next scheduled grand jury appearance, on April 2. In fact, it energized Angiulo and he began to spoil for a fight with his nemesis Quinn and the "bitch" prosecutor Collins. "Tomorrow," he announced, "I will get up at my convenience. And then I will escort my wary underling up to the federal building. And we will look for Miss Collins."

Angiulo ended the pregame planning with a rare paternal moment, giving a maudlin speech to his son from a bad movie: "Before you got this summons, I could call you boy, now I call you a man . . . ain't going to take much for you to be a man . . . you take it easy now. All I just ask is you just stand up. Don't worry about a fucking thing."

But, just before they headed off to the Federal Building, Angiulo had to get one thing straight with Jason. It was as brass-tacks a talk as a father can have with his son. Will you stand up for Dad if it comes to it?

The real danger, as Angiulo saw it, was LaFreniere coming back to convict Jason Angiulo of perjury after Jason had denied all. It came down to the answer to two questions: "Does Jason admit he does this barbooth game? . . . Does he admit that it's not him, it's his father?"

Weeks after the issue first came up, Angiulo finally got to the heart of the matter: Would his son betray

him in a world of traitors and motherfuckers? With all
his wealth and power, Angiulo found himself pacing
back and forth in a ramshackle office and worrying
about whether he could trust his own child. "It's a hell
of fucking theory, isn't it," he said to Jason. "You
wouldn't be the first son that turned in his father. Take
my word for it . . . And on the other hand, you must
remember there're a lot of guys in Leavenworth and a
lot of guys in Lewisburg that protected their sons. They
went, 'he had nothing to do with it. It was me.' There'll
be no such thing here. We will be men or mice."

At the courthouse, Angiulo tried to set the tone for
Jason Angiulo's appearance by having calculated run-
ins with Wendy Collins and Ed Quinn in blatant attempts to intimidate them both. He had been warming
up for the pair of feds for several days.

After listening to some of Angiulo's threatening talk
about where Quinn lives and whether he had a family,
the case agent was alarmed enough to wear a hidden
body wire to work that day. But Collins was not expecting a personal visit. Angiulo took her by surprise
at the morning hearing held to consider the government's challenge to Cintolo's dual representation of
Jason Angiulo and Walter LaFreniere. She argued that
it was a conflict of interest for Cintolo to represent the
latter party, who had been nearly killed to protect the
former. The court ruled that Cintolo could not represent Jason.

At the beginning of the hearing, Collins was sitting
at the counsel's table when she heard a gruff, imperious
voice calling, "Miss Collins, Miss Collins." She thought
to herself, Gee, that sounds familiar. She turned and
looked out over the courtroom, not seeing anyone until

she looked down to find the diminutive Angiulo standing there with his arms crossed, wearing a floral shirt.

"I'm Mr. Angiulo. Gennaro Angiulo," he said, staring at her intently, something he always did when he first met somebody he wanted to intimidate. He basked briefly in his persona and made sure she knew that he knew who she was. "I'm the one you're looking for, aren't I?" he said.

In a resolutely calm and patient voice, she told him, "If you are not a lawyer and you are not a witness, then you can't be here in front of the bar. You will have to go back and sit down over there, behind the bar." She turned to the bench and sat down hard, her heart pounding, unnerved by his boldness and by the disconcerting sensation of having a direct conversation with a man she had been eavesdropping on for weeks. Rebuffed, Angiulo blustered for a while and finally sat down. He had some choice words about Collins when he got back to the office, but nothing she hadn't heard before.

Angiulo's encounter with Quinn was just as short but more menacing, an exchange marked by subdued mutual hostility. From the secret tapes, Quinn knew Angiulo had come to consider him as a personification of the mafioso's troubles. Two days earlier, Angiulo had ruminated in his office about finding out more about Quinn's family. The low-key Quinn had taken to wearing his .38 pistol instead of carrying it in his briefcase, a change that was not lost on his colleagues.

Quinn deliberately appeared in the corridor near the elevator at the time Angiulo was leaving the courthouse, and Angiulo spotted him as he headed out with his son and Cintolo. "You know," he said to Quinn.

"I know that you know me, and most certainly I know that I recognize you, but I can't remember your first name."

"Yeah, well, my name in Agent Quinn."

"You see, I said the first name; Quinn, I know it is, the first one?"

"Well, I think that's how you'll know me though, right?"

"Hey that sounds good. Okay. I call you Mr. Quinn."

"Okay and I'll call you Mr. Angiulo."

"Until the time comes."

"Until the time comes," Quinn repeated.

Angiulo, as he stepped onto the elevator, looked up and said, "Be careful."

Quinn, as the doors closed, said, "Bye now."

Luckily for Angiulo, he made no explicit threat.

And luckily for Jason Angiulo, he was able to duck testifying by citing the dispute over Cintolo's challenged representation. The court decision to bar Cintolo from representing him appeared to have spared Jason a certain perjury indictment had he been required to testify about the barbooth game. When he was recalled later in the month, Jason Angiulo claimed illness and the feds let it slide, overwhelmed with work and confident they had enough on the family anyway. The bumbling Jason simply wasn't worth it.

Angiulo would also have good fortune when LaFreniere appeared before the grand jury at the end of April. LaFreniere read a statement prepared by Cintolo that contended the grant of immunity was flawed and he was really being forced to relinquish his Fifth Amendment protection against self-incrimination.

It was a feisty, revitalized LaFreniere who went into the grand jury room on the nineteenth floor, jamming with Collins over her purported threat to put him in jail for not talking. She bristled and told him the issue was contempt, not necessarily jail. His refusal to testify despite immunity was quickly brought to a federal judge standing by on "emergency." Five weeks later, La-Freniere was indeed in jail and would not get out for eighteen months. He would spurn another offer of witness protection from Quinn with two months left to serve. LaFreniere turned out to be the ultimate stand-up guy.

But it wasn't as if he lacked motivation. There was always Richie Gambale calling to see if he wanted to have a a few drinks. And there were sit-downs with his father-in-law and Skinny Kazonis, another stand-up guy who went away for the cause in the 1970s.

Kazonis met with LaFreniere on the eve of a scheduled grand jury appearance at the Penalty Box, a shot-and-beer bar across from the Boston Garden. It was part pep talk and part reminder of the consequences of talking.

Kazonis, a stoic factotum and Angiulo favorite who would be convicted of obstruction in the LaFreniere case, was the outside reinforcement for Venios's incessant admonitions to stand up or risk Gambale. Kazonis later reported to Angiulo, "Well, I convinced him already, for tomorrow forget about—"

Angiulo interrupted to brag to others in the office: "In fact, what the kid wanted to do was when he got through with Skinny, he wanted to just go home and get his fuckin' underwear and go, go, go away. See? Yeah, good health, gentlemen."

Earlier that week, Angiulo had personally worked over Louie Venios, who had been summoned to 98 Prince Street for a guarded discussion about his son-in-law's reliability. Angiulo was so oblique, Louie had trouble following him. It was no time for crossed signals.

Venios asked, "Now what's your advice? To me?"

That set off alarms for the wary Angiulo, who never had explicit conversations on matters that could come back at him as testimony, even with someone as tried and true as Venios. "I ain't got nothin' to do with it," Angiulo told him. Moving on to safer ground, he told Venios, "You made the best decision you ever made in your fucking life. Let me tell you something. You better know him though."

"I know the cocksucker," Venios assured him.

The meeting ended with Jerry the Magnanimous: "Once he goes to the can, don't you let a fucking day slip, wherever he is, that somebody goes up there to visit." Later, Jerry offered Kazonis a different view of LaFreniere's sacrifice. "Him . . . he'll go away like a jerk."

If Angiulo had failed to intimidate Collins and Quinn, he had been a smashing success with Walter La-Freniere. LaFreniere would spend Christmas in jail that year, residing for most of the sentence in a Manhattan prison, a tough place loaded with killers. He served from June 4, 1981, to December 4, 1982, and never said a word. Not only did he stand up then, he testified for the Angiulos at trials in 1985 and 1986, denying that he was present at a barbooth game or that he ever took a loan from Jason Angiulo or anybody else. He even disputed his own words on tape, including the segment in which he identified himself, correcting Frank Angiulo, who thought Walter was another flunkie from the Mouse Trap. "I'm Walter," LaFreniere had said to Frank.

LaFreniere's court testimony also included a bitter recollection of his visit from Ed Quinn two months before he was to get out of jail. "You come down here and tell me you tried to help me? You tell me a story about a contract on my life, you put me in a house with fifteen hundred killers. He tries to help me!" Later, Quinn, looking back, would remark: "I'd say Walter is home free. He stood up. He went the whole distance, even testifying—if you can call it that—denying his own voice. . . . He did his very best to help the guys who wanted to kill him."

But the last word on the LaFreniere matter belonged, appropriately enough, to Gennaro Angiulo. Near the end of the bugging operation that lasted four months in 1981, when the roof was caving in, when the FBI formally tipped its hand and was running up and down Prince Street kicking down doors and grabbing betting slips to go with the recordings of Frank Angiulo counting the money, Gennaro could only blame fate and Walter LaFreniere. He was right for the wrong reasons. "Soon as that kid got a fuckin' summons, that was the beginning. That was the beginning. We all fell asleep. . . . It was like, it was like God sending us a fuckin' message, and we couldn't read it."

His empire shaken by pinpoint raids, Angiulo brought all the travail back to the laxity that produced Walter LaFreniere as a problem, overwhelmed and disgusted that such big trouble could come from simple complacency, cancer from a small mole. "Why should I go to jail in this fuckin' thing? You know how many fuckin' things I did worse than this shit?" he asked in his office, filled with suddenly taciturn henchmen. No one disagreed with him.

10

THE NOOSE
TIGHTENS

Not long after Walter LaFreniere's life was saved, talk
of another murder came across the FBI wire. "This
Harvey Cohen. I'm going to kill him," Larry Zannino
told his soldiers in a late-night aside.

The line was tucked into a rambling Zannino discourse that suddenly veered to the grisly assertion and
then just as quickly veered back to the main topic—
some malcontent who concerned the Angiulos. "Now
about Jerry," continued Zannino. "Danny's been talking to this guy . . ."

The Cohen reference might easily have been missed,
but it wasn't. Eavesdropping agents rewound the tape
in Charlestown to confirm what they thought they'd
heard.

"This Harvey Cohen. I'm going to kill him."

Later, Zannino explained the hit "is for the family
in New York."

The Zannino aside once again set off a series of FBI countermoves to stymie the Mafia—moves that increasingly frustrated Jerry Angiulo and his men. Angiulo had passed along to Zannino the request that had traveled from New York to Providence to Boston, and the failure to fulfill the contract was a cause for embarrassment and suspicion. Why so long? What the hell is going on here?

The very next day the FBI met with the man the Mafia had marked for death. Harvey Cohen was not an unfamiliar name to the bureau. John Morris's men on the organized crime squad hadn't had much to do with him, but agents on other squads had. Cohen, who'd grown up in Revere, was involved in his family's trucking firm, Camel Trucking.

Cohen's troubles stemmed from the trucking business. Camel Trucking had originally been based in East Boston, but Cohen moved the operation to an old terminal he purchased in an industrial wasteland in Chelsea, a city just north of Boston not far from Logan Airport. No problem there, except that Cohen immediately ousted the prior tenant of the terminal, a firm with mob connections.

The prior tenant was a subsidiary of Pinto Trucking of New York. The owners of Pinto included Philip Giacone and Chubby Bono, two reputed members of one of the crime families in New York City that had longstanding ties with Raymond Patriarca in Providence. Pinto was also one of Cohen's chief competitors in hauling freight from airports in Boston and New York. Cohen, divorced and in his forties, kept an apartment in New York to stay at while there on business.

Even before Zannino's pledge to kill Cohen, word had already filtered up to Boston from the FBI in New

York that Cohen might have Mafia troubles. It was the white-collar crime unit in Boston that got the news, and one of the unit's agents had gone to see him to discuss this possible problem.

At first, Cohen didn't act too worried, but given fresh details of a specific threat, he flushed. "They want you dead," agent Jim Cullen disclosed at the meeting in the rear parking lot of a Woburn restaurant within twenty-four hours of Zannino's remarks. "They want you dead by the end of the weekend."

Morris had instructed Cullen to play it close to the vest so as not to tip his hand about the source of the threat. Morris wasn't so sure he would have jeopardized the secret bugs by warning Cohen if all they'd overheard Zannino discuss was a plan to hijack trucks. But a murder plot—well, you just had to tell the guy before he became a victim.

Cohen made Cullen's job easy. He slipped into a kind of semishock and didn't question the reliability of the threat, so Cullen tried to pry information from him.

"What's this all about?" Cullen asked.

"I'm 1,000 percent sure it involves New York," Cohen replied, going a little bit into the business conflicts that the FBI already knew about. He was visibly upset. Then he began to clam up.

"So what's next?" Cullen asked, to keep things going.

"I think I'll leave."

"Where?"

"I'll let you know."

Three weeks later, Zannino, unaware that Cohen had been warned, began harping about him. He was livid with soldier Dominic Isabella for taking the order to kill so nonchalantly.

"I want to kill Harvey Cohen very shortly," he demanded of Isabella. "You ain't done a fuckin' thing by tellin' me you're going by his fuckin' house and see his car. I want the both of youse start talking to this fucking guy. As a matter of fact, run into each other accidentally. 'Hey, what'd ya say? How are ya?' Get his confidence.

"Shouldn't he be dead by now?" he suddenly posed to his men. "This is for the family in New York. Now I'm responsible."

Dominic Isabella promised to do better. "I think I'm gonna, gonna nail him comin' out of the bar. Cause with that Jew, he's always got four or five guys around him."

"If you get his confidence," encouraged Zannino. "I know where it is. I've been there. Get his confidence and you finally keep talkin' to him and you make him feel he's behind you. And we'll hit him in the fucking head. We'll bring a package behind and fuckin' we'll crack him."

Isabella then confessed he couldn't even find Cohen's home in the swanky North Shore town of Marblehead. "There's no number, Larry."

Instead of chastising Isabella further for his ineptitude, Zannino launched into an emotional pep talk, sensing the soldier needed encouragement in a difficult assignment.

"You are basically a beautiful fuckin' guy. And I'll tell ya. I got the best regime in the fuckin' country. . . . And not only that, we volunteered. And not only that, the boss and the underboss give us the work. Why did they give us the work? Why do they give it to us? Because they've got confidence in us."

Zannino's men never found Cohen. He went underground shortly after meeting with Cullen, resurfacing

eventually in Israel. He never notified the FBI. Nor did
he tell Larry Zannino. It was the kind of setback for
the Mafia that Jerry Angiulo began to string together
during the course of the FBI's secret bugging operation.
There was the Walter LaFreniere debacle, then the Cohen
screw-up.

But if Angiulo was still reluctant to put too much
stock in his apprehensions about "too many coincidences," he no longer was after the FBI's gambling raids
of April 20. Since the FBI had all the evidence it needed
and the electronic surveillance was nearing its end, Ed
Quinn and his men hit Angiulo hard—twenty bookmaking offices in the Boston area, including the main
office at 126 Prince Street managed by nephew "Jimmy
Jones" Angiulo.

"Nicol," Mikey Angiulo called out to his brother as
he rushed into 98 Prince Street in the early afternoon.
"They just nailed Jimmy Jones."

"Jimmy Jones? Where?"

"He was—"

"Up the street?"

"Yeah."

Mike Angiulo cursed the bookmakers for not moving
their operation often enough among different apartments to avoid snooping investigators. "Motherfuckers, I told them last Friday, 'What are youse doing there?
Is that the only place you know where to work?' Fuckin'
nitwits."

The FBI had tapped the telephone at 126 Prince Street
with a pen register—a device that recorded not conversation but telephone numbers dialed for outgoing
calls. Agents then traced the outgoing numbers and
came up with the locations for all of the other
offices—Medford, Chelsea, Boston, Watertown, and

Revere. Quinn chose a Monday to get the records of the extensive weekend gambling activity. Mounds of evidence were seized—mostly betting slips and records—in the raids that had been planned to define the scope of the Angiulo illegal numbers operation, as well as to stoke the gambling talk inside 98 Prince Street.

The only wrinkle in the otherwise smoothly executed busts came when Quinn, leading four agents in the main raid at 126 Prince Street, broke into the wrong apartment—one on the second floor instead of the third floor. Knocking down the door, he startled two women and a young girl.

"Where's James Angiulo?" Quinn barked at two frightened women who stared at him and the other agents as if they were from Mars. Seconds later, an agent tapped his shoulder. "Ed, not this floor, next floor." Quinn stayed long enough to explain the situation to the women after sending three agents upstairs. James Angiulo and John Orlandella were found seated at the kitchen table, unaware of the commotion downstairs, amid piles of gambling receipts and records. Quinn told the women to send the FBI the bill for the shattered door.

News of the gambling raids traveled quickly in the city's underworld. Throughout the afternoon, Mike and Frank Angiulo kept track of their losses. "They grabbed 'G,' " Frank announced two hours after the initial word of the busts. "They grabbed Chelsea." By 4:35 P.M., the results were in. "They grabbed everybody today," Frankie concluded. He also guessed correctly how the FBI did it. "Tapped Jimmy Jones's phone," he told his brothers. "He called all them fuckin' guys."

The main man did not show up at the Mafia headquarters until 7:30 P.M., but when he did, Jerry Angiulo began a tirade that lasted well into the next morning, and was resumed often during the days that followed. He vented anger, but also despair. "Who the fuck gives a fuck?" he claimed at one point, sounding uncharacteristically weary and resigned. For the most part, however, he schemed up ways to get back in business as quickly as possible.

But first, Angiulo had to lash out at everyone around him, remind them he'd suspected all winter long that with so many coincidences of late he knew the feds were circling in. "I remind you I only came in early one fuckin' day, and I said, 'They're here.' Now, they're here." He cursed about how soft they'd all become. "Remember how we beat 'em four years, five years ago? Do you remember how? No phones, no cars, no drivers. We got careless; that's what happened, and we got exactly what we deserved. We have become fuckin' idiots. And in our zeal we fell asleep. Remember the old days when we were in the cellars. Hear a knock here, crash, out the fire escape, over the top. We got . . . What happened? Come in, take what you want, have a party."

He didn't even spare himself. "Fuckin' stupid we became. I'll tell you the truth, I know who fell asleep. Me. You know why? I started listening to some stories from lawyers. 'Feds are giving up on gambling.' "

From his nephew and John Orlandella, Angiulo extracted the details about Quinn's raid of 126 Prince Street. The two told Jerry Angiulo how they had refused to answer any of Quinn's questions and wouldn't sign an FBI inventory list of the evidence the agents had seized under a search warrant. "I'm beginning to hate this fuckin' motherfucker more every minute," Angiulo said. And Quinn wore white gloves to pick up stuff in the apartment, the nephew reported. "He's a cute son of a bitch."

By the next morning, the bookmaking was back on line, although Jerry Angiulo had issued new marching orders. Security was to be beefed up. No more outgoing calls from the main office, only incoming. Arrangements were to be made so that each branch office called in the business. "That stuff has absolutely gotta be done at nighttime. I don't want to hear a fucking thing. You can forget daytime for the next five years. Don't even think about it."

"Better not stop looking in the mirror any more boys," he warned his nephew and John Orlandella. In an effort to throw off the FBI, he ordered James Angiulo to hit the street and keep a high profile, particularly during the hours he used to book the numbers. This way the feds would think he was out of business. Others were assigned to book. "You know what it's all about? Darkness. Well, that's it, Frank. See what you can arrange and if you cannot arrange it, Friday fucking night you're gonna tell everybody that doesn't send stuff in that they're out. Okay?"

In one sense, the raids were history. "Go from here," Angiulo declared. "We'll start brand fucking new." But, in another sense, Angiulo could no longer shake his concerns about security. The network ruptures haunted him. How the FBI knew about every bookmaking branch office became a riddle even he could not solve. "How the fuck can we allow twenty-two fuckin' guys to get caught with one fuckin' telephone?" he asked. "Every motherfuckin' stop. They didn't miss a fuckin' stop. They didn't miss a fuckin' one, did they? That's a very interesting question."

He badgered his brothers and Zannino with the different possibilities. "We got a louse in the middle of us. You understand American?" If it wasn't an informant, Angiulo concluded, it was a bug, coming as close as he would come to the FBI's dark secret. "Frank," Angiulo ordered the day after the FBI raids. "Tomorrow, tonight, call the electrician and give him ladders. Tell him to go outside and take that fan apart. Go all the way into that fan and take the air conditioner out of there and look in the air conditioner too. Okay? Before we wind up in the fuckin' nuthouse." Later, he told his brother, "I ain't had a fuckin' night's sleep, trying to figure out how fucking stupid we got. And I'm not gonna blame me alone."

Angiulo's worry became the FBI's worry, for eavesdropping agents in Charlestown went into a red alert every time Angiulo began talking about looking for bugs in 98 Prince Street. And Angiulo kept coming back to the subject, nagging his brother Frankie to get the electrician in, or to call Mickey Caruana of Peabody, a Patriarca favorite and major drug runner whose hobby was electronic gadgets and bug detection. He could sweep the office.

Finally, Frankie Angiulo climbed up onto a chair himself, lifted ceiling tiles, and poked around. "Look at Frankie," Jerry pointed. "He's looking for the feds on the fucking roof."

Angiulo might make a nervous joke out of it, but Frankie snooping in the dropped ceiling set off a scramble in Charlestown. Within minutes, squad leader Morris and case agent Quinn were notified. Morris raced to the monitoring site and climbed into the jump seat. Quinn assembled a team of agents to descend upon the office if he got word from Morris that Frankie Angiulo had blundered into the battery packs in the ceiling. They would at least recover government property.

Morris had had nightmares about this moment, and in them a bug was always discovered. If it happened, he would have to decide whether to have Quinn leave the second microphone alone. It had been done before in other buggings; some of the most candid lines had been taped after the mobsters thought they'd foiled the feds.

But the scare was a false alarm. Frankie gave up. A few days later, he took apart the fan and found nothing. Caruana came by after a Celtics game at the nearby Boston Garden, but never got around to sweeping the office. It was as if all the Angiulos knew there was a bug but simply did not have the energy or imagination to deal with the possibility of one being in their office, on their street, in their North End. So the hidden microphones remained intact and the FBI got what it wanted: a continuous stream of incriminating talk about gambling and obstructing justice—and an unending series of doomsday monologues from Angiulo. The Mafia boss grew more anxious each day following the raids, and the source of his anxiety was RICO.

Angiulo was obsessed with the law. "See this motherfucker," he snapped at Frankie, waving a copy of the statute at his brother. "This is what they're doing to us. This is RICO. This thing here. They appealed it to the highest fucking court. Now read it." To Jason he complained, "Shoulda stayed single. I was single. I'd be fucking long gone."

"Let me tell you something," Angiulo told Larry Zannino at the end of April. "It's gone. We blew the biggest fucking thing in the country. For fifty fucking

G's we could've got the best argument team in Washington. For fifty cold." But Zannino tried to resist Angiulo's dreary forecast. What if we win? he asked. What if the court upholds Turkette? There was always that chance. What if, as Turkette argued, RICO didn't apply to a criminal outfit until the outfit tried to muscle in on some legitimate business?

Angiulo nibbled at the possibility. If somehow the court did decide in their favor, they'd all come out fine. The FBI would be left holding a gun with no bullets. "What the fuck are the feds gonna do with shylocking?" Angiulo ruminated. "What are they gonna do with numbers? What are they gonna do with horses? What are they gonna do with marijuana? What are they gonna do with junk? They can stick it up their fuckin' ass."

He liked the hypothetical victory and the logic of the Turkette argument claiming RICO didn't apply to him. "It says that if they don't prove that a legitimate business was infiltrated we're off the hook," he went on. "We can do anything we want. They can stick RICO." He felt like his old cocky self. "I wouldn't be in a legitimate business for all the fuckin' money in the world to begin with."

The duet of Angiulo and Zannino suddenly launched into a bizarre, tribal chant for the hometown Mafia club. "The law says that whoever infiltrates legitimate businesses in interstate commerce shall be susceptible to this," opened Jerry.

"That's right," cheered Zannino.

"Our argument is, we're illegitimate business."

"We're a shylock," noted Zannino.

"We're a shylock," repeated Angiulo, as if relishing the sound of it.

"Yeah," gushed Zannino.

"We're a fucking bookmaker," added Angiulo.

"Bookmaker."

"We're selling marijuana."

"We're not infiltrating."

"We're, we're, we're illegal here, illegal there, arsonists!" declared Angiulo, for once sounding almost at a loss for words. "We're every fucking thing."

"Pimps! Prostitutes!"

"The law does not cover us. Is that right?"

Quinn and Morris also worried about the outcome of the Turkette case before the Supreme Court. The concern was part of the reason behind the gambling raids and the pressure from the strike force to accumulate massive amounts of evidence for a major gambling case if they lost the RICO option. Ultimately, the investigation would have to go either way: a series of cases accusing Angiulo and the others of separate crimes or a single RICO case against a Mafia crime family based on the combination of offenses. While they waited for the high court decision they had the comfort of knowing they had the evidence for a solid case—either way. But they all preferred RICO. Much more punch.

For all of the bug's high points, the grueling investigation was beginning to take its toll on the crew. There was a ceiling on the overtime an agent could earn, so no one was getting rich working everyday, all day, on top of a $35,000-a-year salary.

Quinn's day began by 7 A.M., when he stopped off in Charlestown to pick up the tapes, and didn't end until after 10 P.M. He'd make it as far as his couch in the television room of his home south of Boston. The television might be on, or, more often, he'd try to talk with his wife. They didn't much get into the Mafia case, although she knew what he was doing. During their nearly twenty years together, she never really pressed him about his work, which was how Quinn preferred it.

He wanted to know what was going on at home, what their three kids were up to. During the bug probe, he had lost his family life. In the four months it was "up," each of his kids and his wife had celebrated a birthday—well, maybe not celebrated, but had a birthday. By the time he'd get home at night, he would pop a Budweiser and try to reconnect. But he usually caved into fatigue and fell asleep within five minutes.

Pete Kennedy, his muscles in knots from the daily battle to decipher Mafia dialogue, found himself getting more and more edgy as the days wore on, so he found some relief by pounding 2-by-4s in his basement. By the time the bugging was completed, so was a new family room.

The guilt Tom Donlan felt about never being home worsened when his mother-in-law, who lived with his family, learned she had cancer. His pregnant wife not only had to manage the house but now had to take her mother to chemotherapy.

The Donlans weren't the only ones who had a baby during Operation Bostar. Bill Regii's kid, born early on in the bugging, was the first of four "Bostar brats." The Regii's baby was followed by Thomas Gianturco, son of Nick Gianturco, then Brendan Donlan, and finally, Michael Buckley, named after his father, agent Mike Buckley.

The strain on family life was not lost on Quinn and Morris. They understood how taxing the reentries and

video car shuffles were for the agents already belea-
gured by the monotonous monitoring in Charlestown,
but this was the price for staying inside the bureau and
not relying on any outside agencies or utilities. And it
worked, for despite a few scares, there had been no
leaks.

As if juggling these pieces weren't enough, there was
also the installation and maintenance of a second bug
at Larry Zannino's club at 51 North Margin Street to
worry about, a controversial installation within the
bureau because of the drain on manpower and the added
risk of the Mafia uncovering the FBI mission in the
North End. But all along, squad leader Morris had insisted the two-bug strategy was worth it and, despite
setbacks, he prevailed.

Nearly three weeks after the January 19 installation
of the 98 Prince Street bug, Morris sent agent Shaun
Rafferty down to the North End to set up the Zannino
bug. For a while, it appeared the move was a mistake.
Not that Rafferty and his team of agents had any trouble staking out the club. It was actually easier than
Prince Street. North Margin was not as residential as
Prince; it was darker and less traveled. Because of the
card games, dozens of strangers came and left during
the course of an evening, so that undercover agents
approaching the front door late at night did not auto-
matically trigger suspicion even if they were spotted.
People lived in apartments upstairs from the Angiulo
office. The North Margin Street club was above a garage. You could count on not bumping into anyone.
Surveillance of the club had also been easier—you just
had to sit on a stool munching on pizza in the pizza
joint across the street.

Debbie Richard was drafted again to play her role as

decoy, and on the morning of February 11 she and a locksmith made their way to the club entrance posing as a lovestruck couple. At the entryway, they stopped and necked. The locksmith knelt and sprung the door, and four technical agents hurried inside behind them. In less than an hour, two microphones were hidden and working—one in the large gaming room and a second in the small rear room that was Zannino's office.

But North Margin proved to be a technical nightmare. First, there'd been a delay in getting any bugging equipment from Washington. The shelves were bare, with the equipment on loan to other offices around the country. Morris called Washington daily trying to drum up something. But by the time Richard and the others had two mikes to install, the FBI had already watched twelve days pass from the thirty-day bugging period the court had approved back on January 30.

Then came the miscalculation about the bug in the gaming room. The microphone worked, but there was no way to tell who was talking or what was said by the dozens of card players. The room was like an echo chamber. The agents heard eating and drinking noises and even a lot of gambling talk about raising bets and borrowing money. Players lost up to $59,000 in a single night. Many losses were converted into loan-shark debts with weekly interest of 1 to 2.5 percent. The house took its 2.5 percent share of every pot. But it was hard to pin down the voices.

Morris and Rafferty decided the gambling room was a lost cause. They had agents break into the club on February 16 to move the microphone from the card room to Zannino's office, with the one already hidden there.

The Zannino bug was ultimately first-rate, delivering the interplay between the city's two most powerful mafiosi that Morris had so badly wanted. It gave them the plan to kill Harvey Cohen, as well as a third murder plot, and it gave them a Larry Zannino uninhibited by Jerry Angiulo, the only mafioso with a bigger ego.

"I'm a capo regime and I'm talking to you as a soldier," Zannino declared to two of his men early one morning inside the office at 51 North Margin Street, which was his domain. He was the consummate company man, disturbed to learn that in a dispute between a non-Mafia party and a mafioso, one of his soldiers had not been clear about whose side he was on. "Don't you ever dare, in your fuckin' life, ever tell me that you're neutral with an outsider, whether he's right or wrong. Didn't you ever hear Jerry when he made his speech? If you have to give the edge, it's the soldier that's right."

Zannino exuded mafiosi pride. "Remember one thing. I didn't become a capo regime for political reasons. I never asked. I never went and wiped asses. And I never went down to Providence. No one helped me. Jerry, or nobody." And he took seriously his responsibility toward his men.

Throughout the winter, Zannino worried about Carmen Tortora, a soldier who was about to go off to federal prison. Tortora had been secretly taped the year before while trying to collect on an illegal loan. He was a stand-up wiseguy who would take his legal lumps for the family. After reviewing the evidence, Zannino had even advised his man to plead guilty. "He'll get a hundred years if he goes to trial," he told his men one night after giving Tortora a pep talk. "He's dead. Ain't got a fuckin' chance. . . . He's got a fourteen page, 'I'll kill you, you cocksucker . . .' "

Zannino was referring to the transcript of Tortora that was the heart of the government's case. Twice Tortora had confronted Paul Alexander about late payments for a $250 loan. Alexander, secretly cooperating with authorities, had worn a body wire both times.

"Where's my motherfuckin' money?" Tortora had demanded as he approached Alexander on Freeport Street in Dorchester for the second time in two months.

"I don't have any money to come down there to give ya, Carmen!" Alexander replied.

"I'm gonna split your motherfuckin' head open if I don't start getting some money! This fuckin' bullshit, fuckin' hidin'; I'll cut your throat! Now, you get me some motherfuckin' money down there!"

"I haven't been working at all, Carmen."

"I don't give a fuck about your working or not. You can fuckin' work. Go out and fuckin' work and get me my fuckin' money. 'Cause yours is way the fuck up there now. You know that, don't ya?"

"Yeah."

"Yeah." Tortora couldn't believe his ears. "I want motherfuckin' money there this fuckin' weekend! Or the next time I see ya, I'll send the guys out to split your fuckin' head open! I'll tell them to cut your motherfuckin' head off."

The problem was Tortora didn't let up in 13 more pages of transcript. Who would ever have guessed Alexander would go crawling to the feds for such a small loan. "You know, if it was $25,000 I could understand the guy panicking," Zannino said. "He can't get it up. But $250 motherfuckin'. Cocksucker . . . they wired him and oh how he set him up."

But Zannino nevertheless liked his man's style. "You're my fuckin' guy," he told Tortora. "Don't ever forget that. I wish I had three more like you. Three more like you."

Still, Zannino's counsel had been to cop a plea. "Hey, that's part of the game," Zannino explained to his men. "He's 33 years old, he's a big boy, he's got good shoulders, he'll go and do his fuckin' time. If he gets like five or six years, he's in good shape. This way he goes to the farm in four months. 'Cause he's a model prisoner. . . . Then from there we go to work. Once he's on the farm, he'll get parole."

That was the Zannino line on the case. He tried to boost Tortora's sagging spirits as best he could, slipping him a grand as well as later promising Tortora's mother to send the kid a television in prison, because Tortora couldn't read.

The night before his sentencing in late February, Zannino even escorted Tortora to see the top man, Jerry Angiulo. But Angiulo wasn't there, causing Zannino embarrassment.

"Look, Frankie, the reason I want, brought, ah, Carmen here, cause you people are aware how Carmen is close to us. You understand? Carmen might go to jail tomorrow, three, four years. You understand? He wants to say good-bye to Jerry, but Jerry's not here. So he's saying good-bye to the brothers." Then Zannino turned to Tortora. "Ya know they're in your fuckin' corner. Not good-bye, but see you later, ya know . . ."

"Nice meeting ya," remarked Tortora lamely.

Filling in for Jerry, the other Angiulos did their best to join Zannino in stirring up a ceremonial send-off. But it was a hasty, half-hearted effort. Frank, the only

Angiulo to really try to rally Tortora from his slump, said, "You'll be back. What is this, 'Nice meeting you'?"

"Got any white wine in there?" added Danny Angiulo.

Zannino repeated the story of Tortora's awful fate, brought down by a guy who'd borrowed only $250. "What about Skinny Kazonis's case back in 1974?" Frank asked. Carmen shouldn't feel so bad. "Seventy-five dollars," Frank said. "He got eight years."

"Yeah, Skinny," remembered Zannino.

"Seventy-five dollars. Five guys went to the can. The fuckin' fines came to almost $50,000," added Danny.

"You want red?" Mike Angiulo asked Tortora.

"You want white?" Zannino asked his soldier.

"Red or white?" asked Mike.

"Yeah," replied Tortora.

"Carmen, you want red or white?" Mike repeated.

"Red."

Mike poured wine for everyone.

"Carmen," said Danny, raising his glass. "To your health, and a very short stay."

"Any idea where you're going?" asked Mike.

"Lewisburg."

More wine was poured, and Zannino resumed his pep talk to Tortora about how to behave in the can so he could get to the farm quickly. But then, as if on cue, Zannino and another one of his soldiers, Ralph Lamattina, began reminding Tortora about another form of behavior that they all expected of Carmen Tortora while in prison—loyalty to the Mafia.

"Carmen," Lamattina warned. "Within two weeks there'll be a couple of guys say, 'Hey, how are ya?'"

"Yeah," interrupted Zannino. " 'What'd ya say, kid?' "

"That's it," Lamattina said.

"No matter who pats you on the shoulder," explained Zannino, "have no conversation. 'How are ya?' Ah. 'You know Larry?' 'Yeah, I know him casual.' No conversation. Nothing we ever did and nothing we ever discussed."

"That's it, that's it," Lamattina repeated in a kind of refrain, referring to other prisoners looking for "evidence" to trade for sentence reductions.

"Because someone might be trying to get ya," advised Zannino.

"I know," said Tortora.

"That's right," Lamattina said.

"You understand?" asked Zannino.

Then came the zinger, the reminder for Tortora never to doubt for a second the significance of his special relationship with the Mafia.

"Remember Joe Porter, kid," Zannino said.

It was a reference to Joe Porter Patrizzi, one-time trusted Mafia associate, partner to Skinny Kazonis in a loan-shark operation. Patrizzi was even involved in the Kazonis loan-shark case of 1974. But in 1978, after Patrizzi began talking too much, began strutting around the city as if he were bigger than any one of them, well, Joe Porter was executed.

"He was an asshole," Zannino said. "He wasn't you."

11

MAFIA MURDER

For more than a month in early 1981, two young thugs on the outskirts of the Mafia had been circling each other around Boston in a clumsy death dance. They would have coffee together, shoot the breeze at a garage in Revere, all the while looking for just the right chance to slit the other's throat.

Given the odds, it could never be a fair fight. In one corner was Freddie Simone of Waltham, a full-fledged Mafia soldier with a mandate from the bosses to kill a maverick with blood in his eye. In the other corner was the badly outgunned Angelo Patrizzi, an ex-con and petty thief who had just escaped from prison and was subsisting on the fringe of the underworld, nursing his dangerous personal agenda. He was after two made soldiers for killing his brother four years earlier and there was even a hint that he might murder the son of Capo

Larry Zannino, who was believed to have been behind the 1978 slaying of Joseph "Joe Porter" Patrizzi.

It was the kind of mindless mission that marked much of the bloody history of the Mafia in which vendettas wiped out entire families. In the New York wars of the early thirties and the Boston gangland slayings of the mid-sixties, it became almost axiomatic: kill one brother, kill them all. Or be killed. Interfamily fratricide has filled entire graveyards in Sicily.

Such antecedents produced a skulking Angelo Patrizzi, hiding from the law and the mob in a South Boston tenement, determined to even the score on his dead brother's behalf. But he kept tripping over treacherous pals trying to set him up to make points with mob leaders. He was all alone, operating with what one friend reluctantly described as the intelligence of an amoeba.

By the beginning of March 1981, it was literally Angelo Patrizzi against all the soldiers in Revere, a reservoir of unruly mobsters who paid tribute to Gennaro Angiulo but always had leaders who could go over his head to Providence, to Raymond Patriarca.

Patrizzi was too brutish and dim-witted to consider the odds in the cold light of day. He was ruled by his primordial grudge and saddled with an eighth-grade education, a drinking and drug problem, and .32-caliber bullet fragments in his skull from a previous encounter with violence. Nicknamed "Hole in the Head," he had foolishly telegraphed his intentions, publicly vowing vengeance against mob leaders after his brother Joseph was killed for skimming on loan-shark collections.

In March 1981, Patrizzi was being phased out of prison, living in a prerelease center in Boston's South End, having served five years for attempted murder. He had been back in town for more than a month and everyone was getting more nervous as each day went by that he wasn't dead.

The Revere mob leaders knew Angelo was being tracked for a hit but were unsettled when they heard Patrizzi was hiding out after smelling a rat. On March 3, Patrizzi had fled the South End prerelease center and moved in with a girlfriend in South Boston. But not for long. He became a priority matter whose fate would be settled by the top two Mafia men in Boston: Jerry Angiulo and Larry Zannino.

The stacked-deck fate of the 38-year-old Patrizzi is what the Mafia is all about. It's not aging old-world dons who won't sell drugs and only resort to violence to protect their turf. It's nine men dragging one man away from a private club near Suffolk Downs Raceway in Revere, hog-tying his legs to his neck, putting him in a sleeping bag in the trunk of a stolen car, and letting him slowly strangle himself to death at the back of a Lynn motel parking lot. Patrizzi's body was finally found in June because of the smell.

Most of the time, that would have been all there was to it; another gangland slaying. But this one was different. Instead of solving a nettlesome problem for Gennaro Angiulo and part of his mob operation, the 1981 murder became a crucial part of the biggest crisis in Boston Mafia history, a legal quagmire that put all its leaders in a courtroom for two years. For, this time, the FBI was eavesdropping, listening to the secret bugs in two North End sites while the murder was being planned and after the deed was done. And while the FBI may not have tried hard enough to stop the murder, the taped conversations about Patrizzi's fate were coup-de-grâce evidence in the eventual federal and state trials.

It took nearly seven years, but Angelo Patrizzi finally did get his revenge. Jerry Angiulo was given a life sentence in 1987 after being convicted of accessory before the fact of Patrizzi's death.

The case began with the bogus white flag that greeted Patrizzi when he was released from Bridgewater State Prison on January 26, 1981. Freddie Simone, a longtime Mafia soldier in the Revere regime of Capo Sammy Granito, befriended him. Both men knew the other would kill him in a second, but also that this was the best way to keep an eye on each other. Simone got Patrizzi a job at Surf Auto Body in Revere and attempted to gain his confidence to better arrange his demise. Patrizzi played along, needing to be within striking distance of both Simone and Connie Frizzi, an East Boston soldier Patrizzi also suspected of murdering his brother.

In the winter of 1981, plans by Granito's soldiers to kill Patrizzi went awry twice when Patrizzi was wary enough not to go off alone with Simone. On the last attempt, Simone scared him off by foolishly showing up at the Revere garage at 9 A.M.—much too early for the 31-year-old soldier, who, like most peers, worked late and slept late. It was a perquisite of rank. "Why so early?" a suspicious Patrizzi had asked.

Angelo knew something was up, so rather than go for coffee with Simone, he said he was waiting for a call about a truck hijacking; he was going to ride shotgun in the holdup. Simone's plan had been to take him to a nearby men's club, where an assassination team waited to overwhelm Patrizzi and stab him to death.

After the klutsy minuet with Simone at the garage,

Patrizzi disappeared for good. That put Simone on his third strike and he knew it. Instead of being dead, Angelo Patrizzi was missing and still a threat to the likes of Larry Zannino. Simone's boss, the aging Capo Sammy Granito, brought him to the ultimate woodshed: 98 Prince Street.

Granito, whose police mug shot shows a fearsome face with the blunt, brutish features of a death mask, got right to the point on the evening of March 11, telling Angiulo that Patrizzi "has screwed and ran away." He rued the missed opportunity of five days earlier, when they had Patrizzi set up and in their sights at the garage. "We had him ready last Friday. Oh, we had him Friday, 'cause Freddie said, 'C'mon we'll go for coffee.' We had a place. We're gonna take him in a house and strangle him." But from there, the story rolled downhill to a bad ending. Granito turned it over to Simone. "You explain, huh," Granito said, "to him just what happened . . . he wants to know why the kid got away from you."

Things had been going real well, Simone told Angiulo. "I had him with me a couple of times driving around you know, an hour at a time; I got him a suit, I got him a jacket, top coat. Suddenly, he don't want to come around no more."

Angiulo interrupted: "What do you mean all of a sudden?"

Simone explained that he showed up early at the garage and a startled Patrizzi wanted to know, "What are you doing here?"

An exasperated Angiulo interrupted again: "Nobody thinks. Nobody thinks . . ."

While the mob knew that Patrizzi was calling people in Revere who were more than willing to set him up,

Granito had strong reservations about doing business with a double agent who was not "a friend of ours," a Mafia member. "We got him in a trap," Granito said of Patrizzi. "See, we figure he's gonna call Pryce and if he gets hold of Pryce, Pryce will set him up. Now he's been calling the other kid Donny. . . . Now if he calls Donny and makes a meet with Donny, we don't know what to do."

Angiulo asked, "You were going to trust Donny?"

Granito quickly reassured him. "No, no, that's what I was just going to tell you. I don't like that. Because we have to kill him. . . . I don't like leavin' myself open for no son of a bitch sitting around fifty years. And then the son of a bitch could finger me."

Angiulo seconded the motion. "No sir."

"So anyway," Granito continued, "ah, as far as Pryce. Okay. He calls Pryce. He wants to meet with Pryce."

"Beautiful," concluded Angiulo.

To make sure that Angiulo took some action and that his men were not in prolonged jeopardy, Granito deftly dropped a surefire incentive. "Now let me give you this. I, I feel that we have no worry about him whacking Larry's kid."

Angiulo's response was: Get this matter into my hands as fast as you can. After he ascertained there was a telephone number available for Patrizzi that could be used to trace him in South Boston, Angiulo turned tough with Simone. It reflected Angiulo's ancient antipathy for autonomous Revere mobsters who only came to him when they needed a favor.

"Well," Angiulo said of the telephone number, "you make it somebody's business to bring it here . . . you'll find out that's why we sit here." Patrizzi's fate all but sealed, Angiulo moved on to small talk with Granito, who was heading off to Florida. "What else is going on Sammy . . ."

On the next day, March 12, marching orders were given at a meeting that included the paramilitary presence of Larry Zannino. He and Jerry Angiulo agreed that the death of Angelo Patrizzi had now become a matter of duty and honor, a message to those who would threaten the top. It put a noble veneer on crass self-interest.

Angiulo opened the conversation with Zannino by saying "Hey, it's you and I . . . you and I are going to solve a problem here. Not because we want to do it, because it's our fuckin' duty to, okay, tonight?" Zannino, who already knew about the problem from other sources, couldn't agree more: "We gotta kill this guy, you know."

In the strategy session, Angiulo followed a familiar pattern of self-interest in which the top mob leaders would work on underlings with a kill-or-be-killed message. Zannino told Revere mobsters that they better get Patrizzi before he gets them. "Freddie, this kid's gonna kill you," he told Simone about the hapless half-wit in hiding. To another hoodlum, Zannino said of Patrizzi, "Don't think he ran away. He didn't run away. He's layin' and he's waitin' and he'll crack one of you."

The dialogue between Angiulo and Zannino about how best to handle Patrizzi was also a character study in the difference between the two top men. For Zannino, the hardened killer, it was an exciting challenge in pragmatics: Where is this bum now and who can kill him the soonest? Since he acknowledged playing a role in Joe Patrizzi's death, Zannino had a special interest in putting any threat from Joe's brother to rest, especially if it could save his own son's life. Because

Angelo Patrizzi was hiding out in South Boston, Zannino's first instinct was to bring in two hit men from Southie and go along himself.

In contrast, Angiulo was cautious. His first instinct was to insulate himself and get some malleable "suckers" to do the dirty work. Why be indebted to South Boston killers when he had a ton of players dying to prove themselves? The Irish hoodlums owed him $245,000, and he wanted to keep the upper hand in all dealings with them. To use them now would change the relationship ever so slightly. He would owe them a favor, something anathema to him. The chits belonged in his vest pocket, not someone else's. Finally, he was dead set against having Connie Frizzi, a hotheaded made soldier directly under him, participating in the hit in "mixed" company. Rather, Angiulo wanted it done by a group that could not point the finger at anyone in the leadership. Angiulo was always on alert about potential witnesses. "Connie is a Friend of Ours. Therefore, we can never put him with these other people and say 'just tell Connie who he is,' cause I know what he'll do. He'll say 'that's him' and stand back, bam! And now we got a fuckin' problem. What do we need it for?"

The discussion ended with the ball passed to the eager Zannino, who agreed to oversee an orchestrated hit by Revere mobsters who did not deal directly with Angiulo. "Once you give me the number, I know what to do," Zannino told his boss. But, by the end of the macho murder talk, the eavesdropping FBI did not even know who the target was—neither crime boss had mentioned Patrizzi's last name. It was as ticklish as any dilemma law enforcement faced in the investigation: There would be no more incriminating conversation to be had in four months of listening, but what could they do about warning the target? Who was he? Where was he? Could they save him without tipping their hand and exposing the bugging operation?

They had two leads from the rambling conversations. A first name, Angelo, was mentioned, and there was a reference to the target's brother, Joe Porter, a Revere loan shark. Luckily, one of the agents remembered the name Joe Porter from another case and was able to come up with Patrizzi as the last name for the brothers. The book on Angelo Patrizzi was that he was minor league but dangerous and not very bright. Investigators also knew that Simone was banking on that, telling Jerry Angiulo, "He's real dumb . . . dumb, dumb."

Those who knew Angelo Patrizzi, however, said that, in his own unglamorous way, he made an almost heroic stand against the Revere mob, a steadfast resistance going back deep into his adolescence. Three years younger than his brother Joseph, he took a distinctly different view of the Mafia.

Joe Porter, nicknamed after his stepfather, had been very much the hip wiseguy who liked traveling in a flashy crowd and driving a Gran Prix; Angelo was an unpredictable loner who never had a steady job or any money. Even as kids, say friends of the family, the mob had a dramatically opposite effect on the brothers. Joseph was drawn to it instantly, falling in with the local mobsters at age 14. Angelo was put off by what he saw as swaggering bullies who tried to tell him what to do. He always stood his ground. "Angelo was never a joiner. He was a very independent person," recalled one family friend. Yet each would be murdered for Mafia code violations in his thirty-eighth year: one for taking money from the top and the other for threatening the top.

The Patrizzi brothers had shared a hard upbringing in Revere, where the family had moved from Lynn in 1947. There were frequent clashes with the stepfather, and the family never had much money. Angelo's first brush with the law showed his pigheaded determination to do it his way. He was 13 and got caught selling pornographic pictures at the local junior high school. The principal told him he had to either reveal the names of the other students involved or go to reform school. Off he went without a word. He did a year and came back more stubborn than before. "There was no turning back for Angelo then," said a friend. "The die was cast. He went on to lead a really pathetic life. He never had a job because he had no training and was usually in jail. He lived on the street when he was out, drifting from girlfriend to girlfriend."

When he was 28, after leaving a nephew's christening, he and a girlfriend stopped by a Charlestown bar. One of the customers shot up the place, hitting three persons, including Patrizzi. Angelo wound up with a bullet fragment at the base of his brain. It was inoperable and Patrizzi's dependence on alcohol and drugs accelerated with the chronic pain. Four years later, he got his first hard-time sentence in 1975, for attempted murder, and was still serving when his brother Joseph was murdered by Revere mobsters for skimming on some loan-shark collections in 1978.

Patrizzi cried vengeance immediately, naming names with abandon. "Angelo hated the Mafia, always did," said the family friend. "He never liked the big shots who swaggered around. He couldn't stand the thought of anyone having jurisdiction over him. He didn't admire many people. He had his pride and was in fear of no man. There was at least that much."

After the FBI and Organized Crime Strike Force attorneys reviewed the taped conversations about killing
Patrizzi, it was decided that the murder plot should be
turned over to the state police. While it was a sensible
decision, Angelo Patrizzi would always be an unnerv-
ing episode for some of those involved. He was the one
who got away, the one who was killed even though the
FBI knew he was slated for death.

Patrizzi posed special problems: He was in hiding
and the Mafia had a good line on where he was staying.
But while the mob went into high gear it appeared that
law enforcement simply went through the motions. In
the aftermath, some investigators have asked: If Angiulo got a phone number that yielded an address, why
didn't we? If Zannino could leave Prince Street saying
he knew what to do, why was it so hard for us to figure
it out?

Patrizzi dropped out of sight on March 3 and was
last seen alive at the St. Patrick's Day parade in South
Boston on March 15, wearing a shamrock pinned to
the left collar of his blue barracuda-style jacket. When
his body was found June 11 in the parking lot of a Lynn
motel, he was still wearing the shamrock. The 1978
LeSabre had been stolen off a used-car lot in Medford,
the license plate stolen from East Boston.

Patrizzi was found in a white sleeping bag with a red
lining where he had been trussed and left to strangle
himself when he moved. Gradually, the weight of his
legs pulled the rope tight around his neck. The body
was so blackened by decomposition that it was not
possible to determine the victim's race. The bullet fragments from the 1975 shooting incident were used for
identification. Patrizzi had 84 cents in his dungarees
pockets.

For some involved in the case, the putrefied body in the LeSabre reflected a troubling penchant among some in law enforcement to shrug when it learned of murder plots on secret microphones, to let someone get murdered simply because he was a dirt bag on the other side. The Patrizzi matter still gnaws at these agents. Looking back, they said it would have been an easy thing to have gone to Patrizzi's prerelease center in the South End to check for leads to a South Boston address or the name of a girlfriend he was staying with. "More should have been done," said one official. "It would not have been hard or taken much time."

As things turned out, the only positive result of the Patrizzi dilemma was that it resurrected a simmering debate over whether to resume the bugging of Larry Zannino's North End card games. The debate had had an edge to it, the sole discordant note in a harmonious team effort that demanded long hours in close quarters for nearly four years.

Zannino's game, where the poker pots were as high as $35,000 and one loan-shark customer got on the hook for $140,000 in losses, had been bugged for the second half of February. This meant that for two days a week, the FBI had to man two electronic surveillance operations on adjacent streets in the North End. All the troops felt it had become a needless risk that had reached the point of diminishing returns. But squad leader John Morris was unshakeable in his insistence that the dual bugging was worth the trouble. He was determined to bag the top two Mafia figures in Boston by catching them hatching conspiracies at Angiulo's office and then carrying them out at Zannino's game.

When the Zannino bug was abandoned at the end of February with only a couple of nights of mildly incriminating conversations to show for it, Morris begrudgingly acquiesced—and waited for the right moment to revive it. Morale and team effort came first with him. But Morris quickly grabbed the Mafia plan to kill Patrizzi to press his argument that the bug had to be revived. It was the only way to track Zannino's promise of "knowing what to do" when he got the South Boston telephone number.

Even with that new motivation, the North Margin Street bug was star-crossed. Done on the fly, the cumbersome T-3 application to the courts, needed to make the new bugging operation legal and the transcripts admissible as evidence, hit a fatal bureaucratic snafu when it got to Washington on March 14, 1981, two days after Angiulo and Zannino had agreed on a general plan. The Justice Department was in transition from the Carter to the Reagan administration. For close to two weeks, no one could be found to sign the required affidavit to get the ball rolling in Boston.

Strike-force lawyer Wendy Collins, who prepared all the T-3s, even thought fleetingly about putting the bug in anyway to find out when the Mafia was going after Patrizzi so that the FBI could rescue the guy. After all, she figured, wasn't a life more important than bureaucratic red tape? She regained her equilibrium, realizing that nothing good came from illegal acts by law enforcement, aberrations the idealistic woman had always abhorred as an undergrad and law student.

It was one of many unexpected moments of truth that Collins confronted in the grueling march to a major case against the Mafia. The issues had become so much more complicated than they were in law school. The question—Do you do something illegal to save a life?—had never come up before. The best answer she could divine was, Probably not. Suddenly, everything in her life seemed to be in gray tones and she became nostalgic for the simplicity of her earlier life—just a year before.

While she fretted and Morris pushed and chief prosecutor Jeremiah O'Sullivan hollered on the phone with the Justice Department to break the log jam, time was running out for Patrizzi. The strike force finally got the newly sworn attorney general, William French Smith, to sign the affidavit on March 26. It took twice as long as usual.

Yet even after the long-delayed authorization for the Zannino bug came through, there was still more red tape to slash. Morris found that although he had a court approval in hand there was no equipment on the shelf. When the microphones were removed from Zannino's poker hall, they were immediately taken by another field office. Morris had to wait until two microphones became available after an undercover operation in Los Angeles shut down. Both borrowed microphones were installed on April 1 in the back conference room at North Margin Street—the place where Zannino and his closest henchmen played big-money poker. It proved to be a bonanza. "Bing," said Morris. "That first conversation and they started talking about murders. I can remember the chill."

The Patrizzi death announcement was made by Zannino as part of a drunken reverie with his minions on the first night the North Margin Street bug was back in place. The news hit Collins hard. She felt herself becoming numb to the endemic violence of the mob, of closing herself to normal feelings just to get through the day. She was exhausted and confused by the tidal wave of paperwork needed to put a T-3 on some desk in Washington where it could be ignored while some guy in Boston died an unspeakable death. "I think that is when it really snapped for me," she recalled later. "I don't know how many bodies we had by then."

For months Collins had simply lived for the case— it was all she wanted to do, all she cared about. But the Patrizzi murder had forced her to confront how far she had drifted from her initial enthusiasm. She was becoming hardened—even as she fought it. When she learned of Angelo Patrizzi's fate, she found herself thinking One more murder with weary detachment. The emotional toll and the mind-numbing hours were turning her into an automaton who popped diet pills to keep going. She laid off the pills only after someone had to stop her from absently picking at french fries from a trash barrel in the FBI's headquarters. "I don't know what I'm doing," she realized, holding the french fries container in her hands. "Something is very wrong here."

On April 3 at about 4 A.M., Larry Zannino soared past even Morris's high hopes for the dual-bug system. After several rounds of drinks, Zannino solved four open murders by bragging about his role in them. It was as nuts-and-bolts as you can get. The blood-drenched list included the late Angelo Patrizzi, which still stands as the most brutal of any recent mob killings. The others were William and Walter Bennett, who were both killed in turf wars in 1967, and the 1976 retribution killing of Joseph Barboza after he had turned on the mob.

Inarticulate, brutish, barely literate, Ilario Zannino still had a curious charisma, stemming mostly from his physical presence. He had the bearing and features of a movie mafioso, a central casting capo regime with a high, shiny forehead and resonant voice, and the deadly, deep-set eyes of a man who gets genuine respect from wiseguys and abiding disdain from police.

If underboss Gennaro Angiulo was in it for the money, the number two man Zannino was there for the stature the mob offered a South End street kid. Like some of the investigators pursuing him, Zannino was drawn to a fraternal organization with rituals and trappings in which the underlings carry out orders without question or comment and get unflinching loyalty in return. Zannino would kill as a favor to another family or over an insult to a soldier's girlfriend. While there has been no more bloody enforcer in the Boston mob, Zannino was also a hopeless romantic about La Cosa Nostra.

It was his life, producing boundless devotion to the "cause." He even left one of his daughter's funeral services in the 1960s to help Jerry Angiulo settle an escalating turf dispute between Boston and Somerville mobsters over gambling and loansharking rights. Recalling the scene years later, Zannino remembered telling Angiulo, "My poor daughter. I come back from the grave [to meet with you]. My fucking heart is broken. But This Thing comes first." He would extract vows of loyalty from all parties and, at least this once, Zannino appeared to have avoided bloodshed rather than caused it.

But, throughout his career, Zannino was a true believer who jumped at any chance to bloody an opponent. "Just listen to Larry," strike-force chief O'Sullivan said about the hours of conversations secretly recorded by the FBI. "Every time, he's ready to grab a machine gun."

So it was with Angelo Patrizzi. Zannino reported the "clip" as information passed to him by Angiulo. As an afterthought, he related a scene of barbaric brutality to two of his top lieutenants. Speaking matter-of-factly, Zannino covered the murder quickly in a by-the-way aside to John Cincotti and Ralph Lamattina.

Three weeks after he and Angiulo had agreed that Patrizzi had to go like his brother before him, Zannino said to Cincotti, "Johnny, I told you didn't I? About Joe Porter's brother?" "No," Cincotti said.

"Well they clipped him and don't say a fuckin' . . ."

"Did they find him?" Cincotti asked.

"No, they didn't find him. They put him in his trunk. Don't even say . . ."

Lamattina interrupted. "Is that the thing you tried to tell me?"

"Yeah, that's right." Zannino said. "Nine of them. Nine of them. They lugged him from the fuckin' Topcoat [a club]. Nine fuckin' guys."

"We got—we got lucky Friday," Lamattina observed.

"But that's all right," Larry insisted. "They did, John . . . nine of them did it. . . . And he's in the trunk. . . . But they got him. They got him. Freddy was scared to death. The kid would have clipped him in two fuckin' minutes. . . . Freddie fucked him in the ass."

Signaling the end of his interest in Angelo Patrizzi, Zannino changed the subject. "Johnny, you having no more brandy?"

12

THE FALL OF GENNARO ANGIULO

Nearly two and a half years after the Angelo Patrizzi slaying, Gennaro Angiulo and two of his brothers were dining at Francesca's when Ed Quinn made the arrest that rocked Boston's underworld. "I'll be back for my pork chops before they're cold," the surly Angiulo had promised that summer night, September 19, 1983. But it was a promise he never kept. In fact, he hasn't been out of jail since making it.

The Mafia boss and three of his brothers were taken to FBI headquarters a few blocks away. In handcuffs, they rode the elevator to the large FBI squad room on the ninth floor. Even a veteran agent like Nick Gianturco, one of the key lookouts in the van during the break-ins, was taken aback at how small the Angiulos were. From the mobsters' reputation, agents expected them to stand more than 6 feet and weigh in at over 220. But Jerry, Danny, Frankie, and Mikey were all basically the same height—5 feet 4 inches to 5 feet 6 inches. Jerry even wore lifts on his shoes.

Angiulo was on his feet most of the night, screaming and hurling curses in English and Italian. The agents who hung around to witness the ruckus could not recall ever having watched someone in federal custody carry on the way Jerry Angiulo did.

He yelled at his brothers, telling them what they could and could not say. He tongue-lashed any agent within earshot, seeming almost crazed. Mostly, he sought out Quinn, going nose to nose several times, demanding to see his lawyer and insisting he deserved a bail hearing that night. It was as if the cornered Angiulo was tormented by Quinn's refusal to fight with him. You can't be the underboss and feel ignored.

Quinn and the others resisted the bait. Some were tempted to swing past the irate mafioso and say, "Shut up, asshole—it's over." But no one broke character. "You'll get your hearing—tomorrow," Quinn told him.

That news triggered another round of denunciations—nonstop abuse that included raw and vintage Angiulo remarks, such as every agent's mother was a whore. "That's the way it's gonna be," Quinn deadpanned, as his colleagues talked to Boston police about keeping the Mafia family at the District One station for the night.

Angiulo was infuriated. For his arrest, he expected to be summoned to court during working hours, not have his dinner interrupted. He expected to be fingerprinted, photographed, and released all on the same day. But, instead of being treated in the respectful manner he thought befit a Mafia leader, he'd been rounded up like a two-bit bookmaker and was being held overnight.

That he was arrested did not surprise Angiulo. He'd suspected it would happen sooner or later, ever since the end of the FBI's secret bugging of his 98 Prince Street headquarters in May 1981. On May 3 of that year, it took FBI agents less than thirty minutes to make their last surreptitious entry into Angiulo's office to remove the two bugs. The very next day agents swarmed the premises with search warrants to gather evidence to present to a grand jury.

Even after eavesdropping on the Angiulos for nearly four months, Ed Quinn, John Morris, and the others who conducted those raids encountered a couple of surprises.

From their secret surveillance, agents knew that Frankie Angiulo often left the office with cash, went upstairs, and came back without the money. So they had expected to find a huge bankroll. But no funds were in sight when they first inspected the upstairs apartment. A couple of agents began tapping the bricks. Some of them were loose, and there was a hollow sound. They had found a safe. Quinn told Frankie Angiulo to open it. But the Mafia's bookkeeper, who'd been found with $4,000 in cash stuffed in his belt beneath a sweater, adamantly refused. Quinn summoned the Boston police, and for the next three hours police officers using jackhammers pounded away at the concrete encasement. Having pried the safe loose, it took four men to carry it outside and onto a truck. Back at the FBI office, a locksmith that Quinn found by flipping through the yellow pages drilled the safe open. Inside was $327,000 in cash, $300,000 in bonds, and a pile of jewelry.

During the same raid, agents searched 95 Prince Street, which was directly across from the main office. In addition to finding another safe and more cash in Frankie's apartment, they discovered a secret suite on the second floor. The three rooms were completely sealed off from the five-story building's main hallways. Where there should have been an entrance from the landing, there was a wall. Where there should have been a window, there was red brick. You could reach the apartment only from inside two other apartments, on the first and third floors. The rooms were stuffy and without windows. One had a large meeting table. The hallway outside was wired for sound, so anyone inside the secret room would know if someone were approaching. The doors were reinforced with steel. The centerpiece of the apartment was a large gas boiler, its fire perfect for destroying cartons of gambling slips.

To Morris and the others, the apartment was like something out of the movie *The Godfather*—a place to conduct secret meetings to baptize a new Mafia member, or for soldiers to sleep on mattresses placed on the floor in the event of a gang war.

Two weeks later, Nick Gianturco and fourteen others hit Larry Zannino's high-stakes poker game as it was in progress. The microphones hidden at 51 North Margin Street had been removed on May 14, and the FBI wanted to seize gambling evidence from there as well. Gianturco, dressed in street clothes, entered the building and got past the doorman posing as just another card player. Within minutes, the others stormed in. No guns were drawn. No one was arrested, just as no one was arrested the day of the 98 Prince Street raids. But mounds of gambling materials were seized.

For Jerry Angiulo, the two quick hits at the core of his empire served as a harsh confirmation: He was nearing the end of the line. Perhaps the worst blow came on June 17, when the U.S. Supreme Court upheld the use of RICO against the strictly illegal drug enterprise of wiseguy Novia Turkette, Jr.

Contrary to Turkette's view, the court ruled that the government's use of RICO was not limited to instances when a criminal outfit sought to infiltrate a legitimate business. In writing the majority opinion, Justice Byron White assumed an almost mocking tone toward the defense argument—a rationale that Angiulo and Zannino had so heartily embraced. "Insulating the wholly criminal enterprise from prosecution under RICO is the more incongruous position," wrote White. The underboss's back was against the wall.

In the months to follow, Angiulo knew the case against him was building, particularly after official notification that he'd been taped secretly came in August 1982. He just didn't know when the agents would come for him. One persistent question of those at the edge of the mob and among law enforcement itself was: Knowing what he knew, why didn't Angiulo run? He even talked about it but, in the end, it seems he simply had no place to go and could not face an uncertain future in a strange place where no one knew who he was. Besides, he'd fought his way out of trouble many times already.

And so time dragged on. The major reason for a delay in the arrests was that the FBI had to transcribe the Angiulo tapes and study the fine print of what they had for evidence. It took fifteen mind-numbing months.

Within weeks of the May 1981 raids, Ed Quinn, Tom Donlan, Bill Regii, Pete Kennedy, Jack Cloherty, Nick Gianturco, and Joe Kelly were holed up in an office in Waltham, west of Boston, trying to put the words onto paper. First they reviewed 540 tapes, to isolate the criminal conversations and divide them into subjects —like gambling, murder, or loansharking. Once they found they had, say, twenty-five gambling exchanges, they chose the best eight and tossed out the others.

They narrowed the tapes down to 696 separate conversations. These were sent to Washington, D.C., where specialists worked on enhancing the Mafia talk and reducing the background noise from the radio and television. Once the tapes were enhanced, the agents sat down and listened again.

They played and replayed the tapes, writing out their first draft of a transcript in longhand. The draft was then typed, and the agent listened to the tape again. The second draft was typed and then went to Quinn. Quinn matched the transcript against the tape and made further corrections. Sometimes a transcript went through twenty drafts.

The work drove the agents nuts. They'd start off clearheaded on Monday morning—grabbed some coffee and a donut and got comfortable in front of the tape recorders—but by Friday, they were batty. They fought over single words: Was that a "hum" or a "hah"? To break the monotony, most jogged. Donlan and Gianturco played handball. In the end, they listened to 850 hours of Mafia talk.

By the time Angiulo was arrested in 1983, the tapes had been culled, transcribed, and placed into the hands of the prosecutors. For many agents, the arrest marked a turning point in the grueling investigation. It was not only the last piece of unfinished business, but it also meant the case, in a way, was no longer theirs. From then on, it would belong to Jeremiah T. O'Sullivan and his team of attorneys on the Justice Department's Organized Crime Task Force.

With all of this in mind, Quinn and the others didn't find it difficult to tolerate Angiulo's tantrums the night he was booked. He could rant all he wanted; they knew what they had on him. The ranting lasted for a couple of hours, then wound down. Quinn and Angiulo parted company, and Quinn drove home. It was after midnight. He rejected his usual Budweiser and poured himself a Cutty Sark on the rocks. He abandoned the practice of not talking business. He and his wife talked late into the night about the past few years, agreeing that, somehow, all the work had been worth it. The next night, after the media focused on little else but the Angiulo arrest, his neighbors surprised them by bringing over a bottle of champagne in honor of the historic FBI takedown.

Quinn, looking back a few years later, would tell others that what got him through the months of around-the-clock work were the stakes involved. "It didn't take a genius to figure out what we had," he said. "From the very first conversations, we knew we were onto something very big and very important, and after you heard the talk, time became unimportant. You just did what you had to do."

Angiulo, meanwhile, spent a less comfortable evening in a downtown lockup. The air was stale and hot. The temperature, which during the day had climbed into the nineties, at night fell only into the high sixties. The brooding Mafia boss found that his cell block was already occupied by a shirtless drunk with a belly as round as a beer keg who didn't show him proper respect. The drunk had been trying to get the guards to give him a match to light a cigarette when Angiulo arrived. Watching the commotion that Angiulo's appearance created, the drunk stage-whispered, "Now that the Godfather is here, can I get a goddamn match?"

The cell-block chatter continued to pick up as the

night wore on. Several transvestites were brought in and placed in a cell down from Angiulo, his brothers, and Sammy Granito, the capo from Revere who'd also been nabbed. It wasn't long before the transvestites realized that their neighbors included a very distinguished crime figure.

"Oh Godfaaaather, Godfaaaather," they sang.

For once, Jerry Angiulo had little to say.

There were no more New Year's Eve parties thrown by Angiulo at which he serenaded his five hundred guests. From the moment he was arrested at Francesca's, he remained behind bars, even though he continually fought his incarceration starting the night Quinn brought him to FBI headquarters in handcuffs for processing. (The court refused to release him on bail.)

If he'd been caught speechless in the jail cell, he soon regained his fighting spirit during the pretrial wrangling that dragged on for months, through 1984 and into 1985. For the most part, he was merely keeping up appearances. Many of the FBI agents and prosecutors felt they had won the battle as soon as Angiulo lost his bid to suppress the tapes that were the heart of the government's case. "You can murder witnesses, but you can't do anything about the tapes," noted one of the prosecutors. Still, to fully exploit the tapes, the FBI and the strike force had long felt that a jury had to be able to use transcripts to follow the mangled syntax and poor audio of the secretly recorded conversations.

But the government won this battle too, although not before prosecutors spent months worrying which judge would get the case and rule on the critical transcript issue. The government hoped to avoid U.S.

District judges Joseph L. Tauro and Walter Jay Skinner. Both were considered especially tough on the use of transcripts. Tauro was viewed as antiprosecution, especially for having permitted Larry Zannino to escape trial on sports-betting charges in 1977 by accepting Zannino's contention that he was seriously ill. Preferred were either judges Andrew A. Caffrey or David S. Nelson. The Angiulo racketeering case became Nelson's.

In public, meanwhile, Angiulo continued to strut and swagger, bantering with reporters and trying to bait FBI agents or prosecutors into a war of words. As soon as the trial began on June 11, 1985, his court appearances drew packed audiences, with every twist in the biggest crime story that anyone could remember often leading the news.

He once tried to exploit Debbie Richard in one of his demonstrative displays of wit, but the attempt backfired. Angiulo, always leading an entourage of guards, lawyers, reporters, and groupies, was making his way down the hall toward the courtroom. Richard was standing in the hall waiting to testify, decked out in a lavender ultrasuede suit, with a white blouse and a string of pearls. Angiulo immediately spotted the striking blonde. "Well, I can be guaranteed of one thing, honey," he said, breaking stride momentarily to speak to Richard and causing those in his wake to jam on their brakes. "I can be assured of one thing—you certainly are not involved with the government in this, because they couldn't afford you." Fifteen minutes later, as she took the stand as an FBI agent and swore she'd tell the whole truth, Richard saw Angiulo's mouth had dropped.

But Angiulo achieved some satisfaction when he succeeded in his bid to unnerve the chief prosecutor of the strike force, Jeremiah O'Sullivan. Ever since his 1983 arrest, he had begun chiding the intense O'Sullivan by calling him Father Flanagan, a reference to the founder of Boy's Town. He claimed O'Sullivan had missed his calling in life by not entering the priesthood. It was the kind of cutting commentary Angiulo relished and habitually aimed at opponents, most notably Quinn. But the unflappable FBI agent was always unfazed. O'Sullivan, however, lost his cool after the jury left the courtroom one day, complaining Angiulo was playing "mind games" with jurors. Within seconds, the prosecutor, red-faced with anger, and Angiulo were inches apart, yelling. They accused one another of the same thing: that neither the chief prosecutor nor the chief Mafia figure ever showed the other the proper respect. The judge finally had to separate them, warning he was wearing the robes.

But in the contest that mattered—the RICO trial—O'Sullivan prevailed convincingly. He devised the strategy for presenting the evidence, assigning different crimes to different prosecutors. Diane M. Kottmyer concentrated on loansharking and the structure of the Angiulo enterprise. Ernest DiNisco handled the murders. O'Sullivan took the gambling operation.

Concerned about the quality of the tapes, they opened the case with the gambling operation. The gambling tapes tended to be clearer, because Frankie Angiulo was usually alone running the office. There wasn't the crowd of people jabbering away as often happened at night. Besides, if one gambling tape didn't work for the jurors, they could always roll out another. They had plenty on gambling.

Priming the jurors on the gambling tapes was critical when it came to the talk about murder. The murder conversations were few and brief, and the prosecutors did not want to find the jury struggling to decipher those chilling words.

Throughout the irrefutable tapes, Angiulo, his chin jutting forward, persisted in playing the boss, offering few clues that the setbacks he was experiencing daily were not restricted to a federal courtroom. His rank in the Mafia in New England had plummeted. He was no longer the unquestioned underboss. For months, the soldiers on the street were forging new, tentative alliances in an effort to fill the power vacuum. Just as John Morris had hoped when he had targeted the Angiulo family, the Boston underworld was fragmented. Angiulo had no protégé and he'd taken the intimate knowledge of the numbers racket, which had catapulted him to the top, with him to prison. The result was a scramble among younger mafiosi in Boston; they elbowed one another for pieces of the rackets but tried just as hard to avoid being tagged as "up and comers," for fear of drawing the attention of federal investigators. Many of the non-Mafia bookies and loan sharks who had paid Angiulo to do business now found themselves pressured by competing mafiosi to make several payments. Disputes flared and dragged on unresolved. Gone was the orderliness of the Angiulo monolith.

Matters had worsened after the death of the godfather of New England's Mafia, Raymond L. S. Patriarca, on July 7, 1984. Had Angiulo not been been tangling with RICO, he probably would have succeeded Patriarca with little opposition and become the top Mafia man in New

England. Even from jail, he vied for the post, but he was up against his old capo, Zannino, as well as Raymond J. C. "Junior" Patriarca. But by that time, Angiulo never really had a chance. He was not only considered stupid for having gotten caught, but many underworld figures were infuriated at the brazen disrepect he had displayed toward them on the FBI's secret tapes. "Mr. Patriarca gave the Angiulos the rope that they used," said the 84-year-old Henry Tameleo, Patriarca's confidant, who was unable to conceal his disgust toward the Angiulos in an interview he gave shortly before he died in prison in August 1985. "They never did anything right. They did it upside down."

The decades of abuse had come home to roost. Angiulo was disliked in Providence and detested by many of the soldiers who'd suffered his barbs for years. Eventually, Zannino, the diehard organization man, threw his support to the young Patriarca. By 1985, the FBI's intelligence network had determined that the Mafia's national commission, composed of the heads of the major Mafia families, had selected Junior.

Jerry Angiulo, on the eve of his RICO trial in mid-1985, had been reduced to the ignominious rank of soldier. Adding insult to injury, the decision-making for the Boston-area Mafia was put into the veteran hands of Revere-based mafiosi who were longtime rivals of Angiulo's. Junior Patriarca rewarded Zannino for his support by appointing him consigliere to replace the seriously ill and indicted Nick Angiulo.

Jerry Angiulo wasn't alone among leading mafiosi in the pummeling he suffered from the government. Ever since the U.S. Supreme Court backed RICO to fight the mob, the FBI began wreaking havoc within the only known organized crime outfit that operates nationwide and whose gross annual income exceeds an estimated $50 billion.

Between 1984 and 1987, strike forces successfully prosecuted 82 made La Cosa Nostra members and 396 associates. It levied $34 million in fines, obtained $20 million in restitution, and seized more than $800 million in narcotics and $60 million in property from underworld figures.

In early 1985, a federal grand jury in New York City indicted the commission, including the five bosses or acting bosses of the New York families. But the Angiulo tapes offered the richest and most intimate portrait of life inside a Mafia family, illustrating the day-to-day workings graphically and revealing the Boston Mafia's innermost secrets—the attempts to kill Walter LaFreniere and Harvey Cohen, and the brutal murder of Angelo Patrizzi.

On February 26, 1986, after eight months of testimony, the 66-year-old Angiulo, Frank Angiulo, Danny Angiulo, and Sammy Granito were convicted under RICO. Mike Angiulo was found guilty of running an illegal gambling operation. The RICO case against the Angiulo family marked the first time top Mafia bosses were convicted of operating a criminal racket.

Many of the FBI agents who had worked on Operation Bostar were among those who jammed inside the courtroom for the verdict in the historic case. Even after receiving a verdict that meant he would die behind bars, Angiulo didn't break character. Escorted into the hallway from the courtroom by a couple of U.S. marshals, Jerry Angiulo turned to his brothers, all in handcuffs. In his inimitable style, he ordered: "Okay, boys, now follow on behind me and march, hut, two, three, four; hut, two, three, four."

. . .

The outcome in the sensational racketeering case did not mean an end to the legal quagmire for the leaders of the city's underworld. Missing from the lineup the day Angiulo was convicted was Larry Zannino.

The aging capo was tried separately a year after the Angiulo verdict on gambling and loansharking charges, even though he'd been arrested during the same 1983 roundup that netted the Angiulos. FBI agents nabbed him in a North Shore hospital room, where he was a patient, as family members hissed at them.

Zannino went down fighting in court. When the jury, in early 1987, found him guilty, his response sounded like the Zannino of 51 North Margin Street—brash and violent. "I hope the jury dies," he snarled. But prior to his sentencing at a later hearing, he sounded more like the obsequious Zannino of 98 Prince Street—deferential to Mafia boss Angiulo. To Judge Nelson, he made an emotional appeal that lasted twenty minutes. "I'm guilty of swearing . . . but who have I harmed? Why am I the most vicious guy in the world?" he pleaded from a wheelchair, oxygen tubes running to his nose.

Behind him sat his three daughters and his wife. They wept. Seated at the government table with the prosecutors was the impassive Ed Quinn. "I should drop dead in front of my family if I ever shylocked," Zannino continued. "I feel just like a sitting duck being shot at with a double barrel."

Quinn turned his head to look at the mobster, the incredulousness barely showing on his face. But Zannino spotted the agent, saw something, and snapped, "You can grin, Mr. Quinn. You testified you spoke to me for twenty minutes, but I never spoke to you in my life." He rose unsteadily to his feet. "I'm not lily white. . . . I grew up in the South End where you had to fight to live and eat. . . . I'm no altar boy. But who did I hurt? All I'm saying, your honor, is how long do I got? You don't know, only the Guy upstairs knows." He pointed back to his wife seated in the courtroom. "Give my family a little hope, a chance that I might come home. You are sentencing a man who is dying. I'm not afraid to die. What I want is hope for my family, so they can say, We might see Daddy on the street again." He insisted he was not begging and, pounding the table, claimed, "I'm not guilty of these charges. I'm guilty of swearing." He began to ramble and repeat himself. "I'm very, very tired, your honor."

Zannino sat down, leaned to his lawyer, and whispered, "How'd I do?" The lawyer nodded in approval. Judge Nelson then gave Zannino thirty years.

As reporters rushed out to file their stories, Zannino stood to join his family for a moment. "That's the system," he told them. "That's *their* system!" one of his daughter's shouted. "That's *their* system!"

The Zannino family huddled into a fist, giving the prosecutors and Quinn just enough room to get past them to exit the courtroom. "I hope you're happy, Mr. Quinn," Zannino said. "Why don't they just kill you right here in the courtroom?" another daughter shouted, pointing at the government team. "The judge showed no sympathy for you. Shit."

The mercy plea, played and replayed that night on television newscasts across Massachusetts, brought smiles to many of the agents and investigators who'd dogged Zannino. To them, Zannino had made a mockery of the justice system, claiming for ten years he was

on his death bed. Citing an ailing heart had helped him
to avoid prosecution of a pending gambling charge for
a decade. But if he was always so sick how come investigators found him at sporting events? "How you
feeling, Larry?" they'd ask. "I'll outlive you all," Zannino promised sarcastically.

"I loved it," remarked one of the investigators who
watched Zannino's dramatic monologue on the tube.
"Him begging. Screw him. He's a killer."

Zannino became the twentieth casualty of the FBI's
secret bugging operation. Following Angiulo's indictment, the others had gone down in waves of arrests.
Twenty-two mobsters were charged in all, although
two never went to trial. Nicky Angiulo died in 1987.
Ralph LaMattina disappeared.

Jerry Angiulo got 45 years for racketeering; Frankie
got 25; Danny got 20; Mikey got 3; and son Jason got
3 for gambling. William J. Cintolo, the family lawyer,
got 2 years for conspiring to obstruct justice.

Some of the soldiers who fell included Richie Gambale, 12 years for conspiring to murder a witness, racketeering, loansharking, and obstructing justice; James
"Fat Peter" Limone, 12 years for racketeering, loansharking, and conspiring to kill a government witness;
John C. Cincotti, 18 years for racketeering; William J.
"Skinny" Kazonis, 6 years for conspiring to impede a
grand jury investigation; and James "Jimmy Jones" Angiulo, 1 year and a $10,000 fine for running the family's
numbers operation.

Most of the agents on Operation Bostar moved on to
new assignments and other cases. Shaun Rafferty went
to New Hampshire to run a branch office there. John

Connolly hit the street again to track a mob that, having lost its top tier, was struggling to find its footing. Jack Cloherty took over media relations for the Boston office. Pete Kennedy became the firearms instructor. Debbie Richard quit the bureau and went into real estate in Florida. John Morris, long before Jerry Angiulo was even arrested, was assigned to run the office's public corruption unit.

That left Ed Quinn. The steady and unflappable case agent became a fixture in court. With an instant recall of dates, facts, and snatches of conversation, he provided the thread linking the myriad parts in the government's ongoing cases against Jerry Angiulo. And the two had one last dance.

It came in December 1987. Angiulo was brought back to Massachusetts from the federal penitentiary at Leavenworth, Kansas, to face a state trial for ordering the execution of Angelo "Hole in the Head" Patrizzi. Nearly a decade after Morris had handed him the ticket on the Angiulo case, Quinn was on his feet in the witness stand, arms folded. "He's seated at the end of the table there," Quinn pointed, when asked to identify Angiulo. The men's eyes locked briefly, but then Quinn looked back to the prosecutor to field the next question. Angiulo just kept staring, reluctant to let go of the energizing hatred.

Behind and all around Quinn were poster-size photographs revealing the inside world at 98 Prince Street. Across the room, several large tape recorders were hooked up to speakers. Once again, he testified about how he stalked Angiulo, how the team of agents penetrated the Angiulo fortress, how the video cars worked, how the tapes showed that Angiulo was an accessory in the murder of wiseguy Patrizzi.

During cross-examination, Angiulo shook his head and quietly cursed Quinn, then later called another FBI agent who testified a "fucking liar." Angiulo had spent the last four years behind bars and had lost weight, but the Mafia boss still displayed moments of his old combative self. "Fuck you," he told two reporters who approached him during a break in the trial. "Didn't they tell you my answer?" he said, referring to Leavenworth prison officials and his response to a letter the reporters had written months earlier about seeing him. Angiulo had crumpled up the letter and thrown it back at the prison guards. "Go fuck yourself," he told them at the outset of a brief interview in court, but ended it by saying "I'm glad someone is still interested."

During the playing of the tapes, he sat forward at the defense table, galvanized by the proceedings. He took notes and often whispered animatedly to his two attorneys. Turning pages of a document, he licked his fingers. His mannerisms were precise, almost fastidious. In this state trial, he'd been able to block the government request to have jurors use transcripts to follow the voices—a legal victory that gave Angiulo some reason to hope he might win this round.

During the recesses, he was restless. He sought out a photographer from a local newspaper. "Did you take this picture?" he asked, holding up a clip he'd removed from his notebook. "Now that's a very nice picture. I'd like a glossy. That's the kind of picture that should be published." Pointing to the government's poster-size photos of his office, he cracked, "Maybe I should get those pictures. Dress up my cell."

He conferred with his brother Mike, who attended each day of the trial, often bringing Angiulo papers to review. Mike Angiulo was living in a halfway house, completing his sentence. "Pants getting loose, Mike. You eating okay?" Angiulo asked. For several sessions, his son Jason appeared.

But even though Angiulo kept up his swagger, much had changed. His stage had shrunk. He no longer drew the capacity crowds that had attended the federal racketeering trial. Although the Patrizzi murder was the most grotesque material in the FBI's massive case against Boston's La Cosa Nostra, only a dozen or so spectators watched the proceedings.

The numbers swelled only when word spread that the jury had reached a verdict. Dressed in a blue blazer and gray slacks, Angiulo made his way through the lobby, accompanied by two state troopers in plainclothes. "What do you think?" Angiulo asked as he passed Richard J. Connolly, the veteran crime reporter at the *Boston Globe*. "I think it looks good for you," Connolly said, reflecting the view of the reporters covering the case that, without transcripts, a jury would not be able to understand tapes that sounded like a ship-to-shore broadcast.

Noticeably absent from the courtroom was Quinn. Unlike the RICO trial, where he and the other agents assembled for the outcome, Quinn stayed away from this one. Word filtered back to the office that a verdict was in, but he had no intention of racing to the courthouse. Not that he'd lost any interest in the Angiulo case, but, as supervisor of the squad of agents who investigated bank robberies and hijackings, the consummate bureau man had plenty of work to do. Besides, he had a hunch that Angiulo would go down once again. Even if he were acquitted, Quinn knew the underboss would not be going anywhere, not while doing forty-five years for RICO.

Inside the courtroom, Mike and Jason sat in the front row, directly behind Angiulo. The moment Angiulo was seated the cameras started clicking. "Smile," Jason joked feebly. Angiulo frowned at his son. He shrugged his shoulders and made a series of faces to his brother—body language that said, Who the fuck knows?

"Guilty," the foreman declared.

Angiulo, on his feet to receive the verdict, did not blink. He stood straight, without expression. The jurors sat down, and Angiulo did too. He remained still, his hands resting on the table. Finally, he moved a hand, to adjust his glasses, but he moved so deliberately, so tightly, his face was so stiff—these were the slightest tremors from a man who'd spent a lifetime refining the ability to show nothing, to repress everything.

He would not embarrass himself the way a mawkish Larry Zannino had. Instead, he sat watching the judge, his chin resting on his hand, as the judge polled the jurors. He heard each juror repeat the conclusion. Guilty. Guilty. Twelve times. Angiulo's shoulders rose slightly. He burped.

"You were wrong again, Dick," he told Connolly in the lobby during a brief recess prior to sentencing. The recess lasted only ten minutes. The judge had no discretion in sentencing—an accessory to murder was treated under state law as if he committed the murder himself, meaning he got the mandatory life prison term without parole. The state term would begin after he'd served the forty-five years he received from his federal racketeering conviction. He would die in prison.

But even though Angiulo held his tongue, there were other signs that the fight was draining from him. When it came time to leave the courtroom, there was a weary resignation about him. In contrast to his snarling resistance to being handcuffed by Quinn four years earlier in the North End restaurant, Angiulo turned from the defense table and searched out one of the two state policemen assigned to guard him. Using pantomime, he asked the guard if he would have to be cuffed: He held up his arms and crossed them at the wrists, with a question on his face. The trooper nodded. Angiulo shrugged and nodded back.

Two guilty verdicts and a sentence to die behind bars could do that to a wiseguy, even Gennaro J. Angiulo.

"Well, gentlemen, it appears this book is now closed," the judge said as he stood and left. "You want to say anything?" asked the reporters who huddled around the 68-year-old Angiulo. The dethroned mafioso ignored them. He shook hands with his son and then they kissed one another on the cheek. "Take care, now," he said quietly. He repeated the gestures with his brother. "Don't give up."